# ACROSS CULTURES

# ACROSS CULTURES
## Universal Themes In Literature

**WILLIAM SMALZER**

**PHYLLIS L. LIM**
University of Arizona

**Heinle & Heinle Publishers**
A Division of Wadsworth, Inc.
Boston, Massachusetts 02116 U.S.A.

The Publication of *Across Cultures* was directed by the members of the
Newbury House Publishing Team at Heinle & Heinle:

Erik Gundersen, Editorial Director
Susan Mraz, Marketing Manager
Kristin Thalheimer, Production Editor

Also participating in the publication of this title were:

Publisher: Stanley J. Galek
Editorial Production Manager: Elizabeth Holthaus
Associate Editor: Lynne Telson Barsky
Assistant Editor: Karen Hazar
Associate Marketing Manager: Donna Hamilton
Production Assistant: Maryellen Eschmann
Manufacturing Coordinator: Mary Beth Lynch
Interior Designer and Compositor: Paola Di Stefano
Interior Illustrator: Carol O'Malia
Cover Designer: Hannus Design Associates
Project Manager: Kyrill Schabert

**Cover**: Alexej Jawlensky, *Helene with Colored Turban*, 1910, Solomon R. Guggenheim
Museum, New York. Photo: David Heald, copyright The Solomon R. Guggenheim
Museum, New York (65.1773.a, color)
Story Credits: See pages 305–306
Across Cultures: Universal Themes in Literature

Manufactured in the United States of America

**Library of Congress Cataloging-in-Publication Data**

Smalzer, William, 1946–
        Across Cultures: Universal Themes in Literature / William
        Smalzer, Phyllis L. Lim.
              p.      cm.
        ISBN 0-8384-3986-1
              1. English language—Textbooks for foreign speakers.  2. English
        literature. 3. Readers.     I. Lim, Phyllis L.     II. Title.
        PE1128.S5815 1993
        428.6'4—dc20                                          93-27952
                                                              CIP

10   9   8   7   6   5   4   3

# CONTENTS

# PREFACE

## OVERVIEW

**Across Cultures: Universal Themes in Literature** is a high-intermediate to advanced, integrated-skills reading text for students of English as a second or foreign language (ESL/EFL). The readings have been selected from the literature of countries where English is a first or a second language, including the United States, England, Nigeria, India, Australia, and Ireland. A variety of genres, including short stories, novellas, poems, and a short excerpt from a novel are addressed in this text. While the reading skill is emphasized throughout **Across Cultures**, listening, speaking, and writing are integral parts of each lesson.

Reading literature is an excellent and natural way to improve language comprehension and language use. Literary texts lead naturally to student involvement and to a desire to communicate. They provide authentic language and offer cultural and personal insights. In developing **Across Cultures**, we drew upon ideas from the integrated-skills and the communicative approaches to language learning as well as from the whole-language movement. We wanted to provide students with authentic literature which would naturally engage them in the language learning process as well as afford them an opportunity for increased self-understanding. While the approach is academic, the selections themselves are also suitable for students in intensive language programs who are not university-bound. The text has four units, each of which centers on a universal theme. It is not necessary for students to read each work. While it is desirable to proceed through the text in a linear way, most lessons can stand alone quite easily.

The approach of **Across Cultures** is experiential rather than literary. Students are asked to use their own experience as a basis for understanding the works. While the selections are multicultural, they were selected for the universality of their themes rather than as a showcase for different cultural traits or customs. Students will, of course, respond from their own cultural perspectives, and cross-cultural comparisons will arise naturally. Prereading activities are designed to raise students' existing schemata about the themes in the works. Background information is given to students on any cultural, historical, or linguistic areas where lack of knowledge might slow or impede comprehension.

The pedagogy calls for two readings of each work. Students are generally guided through the first reading with questions designed to ensure that they follow the main events of the text. The second reading asks them to focus more on details of the content and on linguistic elements of the text and to bring their own experiences to the reading.

While **Across Cultures** aims to give ESL/EFL students the background, guidance, and help they need to understand works that might otherwise remain inaccessible to them, it also recognizes that most second language students aspire to cope independently with authentic texts. Therefore, to help students become more independent readers, opportunities for students to take responsibility for comprehension themselves are interspersed throughout the text. There are three important ways this is accomplished:

1. Some lessons have a reader-response format in which students negotiate the meaning of the text among themselves.

2. In some lessons students are asked to write their own discussion questions, make predictions, participate in writing comprehension questions, and identify key words in the text.

3. Exercises throughout the text which deal with comprehension, discussion, and responding are largely student-centered because the experiential approach is consistent with a smaller role for the teacher in negotiating the meaning of the works and increased responsibility for the students.

Most activities in the lessons are text-based; that is, they are related to or grow naturally out of the students' interaction with the text and their own experiences which they bring to the text. When the work under study has been mastered, students are asked to extend the ideas in the text, that is, to go beyond the text, to connect ideas in the text with the outer world.

## FORMAT

The general format for the lessons serves the purposes of the book and the need for consistency in a textbook. However, the variety of both text genres and lengths makes it impossible for each lesson to fit perfectly into this format. Following is a discussion of our "prototypical" lesson format. Deviations from the format are noted at the end. Each lesson opens with an illustration and questions for thought and discussion.

### I. Getting Ready

*Getting Ready* ordinarily includes a discussion activity and/or a listening passage from the work to prepare students for the themes of the literary text to be read. It concludes with *Background,* a section with historical, cultural, and/or linguistic information the students are likely to need to understand the text more fully.

### II. Engaging with the Text

Students read the text the first time using *Signpost Questions* in the margin of the text that are designed to help students follow the story line. Students read the story a second time and answer other questions, some of which are content-based and factual and some of which are context-based to get students to relate their experiences and opinions to the text. For many works, students return to the text a third time to focus on specific lines of syntactic, idiomatic, stylistic, or other linguistic interest. Depending on the length and type of text, the activities in the second and third readings may be combined. For most texts, students discuss their answers in small groups before going on to the next reading.

### III. Strengthening Skills Through the Text

Students have an opportunity to respond in writing to the text and to share these responses with each other. *Responding to the Reading* responses can be kept in an ongoing journal. The next activity is the *Global Comprehension Check.* The format of this check varies from lesson to lesson (e.g., a summary-writing exercise, a true-false quiz, sentences to put in chronological order, etc.). Several lessons include *Dramatization,* in which a portion of the text is dramatized by groups of two or three students. The final activity in this section, which also takes students back to the text itself, is the *Text-based Focus on Vocabulary*. The format of the vocabulary exercises varies from lesson to lesson (e.g., finding a word or phrase in the text to match a definition, matching a word or phrase to the correct definition, selecting and explaining key words).

## IV. Moving Beyond the Text

This last section begins with *Discussion and Writing*. The questions help students explore the relevance of the readings in a larger context: to their lives or to people in general. The questions are often more academic in nature, bearing on sociological and psychological issues, or have students make comparisons between the story and similar situations in their countries. The last activity is usually a roleplay, roleplay interview, or a short speech. All of these final oral activities, like the discussion questions, are designed to move beyond the text by asking students to interpret a character's role at a later time or to take a stand on an issue suggested by the text.

Deviation from the prototypical lesson format occurs when the genre or the length of a work calls for it. For example, deviation occurs:

1. in poems, where Sections III and IV (but not Discussion or Responding in Writing) are omitted to accommodate a shorter work;

2. in short stories whose style suits them to a first exposure through listening rather than reading; and

3. in extended readings, where the length requires that stories be divided into parts and the lesson format be changed somewhat to fit the longer works.

## HOMEWORK AND CLASSWORK

We recommend that **Across Cultures** be divided between classwork and homework as follows (the poetry lessons, most of whose elements should be done in class because of their oral nature, are the exception to this distribution of assignments):

**Classwork**
Getting Ready discussions and listening passages
Follow-ups to first and second readings
Dramatizations
Questions to be discussed from Discussion and Writing
Other Moving Beyond the Text oral activities

**Homework**
First and second readings
Text-based Focus on Vocabulary
Questions assigned for writing from Discussion and Writing

**Classwork or homework**
Background
Journal writing from Responding to the Reading
Global Comprehension Check (sometimes collaborative in nature)

## COMPONENTS

In addition to the student text, an audio cassette for **Across Cultures** is also available. The audio cassette includes recordings of selected readings and involves students in the aural dimension of literature. A text/cassette package is also available.

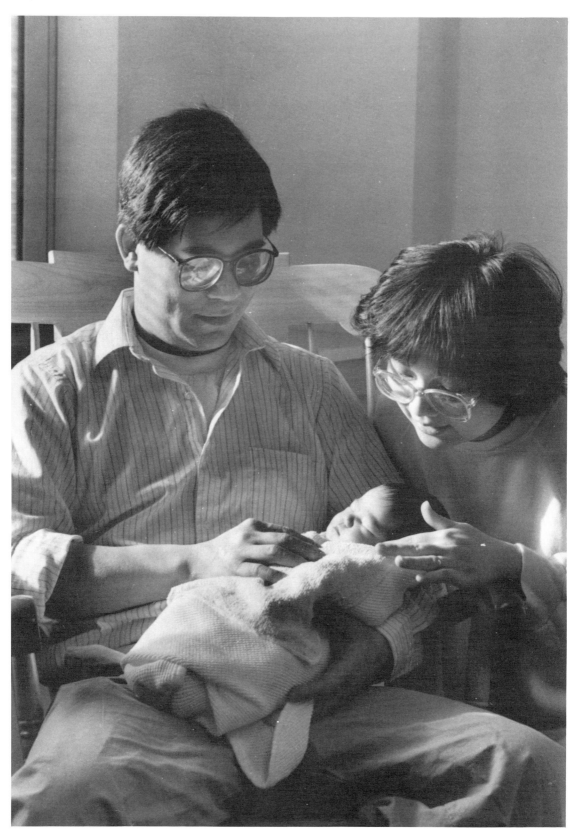

What's happening in this picture?
What's the relationship between the people?

# UNIT I

# Beginnings: Learning About Life

Is the woman hugging the boy or restraining him?
Why do you think so?

# Lesson 1

## THANK YOU, M'AM

### Langston Hughes

### U.S.A.

# I. GETTING READY

## A. Discussion: Proverbs about Bringing Up Children

Proverbs tell us in a few words a lot about the values of a society or culture. Their meaning, however, is not always easy to understand. See if you can match the number of each proverb with the letter of its paraphrased meaning below. Write the letter next to the number.

_____ **1.** To err is human; to forgive divine.

_____ **2.** Make the punishment fit the crime.

_____ **3.** As the twig is bent, so grows the tree.

_____ **4.** Spare the rod and spoil the child.

**a.** A child needs physical punishment in order to grow up properly.

**b.** A punishment should have a relationship to the type of misbehavior being punished.

**FOLLOW-UP**
Check your answers. Do you have any proverbs in your language that are similar to these?

**c.** Making mistakes is part of our human nature; when we forgive others, we are like God.

**d.** Early childhood influences determine how a person will be as an adult.

## B. Entering the Story through a Fable

A fable is a short story intended to teach a "moral" (a lesson about life). The moral is found at the end of the story. Read the following fable and answer the question that follows.

### The Young Thief and His Mother

A young man had been caught in the daring act of theft and had been condemned to be executed for it. He expressed his desire to see his mother and to speak with her before he was led to execution, and of course this was granted. When his mother came to him he said: "I want to whisper to you," and when she brought her ear near him, he nearly bit it off. All the bystanders were horrified and asked him what he could mean by such brutal and inhuman conduct. "It is to punish her," he said. "When I was young I began with stealing little things and brought them home to Mother. Instead of rebuking and punish-

ing me, she laughed and said: 'It will not be noticed.' It is because of her that I am here today."

"He is right, woman," said the Priest; "the Lord hath said:

**Train up a child in the way he should go; and when he is old he will not depart therefrom."**

## Question

Which proverb is most nearly the same as the moral of the fable?

**a.** To err is human; to forgive divine.

**b.** Make the punishment fit the crime.

**c.** As the twig is bent, so grows the tree.

**d.** Spare the rod and spoil the child.

**FOLLOW-UP**
Discuss as a class whether you agree with the moral of the fable.

# C.   Background

Read the following information, noting the italicized words, to help you understand the story more easily and fully.

"Thank you, M'am" is a straightforward story of an attempted purse snatching. There are only two characters, the intended victim and the would-be snatcher. We must infer a lot of information about the characters. For example, we know that Mrs. Jones lives in a **roominghouse** because the other "roomers" are mentioned. A roominghouse rents rooms to individual tenants who are ordinarily not related to each other. In some cases the roomers may share a common dining room and eat together. In Mrs. Jones's case, she has her own very tiny kitchen **(kitchenette).**

The two characters use some language with features that come from Black English. This colorful, expressive dialect adds to the reader's enjoyment of the story. It should be pointed out, however, that some features deviate from formal Standard English. For example:

**"You a lie!"** *(line 20)* You're a liar!

**"Ain't you got nobody home...?"** *(line 29)* Don't you have anybody at home...?

**"...you got..."** *(line 44)* ...you have...

*"I would not take you nowhere...."* (line 65)  I wouldn't take you anywhere....

*"Maybe you ain't been to your supper...."* (line 67)  Maybe you haven't had your supper...

*"You could of asked me."* (lines 74–75)  You could have asked me.

*"I were young once...."* (lines 82–83)  I was young once....

*"So you set down...."* (lines 90–91)  So you sit down....

*"...nor nobody else's"* (lines 117–118)  ...or anybody else's....

*"I got to...."* (lines 118–119)  I have to....

# II.  ENGAGING WITH THE TEXT

# A.  First Reading: Following the Story Line

To gain a general idea of how the story develops, read all the Signpost Questions in the margin before you begin to read. Then concentrate on answering the questions as you read the story.

**1.**

What does the boy do to make the woman angry?

### Thank You, M'am

1    She was a large woman with a large purse that had everything in it but a hammer and nails. It had a long strap, and she carried it slung across her shoulder. It was about eleven o'clock at night, dark, and she was walking alone, when a boy ran up behind her and tried to snatch
5    her purse. The strap broke with the sudden single tug the boy gave it from behind. But the boy's weight and the weight of the purse combined caused him to lose his balance. Instead of taking off full blast as he had hoped, the boy fell on his back on the sidewalk and his legs flew up. The large woman simply turned around and kicked him right
10   square in his blue-jeaned sitter. Then she reached down, picked the boy up by his shirt front, and shook him until his teeth rattled.

After that the woman said, "Pick up my pocketbook, boy, and give it here."

She still held him tightly. But she bent down enough to permit him
15   to stoop and pick up her purse. Then she said, "Now ain't you ashamed of yourself?"

Firmly gripped by his shirt front, the boy said, "Yes'm."

The woman said, "What did you want to do it for?"

The boy said, "I didn't aim to."

20 She said, "You a lie!"

By that time two or three people passed, stopped, turned to look, and some stood watching.

"If I turn you loose, will you run?" asked the woman.

"Yes'm," said the boy.

25 "Then I won't turn you loose," said the woman. She did not release him.

"Lady, I'm sorry," whispered the boy.

"Um-hum! Your face is dirty. I got a great mind to wash your face for you. Ain't you got nobody home to tell you to wash your face?"

30 "No'm," said the boy.

"Then it will get washed this evening," said the large woman, starting up the street, dragging the frightened boy behind her.

He looked as if he were fourteen or fifteen, frail and willow-wild, in tennis shoes and blue jeans.

35 The woman said, "You ought to be my son. I would teach you right from wrong. Least I can do right now is to wash your face. Are you hungry?"

"No'm," said the being-dragged boy. "I just want you to turn me loose."

40 "Was I bothering *you* when I turned that corner?" asked the woman.

"No'm."

"But you put yourself in contact with *me,*" said the woman. "If you think that that contact is not going to last awhile, you got another
45 thought coming. When I get through with you, sir, you are going to remember Mrs. Luella Bates Washington Jones."

Sweat popped out on the boy's face and he began to struggle. Mrs. Jones stopped, jerked him around in front of her, put a half nelson about his neck, and continued to drag him up the street. When she got
50 to her door, she dragged the boy inside, down a hall, and into a large kitchenette-furnished room at the rear of the house. She switched on the light and left the door open. The boy could hear other roomers laughing and talking in the large house. Some of their doors were open, too, so he knew he and the woman were not alone. The woman
55 still had him by the neck in the middle of her room.

She said, "What is your name?"

"Roger," answered the boy.

"Then, Roger, you go to that sink and wash your face," said the woman, whereupon she turned him loose—at last. Roger looked at
60 the door—looked at the woman—looked at the door—*and went to the sink.*

"Let the water run until it gets warm," she said. "Here's a clean towel."

"You gonna take me to jail?" asked the boy, bending over the sink.

65 "Not with that face, I would not take you nowhere," said the woman. "Here I am trying to get home to cook me a bite to eat and

## 2.

Where will she take the boy—to the police?

## 3.

Will the boy try to escape?

you snatch my pocketbook! Maybe you ain't been to your supper either, late as it be. Have you?"

"There's nobody home at my house," said the boy.

70    "Then we'll eat," said the woman. "I believe you're hungry—or been hungry—to try to snatch my pocketbook!"

"I want a pair of blue suede shoes," said the boy.

"Well, you didn't have to snatch *my* pocketbook to get some suede shoes," said Mrs. Luella Bates Washington Jones. "You could of

75    asked me."

"M'am?"

The water dripping from his face, the boy looked at her. There was a long pause. A very long pause. After he had dried his face, and not knowing what else to do, dried it again, the boy turned around, won-

80    dering what next. The door was open. He could make a dash for it down the hall. He could run, run, run, *run!*

The woman was sitting on the daybed. After a while she said, "I were young once and I wanted things I could not get."

There was another long pause. The boy's mouth opened. Then he

85    frowned, not knowing he frowned.

The woman said, "Um-hum! You thought I was going to say *but,* didn't you? You thought I was going to say, *but I didn't snatch people's pocketbooks.* Well, I wasn't going to say that." Pause. Silence. "I have done things, too, which I would not tell you, son—neither tell God, if

90    He didn't already know. Everybody's got something in common. So you set down while I fix us something to eat. You might run that comb through your hair so you will look presentable."

In another corner of the room behind a screen was a gas plate and an icebox. Mrs. Jones got up and went behind the screen. The woman

95    did not watch the boy to see if he was going to run now, nor did she watch her purse, which she left behind her on the daybed. But the boy took care to sit on the far side of the room, away from the purse, where he thought she could easily see him out of the corner of her eye if she wanted to. He did not trust the woman *not* to trust him. And he

100    did not want to be mistrusted now.

"Do you need somebody to go to the store," asked the boy, "maybe to get some milk or something?"

"Don't believe I do," said the woman, "unless you just want sweet milk yourself. I was going to make cocoa out of this canned milk I

105    got here."

"That will be fine," said the boy.

She heated some lima beans and ham she had in the icebox, made the cocoa, and set the table. The woman did not ask the boy anything about where he lived, or his folks, or anything else that would embar-

110    rass him. Instead, as they ate, she told him about her job in a hotel beauty shop that stayed open late, what the work was like, and how all kinds of women came in and out, blonds, redheads, and Spanish. Then she cut him a half of her ten-cent cake.

"Eat some more, son," she said.

115    When they were finished eating, she got up and said, "Now here, take this ten dollars and buy yourself some blue suede shoes. And next

**4.**

How will Mrs. Jones teach Roger a lesson about stealing?

120    time, do not make the mistake of latching onto *my* pocketbook *nor nobody else's*—because shoes got by devilish ways will burn your feet. I got to get my rest now. But from here on in, son, I hope you will behave yourself."

She led him down the hall to the front door and opened it. "Good night! Behave yourself, boy!" she said, looking out into the street as he went down the steps.

125    The boy wanted to say something other than, "Thank you, M'am," to Mrs. Luella Bates Washington Jones, but although his lips moved, he couldn't even say that as he turned at the foot of the barren stoop and looked up at the large woman in the door. Then she shut the door.

**FOLLOW-UP**
Check your answers as instructed by your teacher.

# B.    Second Reading

## Taking a Closer Look

Read the story a second time. Use the questions to gain a better understanding and to bring your experience to the story.

1.    Why was Roger unsuccessful in his purse snatching attempt?

2.    What was Roger's lie? Were you surprised when he told the truth in line 24?

3.    What kind of life do you think Mrs. Luella Jones had?

4.    What kind of life do you think Roger had? Have you ever known anyone like Roger?

5.    What kind of attitude did Luella show towards Roger? How did she teach him a lesson this way? Do you know anyone like Luella?

6.    Do you think Roger will ever see Mrs. Jones again?

## Delving More Deeply

Find the following text in the lines indicated. Use the surrounding text and your experience to give an informed answer.

1.    *"When I get through with you, sir, you are going to remember Mrs. Luella Bates Washington Jones."* (lines 45–46) Why do you think she introduced herself this way, i.e., using her full four names? Can we tell anything about her from these four names?

2.    When Mrs. Jones said, *"You could of asked me"*, (lines 74–75) what did she mean? How does Roger feel when he replies *"M'am?"* (line 76)

3. ***Then he frowned, not knowing he frowned.*** *(lines 84–85)* Why do you think Roger frowned?

4. Mrs. Jones tells Roger, ***"I have done things, too..."*** *(lines 88–89)* What kinds of "things" did she mean? Why do you think she said this to Roger?

5. ***He did not trust the woman* not *to trust him.*** *(line 99)* Why is it so important that she not mistrust him now?

6. Why didn't Roger say "Thank you, M'am" to Mrs. Jones as he left? *(line 124)*

**FOLLOW-UP**
Check your answers as instructed by your teacher.

# III. STRENGTHENING SKILLS THROUGH THE TEXT

## A. Responding to the Reading

Write at least 75 words on *one* of the following topics. When you finish, choose a classmate to listen to what you have written.

1. Did you like this story? Why or why not?

2. Does this story remind you of a related incident in your own experience? Describe the incident.

_____

_____

_____

_____

_____

_____

_____

_____

_____

_____

_____

_____

_____

_____

_____

# B.   Global Comprehension Check: Pivotal Points

Each event in a story is tied to what happens before it and, in turn, will affect what happens after it. For each of the following events, briefly summarize:

**a.**   what happened before it that causes or connects to it; and

**b.**   what happens after it as a result or consequence.

**1.   *Instead of taking off full blast as he had hoped, the boy fell on his back on the sidewalk and his legs flew up.*** (lines 7–9)

**a.**   _____

_____

**b.**   _____

_____

**2.   *Roger looked at the door—looked at the woman—looked at the door*—and went to the sink.** (lines 59–61)

**a.**   _____

_____

**b.**   _____

_____

3. **The woman did not watch the boy to see if he was going to run now, nor did she watch her purse...** *(lines 94–96)*

a. _____

_____

b. _____

_____


4. **...she got up and said, "Now here, take this ten dollars and buy yourself some blue suede shoes."** *(lines 115–116)*

a. _____

_____

b. _____

_____


# C.    Text-based Focus on Vocabulary

## The Vocabulary of Physical Confrontation

The following vocabulary comes from the depiction of the physical confrontation of the purse snatching, Mrs. Jones's restraint of Roger, and his reaction to all this. Find the italicized word or expression in the line(s) indicated. Check the context, and decide which answer means most nearly the same as the italicized word. Circle **a, b,** or **c.**

1.  *tug* (line 5)

    a.  sneaky glance
    b.  quick, hard pull
    c.  attempt

2.  *taking off full blast* (line 7)

    a.  running away as fast as possible
    b.  keeping the purse in his hands
    c.  returning the purse

3.  *rattled* (line 11)

    a.  fell on the ground
    b.  made a fierce, threatening expression
    c.  made short, sharp sounds like a loose window in the wind

4. **gripped** *(line 17)*

   a. held or seized tightly
   b. picked up off the ground
   c. shaken violently

5. **turn you loose** *(line 23)*

   a. don't call the police
   b. let you go
   c. let you turn around

6. **dragging** *(line 32)*

   a. pulling along against resistance
   b. pushing along in front
   c. carrying off the ground

7. **popped out** *(line 47)*

   a. was wiped away with a cloth
   b. disappeared by itself
   c. appeared suddenly

8. **jerked him** *(line 48)*

   a. kicked him with her foot
   b. pulled him with a sudden movement
   c. gently placed him

9. **make a dash for it** *(line 80)*

   a. take a long look
   b. rush out suddenly
   c. walk calmly away

**FOLLOW-UP**
Check your answers as
instructed by your teacher.

# Application: Vocabulary in a New Context

After you have checked your answers to the exercise above and are
familiar with the new words, think about the phrases or expressions
below, each of which contains a word from the previous exercise. The
word is used in a different context, with a slightly different meaning.
Explain what each phrase or sentence might mean from your current
understanding of the italicized words.

1. a **tug**boat _____

   _____

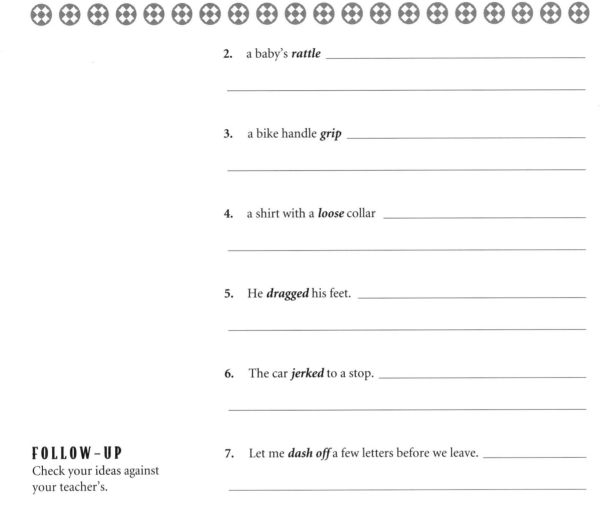

**2.** a baby's *rattle* _____

_____

**3.** a bike handle *grip* _____

_____

**4.** a shirt with a *loose* collar _____

_____

**5.** He *dragged* his feet. _____

_____

**6.** The car *jerked* to a stop. _____

_____

**FOLLOW-UP**
Check your ideas against
your teacher's.

**7.** Let me *dash off* a few letters before we leave. _____

_____

# IV.  MOVING BEYOND THE TEXT

## A.  Discussion and Writing

Discuss the following topics as a class or in groups. Your teacher may
assign a different topic to each group and ask a group leader to summarize its discussion for the class. Write on one or more of the topics
as instructed by your teacher.

**1.** What lesson did Mrs. Bates teach Roger? How effective was this
lesson? Can one lesson or experience have a lasting impact on a person?

**2.** Should punishment be the same for all persons committing the
same crime, or should other factors be taken into consideration? (For

example, should young criminals be treated differently from older criminals? Should a poor person who steals to feed his family be punished the same as a thief with money? Should a woman be punished the same as a man? etc.)

**3.** Both Langston Hughes's story and the fable, "The Young Thief and His Mother," deal with wrongdoing by young people. Both contain a message about adults' responsibility towards young wrongdoers. Are the messages the same or different? Explain. Do you agree with the message(s)?

**4.** Do you agree with this proverb: **Spare the rod and spoil the child** ? Should children be punished physically when they misbehave or do wrong, as Roger did?

# B.   Roleplay

Prepare the following roleplay orally, without writing. The first line is given to help you begin.

*[Two students—**Roger and his 10-year-old son**] It's 15 years later. Roger has a good job in construction, is married, and has a young son. The boy has been caught stealing candy from the local grocery store, but he is denying it. Roger is talking to his son.*

ROGER: Son, we have to have a serious talk. I want you to tell me what happened.

Do you think these people are enjoying themselves?

# Lesson 2

## MY PAPA'S WALTZ

### Theodore Roethke

### U.S.A.

# I.  GETTING READY

## A.  Discussion: Exploiting the Picture

Using the title of the poem and the illustration, discuss the following questions with a partner or in a small group.

1.  Who are these people?

2.  Where are they?

3.  What are they doing?

4.  Look at the definitions of these words; then find an example of each one in the illustration.

    *dizzy*  feeling as if everything is turning around

    *countenance*  face, including the expression on it

    *wrist*  the joint between the hand and arm

    *knuckle*  the joint in a finger

    *buckle*  the fastener that holds a belt together

    *clinging*  holding tightly, like a vine on a wall

**FOLLOW-UP**
Discuss your answers to the questions with another group or with the whole class.

5.  Using your imagination, make up a short story of a few sentences to *explain* what is happening in this picture. Be sure to include how each person feels.

# II.  ENGAGING WITH THE TEXT

## A.  First Exposure: Listening

Listen to the poem as your teacher reads it. Then write down as many words as you can remember from the poem, excluding the ones in question 4 above. Then share your words with the class. From the words you have together, decide if this is mostly a happy poem or a sad poem.

# B.   Second Exposure: Reading

Read the poem carefully to answer these questions.

1.   What had the father been doing before he began dancing with his son?

2.   What in the poem tells us that this was not a completely pleasant experience for the little boy?

3.   How do you know that the mother was not happy?

4.   How old do you think the little boy was? Why do you think so?

**FOLLOW-UP**
Discuss your answers with your classmates.

**My Papa's Waltz**


The whiskey on your breath

Could make a small boy dizzy;

But I hung on like death:

Such waltzing was not easy.


We romped until the pans

Slid from the kitchen shelf;

My mother's countenance

Could not unfrown itself.


The hand that held my wrist

Was battered on one knuckle;

At every step you missed

My right ear scraped a buckle.


You beat time on my head

With a palm caked hard by dirt,

Then waltzed me off to bed

Still clinging to your shirt.

## C.  Discussion Questions

Discuss the following questions with your partner or in small groups.

1.  What might have caused the father to behave the way he did?

2.  Do you think the little boy enjoyed this dance with his father at all?

3.  Why didn't the little boy try to escape from his father?

4.  Why didn't the mother try to stop the father?

5.  What do you think happened between the mother and father after the little boy went to bed?

6.  Circle the adjectives that you think best describe how the little boy felt during the dance:

**FOLLOW-UP**
Share your ideas with another group or with the whole class.

| | | | |
|---|---|---|---|
| confused | excited | happy | proud |
| lonely | sad | frightened | angry |
| jealous | terrified | loving | guilty |
| embarrassed | | | |

# III. STRENGTHENING SKILLS THROUGH THE TEXT

## A.  Responding to the Reading

Write at least 75 words on *one* of the following topics. When you finish, choose a classmate to listen to what you have written.

1.  Did you like this poem? Why or why not?

2.  Write a letter to the father in the poem, telling him what you think about him.

_____

_____

_____

## B.   Rhyme

**FOLLOW-UP**
Check your answers with
your teacher.

Listen to the poem again as your teacher reads it. Indicate the line
numbers of the final words that rhyme perfectly to the ear, e.g.,
lines 1 and 3 (*breath* and *death*).

## C.   Choral Repetition

**FOLLOW-UP**
Think about how you feel
this time in comparison to
the first time you heard the
poem. Do you feel the
same or different?

Divide into four groups. Each group will take one stanza of the poem
to prepare for choral reading. When each group is ready, read the
poem chorally as a class.

It's easy to think of these dolls as different generations in the same family.
What might they represent if we take them all as the same person?

# Lesson 3

## ELEVEN

### Sandra Cisneros

### U.S.A.

# I. GETTING READY

## A. Recollection and Reflection: School Days

Think back to the time in your life when you were eleven years old.

✦ What grade were you in when you were eleven years old?

✦ What did your classroom look like?

Now close your eyes and listen as your teacher reads a few questions. Just listen and think about that time of your life. When you are ready, open your eyes.

✦ Who was your teacher when you were eleven?

✦ Did you like him or her?

✦ Did your teacher ever make you do something you really didn't want to do?

✦ Can you remember some of your classmates? Who?

✦ Was there someone you especially liked?

**FOLLOW-UP**
Tell your partner what you remember about your classroom, your teacher, and your classmates when you were eleven. Use the questions to prompt your memory.

✦ What was he or she like?

✦ Was there someone you particularly disliked?

✦ What was he or she like?

✦ Did you like school? Why or why not?

## B. Background

Read the following information, noting the italicized words, to help you understand the story more easily and fully.

The author of "Eleven" is an adult, but she has skillfully conveyed the feelings of an eleven-year-old by writing the story as if it were being told by a child that age. She writes the way a young girl that age might think and talk to herself. While the incident in the story is a minor one from the perspective of an adult, it is a major, painful event in the life of young Rachel. The incident takes place on her eleventh birthday.

The language here is childlike and colloquial (informal, spoken language), just as an 11-year-old might speak. For example, **kind of** (line 15: "kind of like an onion") is normal, spoken language, whereas **rather** would normally be preferred in writing. Rachel also uses the preposition **like** as a conjunction (lines 36–37: "like you could use it for a jump rope"; also in lines 50, 68, and 76). This is a very colloquial usage. Many native speakers would prefer **as though** or **as if.**

# II. ENGAGING WITH THE TEXT

## A. First Exposure: Listening to the Story

Read the following questions before listening to each section of the story. Stop the tape to discuss each question before listening to the next section.

**Section 1.** *(lines 1–47)* Why does Rachel end up with the red sweater on her desk when she says the sweater isn't hers?

**Section 2.** *(lines 48–78)* Will Rachel finally accept the sweater as hers and put it on?

**Section 3.** *(lines 79–end)* How will the story end? Who does the sweater belong to?

## B. Second Exposure: Reading

### Taking a Closer Look

Read the story. Use the questions that follow the story to gain a better understanding and to bring your experience to the story.

#### Eleven

1    What they don't understand about birthdays and what they never tell you is that when you're eleven, you're also ten, and nine, and eight, and seven, and six, and five, and four, and three, and two, and one. And when you wake up on your eleventh birthday you expect to

5    feel eleven, but you don't. You open your eyes and everything's just like yesterday, only it's today. And you don't feel eleven at all. You feel like you're still ten. And you are—underneath the year that makes you eleven.

Like some days you might say something stupid, and that's the part
of you that's still ten. Or maybe some days you might need to sit on
your mama's lap because you're scared, and that's the part of you
that's five. And maybe one day when you're all grown up maybe you
will need to cry like if you're three, and that's okay. That's what I tell
Mama when she's sad and needs to cry. Maybe she's feeling three.

Because the way you grow old is kind of like an onion or like the
rings inside a tree trunk or like my little wooden dolls that fit one
inside the other, each year inside the next one. That's how being
eleven years old is.

You don't feel eleven. Not right away. It takes a few days, weeks
even, sometimes even months before you say Eleven when they ask
you. And you don't feel smart eleven, not until you're almost twelve.
That's the way it is.

Only today I wish I didn't have only eleven years rattling inside me
like pennies in a tin Band-Aid box. Today I wish I was one hundred
and two instead of eleven because if I was one hundred and two I'd
have known what to say when Mrs. Price put the red sweater on my
desk. I would've known how to tell her it wasn't mine instead of just
sitting there with that look on my face and nothing coming out of my
mouth.

"Whose is this?" Mrs. Price says, and she holds the red sweater up
in the air for all the class to see. "Whose? It's been sitting in the coat-
room for a month."

"Not mine," says everybody. "Not me."

"It has to belong to somebody," Mrs. Price keeps saying, but
nobody can remember. It's an ugly sweater with red plastic buttons
and a collar and sleeves all stretched out like you could use it for a
jump rope. It's maybe a thousand years old and even if it belonged to
me I wouldn't say so.

Maybe because I'm skinny, maybe because she doesn't like me, that
stupid Sylvia Saldívar says, "I think it belongs to Rachel." An ugly
sweater like that, all raggedy and old, but Mrs. Price believes her. Mrs.
Price takes the sweater and puts it right on my desk, but when I open
my mouth nothing comes out.

"That's not, I don't, you're not… Not mine," I finally say in a little
voice that was maybe me when I was four.

"Of course it's yours," Mrs. Price says. "I remember you wearing it
once." Because she's older and the teacher, she's right and I'm not.

Not mine, not mine, not mine, but Mrs. Price is already turning to
page thirty-two, and math problem number four. I don't know why
but all of a sudden I'm feeling sick inside, like the part of me that's
three wants to come out of my eyes, only I squeeze them shut tight
and bite down on my teeth real hard and try to remember today I am
eleven, eleven. Mama is making a cake for me for tonight, and when
Papa comes home everybody will sing Happy birthday, happy birthday to you.

But when the sick feeling goes away and I open my eyes, the red
sweater's still sitting there like a big red mountain. I move the red

sweater to the corner of my desk with my ruler. I move my pencil and books and eraser as far from it as possible. I even move my chair a
60 little to the right. Not mine, not mine, not mine.

In my head I'm thinking how long till lunchtime, how long till I can take the red sweater and throw it over the schoolyard fence, or leave it hanging on a parking meter, or bunch it up into a little ball and toss it in the alley. Except when math period ends Mrs. Price says
65 loud and in front of everybody, "Now, Rachel, that's enough," because she sees I've shoved the red sweater to the tippy-tip corner of my desk and it's hanging all over the edge like a waterfall, but I don't care.

"Rachel," Mrs. Price says. She says it like she's getting mad. "You put that sweater on right now and no more nonsense."
70 "But it's not—"

"Now!" Mrs. Price says.

This is when I wish I wasn't eleven, because all the years inside of me—ten, nine, eight, seven, six, five, four, three, two, and one—are pushing at the back of my eyes when I put one arm through one sleeve
75 of the sweater that smells like cottage cheese, and then the other arm through the other and stand there with my arms apart like if the sweater hurts me and it does, all itchy and full of germs that aren't even mine.

That's when everything I've been holding in since this morning,
80 since when Mrs. Price put the sweater on my desk, finally lets go, and all of a sudden I'm crying in front of everybody. I wish I was invisible but I'm not. I'm eleven and it's my birthday today and I'm crying like I'm three in front of everybody. I put my head down on the desk and bury my face in my stupid clown-sweater arms. My face all hot and
85 spit coming out of my mouth because I can't stop the little animal noises from coming out of me, until there aren't any more tears left in my eyes, and it's just my body shaking like when you have the hiccups, and my whole head hurts like when you drink milk too fast.

But the worst part is right before the bell rings for lunch. That stu-
90 pid Phyllis Lopez, who is even dumber than Sylvia Saldívar, says she remembers the red sweater is hers! I take it off right away and give it to her, only Mrs. Price pretends like everything's okay.

Today I'm eleven. There's a cake Mama's making for tonight, and when Papa comes home from work we'll eat it. There'll be candles and
95 presents and everybody will sing Happy birthday, happy birthday to you, Rachel, only it's too late.

I'm eleven today. I'm eleven, ten, nine, eight, seven, six, five, four, three, two, and one, but I wish I was one hundred and two. I wish I was anything but eleven, because I want today to be far away already,
100 far away like a runaway balloon, like a tiny *o* in the sky, so tiny-tiny you have to close your eyes to see it.

## Questions

**1.** How did Rachel explain an eleven-year-old's saying something stupid? An adult's feeling like crying?

**2.** Rachel probably didn't speak up more strongly about the sweater because she:

    **a.** didn't know English very well
    **b.** was shy and afraid
    **c.** thought it might be hers.

**3.** Should Rachel have insisted very loudly that the sweater wasn't hers? Why or why not?

**4.** How did the red sweater make Rachel feel? Why do you think she felt so strongly? Was she overreacting or were her feelings normal? Have you ever had this kind of reaction to a *thing*?

**5.** What strategies did Rachel use to try to distance herself from the sweater? What plans did she have to get rid of the sweater? Why couldn't she carry out these plans?

**6.** Why did Rachel put the sweater on when it wasn't hers? Should she have refused to do this?

**7.** Why do you think that wearing the sweater was so repugnant to Rachel?

**8.** How did Mrs. Price act when another student remembered that the sweater was hers?

## FOLLOW-UP

Discuss your answers with your classmates in small groups.

**9.** How was Rachel's birthday going to be celebrated later that evening? Do you think Rachel will enjoy this party? Why? If this incident had happened on another day, would Rachel have reacted as strongly? Explain.

## Delving More Deeply

Find the following text in the lines indicated. Use the surrounding text and your experience to give an informed answer.

**1.** At the beginning of the story Rachel talks about **they** and **you** without explaining who **they** and **you** are. Read lines 1–22 and notice how she uses **they** and **you.** Who is **they**? Who is **you**?

**2.** *...the worst part is right before the bell rings for lunch.* What happened, and why was this the "worst part" of the whole experience for Rachel? *(line 89)*

**FOLLOW-UP**
Discuss your answers in
small groups.

**3.** What was Rachel talking about when she said, ***...only it's too late***? Why do you think she felt this way? *(line 96)*

# III. STRENGTHENING SKILLS THROUGH THE TEXT

## A. Responding to the Reading

Write at least 75 words on *one* of the following topics. When you finish, choose a classmate to listen to what you have written.

1. Did you like this story? Why or why not?

2. When you were a young pupil at school, did you ever have an experience similar to Rachel's? Explain what happened and how you felt. How do you feel about what happened now that you are older?

_____

_____

_____

_____

_____

_____

_____

_____

_____

_____

_____

_____

_____

_____

_____

_____

## B.    Global Comprehension Check: Comparing Summaries

Read the two summaries of "Eleven" carefully. Then decide which one is better. Which summary gives a clearer account of the main events of the story *and* interprets the events more accurately?

### Summary 1

Sandra Cisneros's "Eleven" paints an accurate picture of a girl on her 11th birthday. Rachel learns on that day that she is not only 11, but all her previous ages as well. Something happens that day involving her teacher, two of her classmates, and a red sweater that makes Rachel feel bad. Rachel gets so upset that she cries. The incident makes such a strong impression on Rachel that she will not be able to enjoy the birthday party her parents are planning for her later that day. Rachel learns that being eleven is different from what she expected.

### Summary 2

In "Eleven," Sandra Cisneros relates the humiliation and anguish a young girl feels at being forced to claim and wear a sweater that is not hers. Rachel's teacher makes Rachel take a red sweater that was left at school because another pupil said it was Rachel's. Too shy to speak up, Rachel accepts the sweater but begins to push it away. Noticing this, the teacher insists that she put it on. When she does, Rachel feels revolted at the sweater, embarrassed by her tears, and exasperated by the realization that though she is 11, she is acting like a much younger Rachel who is still part of her.

**FOLLOW-UP**
Discuss your choices.

## C.    Text-based Focus on Language

*Figurative language* is a way of saying something differently from the ordinary way. Figurative language is enjoyable because it gives us the opportunity to use our imagination, and it increases the emotional intensity of what is written or said. Figurative language often appeals to our senses of sight, hearing, smell, and touch, and this appeal helps to make an abstract idea more concrete. It is also very efficient language because a lot can be expressed with few words.

"Eleven" is particularly rich in figurative language. In this exercise, you will learn what **similes, overstatements,** and **images** are and look *at* and *for* examples of each.

Use the line numbers to find the examples in the text. Then answer the questions.

**1.** A *simile* seeks to help us understand something by comparing it to something different. Similes contain a comparison word (e.g., *as, than, similar to, like*).

"...today I wish I didn't have only eleven years rattling inside me *like pennies in a tin Band-Aid box*" *(lines 23–24)*. The simile in bold expresses how Rachel felt about herself that day. Circle the adjectivals that the simile makes you think of *in this context*.
Rachel feels . . .

noisy and disruptive          conspicuous          hidden          awkward

valuable                              special               useful

**2.** Find three similes Rachel uses to explain **the way people age or become older** *(lines 15–18)*. Write them below.

**a.** (3 words)_____

**b.** (7 words)_____

_____

**c.** (11 words)_____

_____

_____

Which of these three similes do you like the best? Why?

**3.** Find the simile in line 57. Write it below.

_____

_____

What two things are being compared?_____

_____

What does this simile mean?_____

_____

**4.** An *overstatement* is an exaggeration. Rachel says, "Today I wish I was one hundred and two instead of eleven..." *(lines 24–25)*. Does this overstatement add a humorous or sad touch to the story? Why?

**5.** Find the overstatement which helps us to understand how awful the sweater is to Rachel *(lines 34–38)*. Write it below.

_____

How would you feel if someone applied this overstatement to your car?

**6.** An *image* is a representation in language of what we can sense, i.e., see, hear, smell, or feel. Rachel says, "...the part of me that's three wants to come out of my eyes..." *(lines 50–51)*. She repeats, "...all the years inside of me...are pushing at the back of my eyes..." *(lines 72–74)*. These images help us *feel* the pressure building behind her eyes. What is causing this pressure? Fear? Anger? Tears? Explain why you think so.

**7.** "I put my head down...and bury my face in my stupid clown-sweater arms. My face all hot and spit coming out of my mouth because I can't stop the little animal noises from coming out of me..." *(lines 83–86)* Underline the images, which are both visual and auditory (related to hearing). What feelings is Rachel having at this moment? Which images have a stronger impact on you, the visual or the auditory?

**FOLLOW–UP**

Check your answers as instructed by your teacher.

# IV. MOVING BEYOND THE TEXT

# A. Discussion and Writing

Discuss the following topics as a class or in groups. Your teacher may assign a different topic to each group and ask a group leader to summarize its discussion for the class. Write on one or more of the topics as instructed by your teacher.

**1.** Are some ages more difficult than others? Do you remember any particular age that was especially difficult for you? Why?

**2.** If you were Rachel's older brother or sister who was writing a letter to Rachel trying to make her feel better, what would you say to her?

**3.** If the main character of the story were a young boy instead of a young girl, would the story be the same? Would the teacher have treated him the way she treated Rachel? Would the boy have reacted differently from Rachel? How?

4. Do you feel other, younger ages inside of you that continue to exist with your present age? Do you see this in other people? Or are you and others simply the age you are at the moment? Support your view with examples.

5. Why didn't Mrs. Price apologize for her mistake? Should parents and teachers apologize to a child when they make a mistake that hurts the child's feelings? Why or why not?

# B.   Roleplay

Prepare one or more of the following roleplays orally, without writing. The first line is given to help you begin.

1. *[Two students: Rachel and Mrs. Price]* *It's ten years later when Rachel goes back to her school to visit.*

RACHEL: You probably don't remember that incident with the sweater, but it was important to me at the time.

2. *[Three students: Rachel, Sylvia, and Phyllis]* *It's a few minutes after school gets out and the three girls are just leaving the school yard.*

RACHEL: I hate you, Sylvia Saldivar! And, Phyllis, you're stupid. And, and, you're both liars!!!

Is this boy off on a vacation?
Where might he be going?

# Lesson 4

excerpts from

## THE ADRIAN MOLE DIARIES

### Sue Townsend

### England

# I. GETTING READY

## A. Discussion: Teenage Problems

Look at 15-year-old Adrian Mole's journal entry, in which he contemplates reasons for living as well as reasons for not living. Then answer the questions about them. (Note: "O" levels are standardized secondary exams in England).

**Tuesday, March 15th**

*Reasons for living*
Things might get better

*Reasons for not living*
You die anyway
Life is nothing but anguish
There is too much cruelty in the world
"O" levels in June
My parents hate me
I've lost Pandora
Nobody leaves Barry Kent's gang alive

### Questions

1.  What kind of mood is Adrian in?

2.  Is he worried about school?

3.  Do you think his parents really hate him? Why might he think so?

4.  Who do you think Pandora is?

5.  What kind of person do you suppose Barry Kent is?

**FOLLOW-UP**
Share your ideas with
the class.

6.  Which of Adrian's reasons for not living do you think he might change his mind about in the future?

7.  How normal do you find Adrian's problems?

## B. Entering the Story through Listening

On the tape, listen to early passages from "The Adrian Mole Diaries" and answer the questions that follow each passage.

**Passage 1.** *(Entry for Monday, March 7th)*
In this passage we learn about Adrian's evening with the gang.

1. What did Barry Kent do?
2. Did Adrian think it was funny? Why or why not?

**Passage 2.** *(Entry for Saturday, January 29th)*
In this passage we learn about Bert Baxter, an old man whom Adrian helps out as part of a volunteer program at his school.

1. Why did Adrian invite Bert for dinner the next day?
2. Why do you think Adrian was angry with his parents?

**Passage 3.** *(Entry from Sunday, December 26th)*
In this passage we learn about Pandora, Adrian's sometime-girlfriend.

1. Did Adrian and Pandora like the presents they received?
2. Did you find anything amusing in this entry? If so, what?

**Passage 4.** *(Entries from January 3rd, 4th, 5th, 6th, 7th)*
In this passage we hear about Adrian's parents and their marital problems.

1. What did you learn about Adrian's parents?

**FOLLOW-UP**
Discuss your answers with
your teacher.

# C. Background

Read the following information, noting the italicized words, to help you understand the story more easily and fully.

Adrian is a teenager growing up in a contemporary English town. He feels overwhelmed by his problems and believes his parents are indifferent to him. Adrian keeps a daily diary, or journal, in which he records his feelings and observations about his problems and the people and events in his life. The period from Tuesday, March 22nd to Sunday, April 16th covers the period in his life when he runs away from home and turns sixteen years old.

Some references and vocabulary are explained below. If a word is specifically British, it is followed by the abbreviation *(Br.)*. If it is slang, it is followed by the abbreviation *(sl.)*. Also there are a few references to people that need explaining since the reading is an excerpt from a novel, and some characters have been introduced earlier.

*(3/22)*    **Building Society** a financial institution similar to a savings bank

*(3/23)*    **Bob Martins** vitamin tablets for dogs
**pigs** *(sl.)* derogatory term for the police (also American)
**gay** *(sl.)* homosexual (also American)

*(3/27)*    **crumblies** *(sl.)* parents, older people

*(3/28)*    **bloke** *(Br. sl.)* guy
**Wellingtons** rubber boots
**Doc Marten's** kind of street shoe
**Plimsolls** athletic shoes; also, sneakers (Br. and American.)
**serviettes** *(Br.)* napkins

*(3/29)*    **sodding** British obscenity
**spots** *(Br.)* pimples
**tin opener** *(Br.)* can opener
**lead** *(Br.)* leash for a dog

*(3/30)*    **lorry** *(Br.)* truck

*(3/31)*    **Chief Constable** police officer
**put-u-up** *(Br.)* cot, foldaway bed

*(4/1)*    **All Fools' Day** April Fools' Day
**pound** British currency (approximately $1.60 U.S. in 1993)

*(4/4)*    **vicar** an Anglican (British) priest of a parish
**existentialist nihilist** philosophical terms Adrian borrows to describe his sad, skeptical mood
**Monophysitism, Lamaism** kinds of religions or doctrines

*(4/5)*    **Calvinism, Shakers, Quietism** kinds of religions or doctrines

*(4/9)*    **"Bloody Camille"** Camille is a character in a play who dies dramatically and slowly

*(4/11)*    **bugger** British obscenity.

*(4/15)*    **CND** Campaign for Nuclear Disarmament, a British anti-nuclear organization

# II.  ENGAGING WITH THE TEXT

# A.  First Reading

Read to answer the following questions.

1.    Why does Adrian run away from home?

2.    What does he hope to accomplish by this act?

3. What happens to him while he is on his own?

4. What happens when he finally gets home?

excerpts from
### The Adrian Mole Diaries

**Tuesday March 22nd**

I have decided to leave home.

Nobody will care. In fact my parents probably won't notice that I've gone. I have given the Building Society one week's notice of my intention to withdraw £50. There is no point in losing interest unnecessarily.

**Wednesday March 23rd**

I am making preparations to leave. I have already written my goodbye letters.

Pandora,
I may be gone for some time.
    Adrian

Dear Mum and Dad,
By the time you read this I will be far away. I know I am breaking the law in running away before my 16th birthday, but, quite honestly, a life as a fugitive is preferable to my present miserable existence.
    From your son,
    A. Mole

Dear Bert,
I've taken your advice and gone off to see the world. You don't need me now that you've got all those wimpy volunteers hanging around you. But watch out, Bert, you are only popular because they think you are a character. Any day now they will find out that you are bad-tempered and foul-mouthed. I will send you a postcard from one of the corners of the world.
    Adios Amigo,
P.S. Give my love to Sabre, and don't forget to give him his Bob Martins.

Dear Grandma,
Sorry to worry you but I have gone away for a bit. Please stop feuding with Mum and Dad. "They know not what they do." Rosie is lovely now, she would really like to see you.
    Lots of love,
    Adrian

35 Dear Mr. Scruton,
By the time you read this I will be miles away from your scabby
school. So don't bother sending the truant officer round. I intend to
educate myself in the great school of life, and will never return.
    A. Mole

40 P.S. Did you know that your nickname is "Pop-Eye"? So-called
because of your horrible manic sticking-out eyes. Everybody laughs at
you behind your back, especially Mr. Jones the PE teacher.
P.P.S. I think you should be ashamed of the fact that Barry Kent *still
can't read* after spending five years in your school.

45 Dearest Elizabeth,
I'm sorry that I have to leave just as our love was bursting into bud.
But a boy has to do what a boy has to do.
    Don't wait for me, Elizabeth. I may be gone for some time.
    Yours with regrets and fondest memories,
50    Aidy Mole

Baz,
I've blown town. The pigs will be looking for me. Try and put 'em off
the scent will you?
    Brains

55 Nigel,
Good luck with being gay. I, too, am different from the herd; so I
understand what it is like to be always out of step.
    It's the ordinary people who will have to learn to accept us.
    Any road up as we say in these parts.
60    Rock on tommy!
    Your old mate,
    Aidy

### Thursday March 24th

Five days to go. I am growing a beard.
65    I have borrowed my dead granddad's suitcase. Luckily he had the
same initials as me. His name was Arnold.
    Grandma thinks I am using it for a camping trip with the Youth
Club. The truth would kill her.

### Friday March 25th

70 I have started packing my case. A certain amount of rationalization
has had to take place regarding clean socks and underwear.
    I will have to lower my standards and only change them every other
day. No sign of the beard yet.

### Sunday March 27th

75
The crumblies spent three hours forcing Rosie to sit up on her own.
But she kept sliding down the cushions and laughing. If she could talk
I know what she would say, "Stop interfering in my development, I'll
do it when I'm ready!"

80
I pointed out that her back muscles are not strong enough yet, but
the crumblies wouldn't listen. They said things like, "Rosie is excep-
tionally forward," and "You were nowhere near as advanced as she is
at five months!"

They will be sorry for these cutting words on Tuesday.

85
### Monday March 28th

An old American bloke called Ian MacGregor has been put in charge
of the National Coal Board. It is a disgrace!

England has got loads of ruthless, out-of-work executives who
would be delighted to be given a chance to close their own country's
90
coalmines down. Mr. Scargill is quite right to protest, he has my full
support on this issue.

Packed my pajamas and dressing gown.

It is RA day tomorrow. I have made out a list of vital equipment,
clothing etc.

95
| | |
|---|---|
| Roller skates | *Penguin Medical Dictionary* |
| Shaving kit | Junior aspirins |
| 3 jumpers | First aid box |
| 2 shirts | Sleeping bag |
| 3 pair trousers | Camping stove |
| 5 pairs socks | Matches |
| Wellingtons | 6 tins beans |
| Doc Marten's | Spoon |
| Plimsolls | Knife |
| Orange waterproof trousers | Fork |
| 4 pairs underpants | Cruet |
| 4 vests | Serviettes |
| Diary | Transistor radio |
| Survival handbook | The dog |
| *Robinson Crusoe* | |
| *Down and Out in Paris and London* | |

100

105

110

### Tuesday March 29th

| | |
|---|---|
| *6 a.m.* | Packed everything on list apart from the dog. |
| *6:05* | Took everything out. |
| *6:10* | Repacked. |
| *6:15* | Took everything out. |
| *6:30* | Repacked, but no good. Still can't get suitcase lid to shut. Decide not to take roller skates. |
| *6:33* | Ditto Wellingtons |

115

| | 6:35 | Ditto camping stove. |
|---|---|---|
| 120 | 6:37 | Suitcase lid shuts. |
| | 6:39 | Try to pick up suitcase. Can't. |
| | 6:40 | Take out tins of beans. |
| | 6:44 | Repack. |
| | 6:45 | Get in a rage. |
| 125 | 6:48 | Take cruet and serviettes out. |
| | 6:55 | Take Doc Marten's out of suitcase. Decide to wear them instead. Spend fifteen precious minutes in doing the sodding laces up. |
| | 7:10 | Examine spots in bathroom. |
| 130 | 7:13 | Check farewell letters have got stamps on. |
| | 7:14 | Pick suitcase up. Not bad. Not good. |
| | 7:15 | Repack suitcase with half previous clothes. |
| | 7:19 | Pick suitcase up. Better. |
| | 7:20 | Remember sleeping bag. Try to pack it in suitcase. |
| 135 | 7:21 | Get in another rage. |
| | 7:22 | Kick suitcase across bedroom floor. |
| | 7:22.30 secs. | Crumblies shout from their bedroom. Demanding to know what all the noise is about. |
| | 7:24 | Make tea. Crumblies ask why I have got a tin opener in the breast pocket of my blazer. I lie and say that I've got Domestic Science for my first lesson. |
| 140 | | |
| | 7:31 | Feed dog, make baby's breakfast slops. |
| | 7:36 | Check Building Society account book. |
| | 7:37 | Groom dog. Pack its personal possessions in suitcase: dog bowl, brush, vaccination certificate, worm tablets, lead, choke chain, 5 tins chum, bag of Winalot. |
| 145 | | |
| | 7:42 | Try to pick up suitcase, can't. |
| | 7:47 | Decide to leave dog behind. Break the news to it. |
| | 7:49 | Dog cries. Crumblies shout at it to be quiet. |
| 150 | 7:50 | Decide to take the dog after all. |
| | 8:00 | Pack minimum amount of stuff in Adidas bag. |
| | 8:10 | Hide Granddad's suitcase in wardrobe. |
| | 8:15 | Say goodbye to Rosie. |
| | 8:20 | Put dog on lead. |
| 155 | 8:21 | Wait until crumblies are distracted. |
| | 8:25 | Leave house with dog. |
| | 8:30 | Post farewell letters. |
| | 9:00 | Draw £50 out of Building Society, and head North. |

**Wednesday March 30th**

160 *3 p.m. Watford Gap Service Station. M1 Motorway.*
My first mistake was waiting for a lift on the southern bound side of the motorway approach road.

My second mistake was bringing the dog.

*7:31 Sheffield.*

165 Got a lift in a pig delivery lorry. This is just my luck!

I had a very long conversation with the driver, which is a miracle really, because I couldn't hear a word he was saying over the noise of the engine. I am having to keep a low profile. Sheffield is rat fink Lucas's stamping ground.

170 Why doesn't my beard hurry up and grow?

*9:30 p.m. Leeds.*

Tuned into the Radio Four nine o'clock news. But no mention was made of my mysterious disappearance. I am writing this at the side of the canal. A man has just come up and asked me if I want to sell the

175 dog. I was tempted but said no.

*11:00 p.m.* Rang home, but the phone wasn't snatched up immediately like it is in the films about runaway children.

Another sign of their indifference.

**Thursday March 31st**

180 *1 a.m.* The man who asked about the dog has just approached me and asked me if I want to sell *myself*. I said, "No," and told him my father was the Chief Constable of Wales.

He said, "Why are you sleeping rough in Leeds?"

I told another lie, I said, "My father has sent me on an initiative

185 test. If I survive this he'll put me down for Hendon Police College."

Why did I tell him such an elaborate lie? Why? I had to listen while he told me his many grievances against the police. I promised to pass them on to my father and copied his name and address into my diary:

Stanley Gibbons

190 c/o Room 2,

The Laurels Community Care Hostel,

Paradise Cuttings,

Leeds

He invited me to spend the night on his put-u-up, but I demurred,

195 saying that my father was checking up on me via a long-distance telescope. He went then.

**Friday April 1st**

GOOD FRIDAY, ALL FOOLS' DAY

*10 a.m. Leeds. (A Launderette.)*

200 Thank God for launderettes, if they hadn't been invented I'd be dead of hydrophobia by now. Nowhere else is open.

It cost a *pound* to dry my sleeping bag. But I was so wet and cold that I didn't care at the time.

I am waiting for the dog to wake up. It was on guard duty last night

205 protecting our respective bodies from Stanley Gibbons. I am sixteen tomorrow. But still no sign of a beard. Good Friday!

**Saturday April 2nd**

*Manchester Railway Station.*

210 Got here by fish lorry. Pretended to be asleep in order to avoid driver's conversation.

*10:31 a.m.* I wonder what my mum and dad have bought me for my birthday. I hope they are not too worried. Perhaps I ought to ring them and convince them that I am well and happy.

*12:15 p.m.* We have been ordered out of the railway station café by a
215 bad-tempered waitress. It's the stupid dog's fault. It kept going behind the counter and begging for bits of bacon.

Yet I bought it a bacon roll all to itself this morning.

*3 p.m.* Nobody has said "Happy Birthday" to me.

*3:05* I'm not well (I've got a cold) and I'm not happy. In fact I'm
220 extremely unhappy.

*5:30 p.m.* Bought myself a birthday card. Inside I wrote:

> To our darling first-born child on his sixteenth birthday.
> With all the love it is possible to give,
> From your admiring and loving parents.
225 > P.S. Come home son. Without you the house is devoid of life
> and laughter.

*6:15 p.m.* There was nothing about me on the six o'clock news.

*7:30 p.m.* Can't face another night in the open.

*9 p.m. Park bench.*
230 I have asked three policemen the time, but none of them have spotted me as a runaway. It's obvious that my description hasn't been circulated.

*9:30 p.m.* Just rang the police station, using a disguised voice. I said "Adrian Mole, a sixteen-year-old runaway, is in the vicinity of the
235 Blood Transfusion Headquarters. His description is as follows: small for his age, slight build, mousey hair, disfigured skin. He is wearing a green school blazer. Orange waterproof trousers. A blue shirt. Balaclava helmet. Brown Doc Martens. With him is a mongrel dog, of the following description: medium height, hairy face, squint in left
240 eye. Wearing a tartan collar and matching lead."

The desk sergeant said, "April Fool's Day was yesterday, sonny."

*10:00 p.m.* Waited outside the Blood Transfusion place but there wasn't a policeman in sight. There is never one around when you need one.

245 *11:39 p.m.* I have walked past the police station twenty-four times, but none of the cretins in blue have given me a second glance.

*11:45 p.m.* I have just been turned away from an Indian Restaurant on the grounds that I wasn't wearing a tie, and was accompanied by a scruffy dog.

250

### Sunday April 3rd
EASTER SUNDAY

*Still in Manchester. (St. Ignatius's church porch.)*
*1 a.m.* It is traditional for the homeless to sleep in church porches so why don't vicars make sure that their porches are more comfortable?
255 It wouldn't kill them to provide a mattress, would it?

*7:30 a.m.* Got up at six. Had a wash in a bird bath. Read the inscriptions on the gravestones. Then went in search of a shop. Found one; bought two Cadbury's creme eggs. Ate one myself, gave the other to the dog. The poor thing was so hungry it ate the silver paper as well. I
260 hope it won't be ill; I can't afford to pay for veterinary attention. I've only got £15.00 left.

### Monday April 4th
*St. Ignatius's church porch, Manchester.*
*6 a.m.* For two days I have had the legal right to buy cigarettes, have
265 sex, ride a moped, and live away from home. Yet, strangely, I don't want to do any of them now I'm able to.
   Must stop. A woman with a kind face is coming through the gravestones.

*9 a.m.* I am in the vicar's wife's bed. She is a true Christian. She
270 doesn't mind that I am an existentialist nihilist. She says I'll grow out of it. The dog is downstairs lying on top of the Aga.

*10 a.m.* Mrs. Merryfield, the vicar's wife, has phoned my parents and asked them to come and fetch me. I asked Mrs. Merryfield for my parents' reactions. She crumpled her kind face up in thought then said,
275 "Angry relief is the nearest I can get to it, dear!"
   I haven't seen the vicar yet. He is having a lie-in because of being so busy yesterday. I hope he doesn't mind that a stranger is occupying his wife's bed.

*12:30 p.m.* The vicar has just gone. Thank God! What a bore! No won-
280 der poor Mrs. Merryfield sleeps apart from him. I expect that she is scared he'll talk about comparative religions in his sleep. I have just spent a week living rough. The last thing I want is a lecture on "Monophysitism."

*2:30 p.m.* The Reverend Merryfield brought my dinner in at 1:30, then
285 gabbled on about "Lamaism," the Tibetan religion, while my dinner got cold, and eventually congealed.

*6 p.m.* I notice my parents are not breaking their necks to get here. I wish they would hurry up. I've had "Mithraism," "Orphism" and "Pentecostalism" up to here.

290      I'm all for a man having outside interests, but this is ridiculous.


### Tuesday April 5th

*Bedroom. Home.*

Well, there were no banners in the street, or crowds of people jostling to get a view as I got out of my father's car. Just my mother's haggard
295 face at the lounge window, and Grandma's even haggarder one behind her.

     My father doesn't talk when he's driving on motorways, so we had hardly said a word to each other, since leaving St. Ignatius's vicarage. (And Reverend Merryfield saw to it that we didn't talk *at* the vicarage,
300 what with his rabbiting on about Calvinism and Shakers. Mrs. Merryfield tried to stop him: she said, "Please be quiet, darling," but it just set him off on Quietism.)

     But my mother and Grandma said a great many things. Eventually I pleaded for mercy and went to bed and pulled the crispy white sheets
305 over my head.


### Wednesday April 6th

Dr. Grey has just left my bedside. He has diagnosed that I am suffering from a depressive illness brought on by worry. The treatment is bedrest, and no quarreling in the family.
310      My parents are bowed down by guilt.

     I can't rest for worrying about the letter I wrote to "Pop-Eye" Scruton.


### Thursday April 7th

The dog is at the vet's, having the blisters on its paws treated. I got up
315 for five minutes and looked out of my bedroom window today. But there was nothing in the urban landscape to interest me, so I got back into bed.

     I haven't opened my birthday presents yet.


### Friday April 8th

320 Ate a Mars bar.

     I can feel my physical strength returning, but my mental strength is still at rock bottom.

### Saturday April 9th

*10 a.m.* I suffered a relapse so Dr. Grey called round.
325   I lay back listlessly on the pillows and let him feel my pulse etc.
He muttered, "Bloody Camille," as he left the room.
Perhaps Camille is a drug that he's thinking of using on me.

*12 noon* I asked my mother to draw the curtains against the sun.

### Sunday April 10th

330   Lay all day with my head turned to the wall. Rosie was brought in to
cheer me up, but her childish gibbering merely served to irritate so she
was taken away.

### Monday April 11th

Bert Baxter was carried up to my bedside, but his coarse exhortation,
335   "Get out of your pit, you idle bugger!" failed to stir me from my
nihilistic thoughts.

### Tuesday April 12th

Nigel has just left, after trying to arouse me by playing my favorite
"Toyah" tapes at a discreet volume.
340   I signalled that I would prefer both his and Toyah's absence.

### Wednesday April 13th

A sign that my parents are now frantic with worry about me; Barry
Kent was allowed into the house.
His inarticulate ramblings about the gang's activities failed to
345   interest or stimulate me, so he was led out of the darkened room.

### Thursday April 14th

A consultant psychologist has been ordered.
Dr. Grey has admitted his failure.

### Friday April 15th

350   Dr. Donaldson has just left my bedside after listening to my worries
with grave attention.
When I'd sunk back onto my pillows he said, "We'll take them one
by one."
1.   Nuclear war *is* a worry, but do something positive about your
355      fear—join CND.
2.   If you fail your "O" levels you can retake them next year, or
never take them—like the Queen.
3.   Of course your parents love you. They didn't sleep during the
time you were away.

360   4.  You are *not* hideously ugly. You are a pleasant, average-looking boy.

5.  Your sister's paternity problems are nothing to do with you, and there is nothing you can do to help.

6.  I've never heard of a sixteen-year-old having their own poetry
365       program on Radio Four. You must set yourself realistic targets.

7.  I will write to Mr. Scruton ("Pop-Eye") and inform him that you were under great stress at the time you wrote the letter.

8.  Pandora comes under the heading of insoluble problems.


**Saturday April 16th**

370   Grandma came to my room at 8 a.m. this morning and ordered me out of bed!

She said, "You've been pampered enough. Now pull yourself together, and go and shave that bum-fluff off your face!"

I weakly protested that I needed more time to find myself.
375   Grandma said, "I need to wash those sheets so get out of bed!"

I said, "But I'm angst-ridden."


# B.   Second Reading

**FOLLOW-UP**
Discuss your answers to the *First Reading*. Then take turns sharing your questions about places in the text you marked during *Second Reading*.

Reread the diaries and mark any places that are still difficult to understand or confusing to you.


# III. STRENGTHENING SKILLS THROUGH THE TEXT

# A.   Responding to the Reading

On a separate sheet of paper, write steadily for 20 minutes about your reaction to what you have read. Write about:

**1.**  Adrian and his problems and how he tries to solve them;

**FOLLOW-UP**
After each person reads, other group members should respond with comments, questions, or help in understanding unclear portions of the text.

**2.**  the things that happen to Adrian; and/or

**3.**  what you still don't understand or find confusing in the text.

Work in small groups. Take turns reading what you have written to the other members of the group.

# B. Global Comprehension Check: Collaborative True/False Questions

Work in pairs. One partner will close the book while the other partner *reads* each of the following true/false statements aloud. The person who is listening will say whether the statement is true or false. When you finish, discuss the answers and look up any in the text that you and your partner disagree about.

_____ 1. One of the reasons Adrian ran away was because he had failed his "O" level exams.

_____ 2. Adrian didn't expect to see Mr. Scruton ever again when he wrote him his farewell letter.

_____ 3. Adrian was gay like his friend Nigel.

_____ 4. Adrian had to leave out of his suitcase some things he had believed at first to be essentials.

_____ 5. Adrian finally decided to leave his dog behind.

_____ 6. Adrian (and the dog) spent a comfortable first night in Adrian's sleeping bag.

_____ 7. Adrian wrote himself the loving birthday message he would have liked to receive from his parents.

_____ 8. Adrian tried in several ways to get the police to notice him as a runaway.

_____ 9. Mr. Merryfield, the vicar of the church, talked to Adrian about Adrian's problems.

_____10. The psychologist who was called in to talk to Adrian gave Adrian realistic advice.

_____11. Grandma threw Adrian out of bed so that she could wash the sheets.

# C. Text-based Focus on Vocabulary

Find the word or phrase in the story which means the same as the definition. (14–16, 1) in item 1 means you should look between lines 14 and 16 for *one* word meaning "a person running away from danger." Write the word or phrase in the space provided.

⊗ ⊗ ⊗ ⊗ ⊗ ⊗ ⊗ ⊗ ⊗ ⊗ ⊗ ⊗ ⊗ ⊗ ⊗ ⊗ ⊗ ⊗ ⊗ ⊗

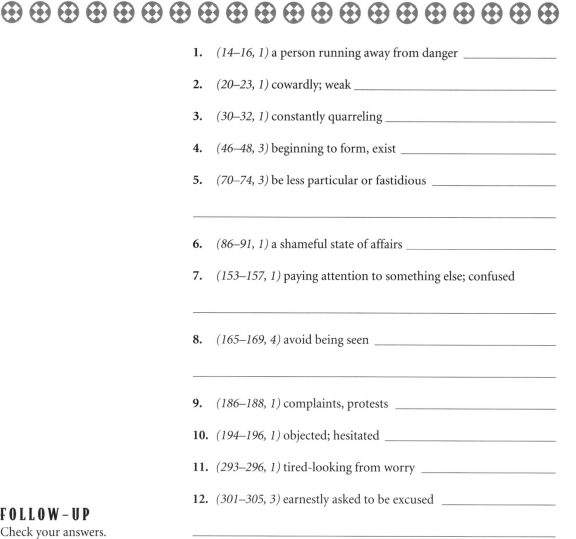

1.  *(14–16, 1)* a person running away from danger _____

2.  *(20–23, 1)* cowardly; weak _____

3.  *(30–32, 1)* constantly quarreling _____

4.  *(46–48, 3)* beginning to form, exist _____

5.  *(70–74, 3)* be less particular or fastidious _____

    _____

6.  *(86–91, 1)* a shameful state of affairs _____

7.  *(153–157, 1)* paying attention to something else; confused

    _____

8.  *(165–169, 4)* avoid being seen _____

    _____

9.  *(186–188, 1)* complaints, protests _____

10. *(194–196, 1)* objected; hesitated _____

11. *(293–296, 1)* tired-looking from worry _____

12. *(301–305, 3)* earnestly asked to be excused _____

**FOLLOW-UP**
Check your answers.

    _____

# IV.  MOVING BEYOND THE TEXT

# A.  Discussion and Writing

Discuss the following topics as a class or in groups. Your teacher may assign a different topic to each group and ask a group leader to summarize its discussion for the class. On a separate sheet of paper, write on *one or more* of the topics as instructed by your teacher.

1.  What should Adrian's parents do differently, if anything, now that he is home?

2. Do you think teenage years are the most difficult years for most people? What are the special problems that teenagers have? Compare these problems to those of a pre-teen like Rachel from the story "Eleven."

3. What are Adrian's real problems, in your opinion? Are his problems caused by Adrian himself, his family and friends, his society? How is it that we often find ourselves laughing when Adrian takes these problems very seriously?

4. What do you think about the way Adrian handled the situations he met while he was a runaway? Do you think he got anything positive out of his experiences?

5. Compare Adrian Mole's problems to the typical problems of a teenage boy in your country. Are the problems similar? Would an average teenager handle his problems the way Adrian did?

6. Do you think Adrian's mood and life will change as the story continues? How will he view his parents, his exams, his appearance, and his girlfriend a year from now? Ten years from now?

# B.    Taking a Stand: A Short Speech

Read the questions below. Take a position on *one* of the issues, and be prepared to speak for two minutes on the issue in front of the class. (Do *not* write out the speech; *do* prepare a note card with the main ideas of your speech. Practice delivering your speech to a partner in class.)

1. Is Adrian a normal teenager or a little abnormal? Why?

2. What are the causes of Adrian's problems?

Did this little boy spend the night in his parents' bed,
or is he making an early-morning visit?

# Lesson 5

## MY OEDIPUS COMPLEX

### Frank O'Connor

### Ireland

# I.   GETTING READY

## A.   Entering the Story through Listening

Listen as your teacher reads two paragraphs from "My Oedipus Complex," a story about a little boy named Larry, whose father was not home much because of the war. Answer the questions below.

**FOLLOW-UP**
Discuss the answer as a class.

**Passage 1.** *(lines 1–7)*

1.   In what ways was Father like Santa Claus?

**FOLLOW-UP**
As a class or in small groups, discuss the questions as well as *why* Mother and the little boy might not have had the same reaction to Father's coming home for good.

**Passage 2.** *(lines 62–68)*

1.   How did Mother feel when Father returned home for good?
2.   How did Larry feel?

## B.   Background

Read the following information, noting the italicized words, to help you understand the story more easily and fully.

The title of the story, "My Oedipus Complex," is meant humorously by the author. The term Oedipus Complex refers to a psychological state in which a young boy has such strong love for his mother that he feels very hostile to his father because of jealousy. Some very serious literature has been written on this topic. However, this story is written in a light, humorous tone.

The humor may not be easy to see unless you pay attention to who is telling the story. Remember that the narrator is a five-year-old boy who sees life very differently from adults. His five-year-old understanding and interpretation of events makes Larry's problems amusing to us as adult readers.

The story, set in Ireland at the time of World War I, has a few cultural and linguistic elements that might be new to you. For example, at one point when the little boy Larry is thinking about what to do to solve his problem with his father, he thinks of sending him to the *Home*, a place this five-year-old doesn't really understand but has heard of. The *Home* he mentions is probably a home provided by the government or the church where old or poor people who are unable to take care of themselves, or who do not have family they can live with, can live together and be taken care of.

Larry's mother in the story mentions *pennies from the Post Office,* a reference to money she receives at the post office from her husband's military pay. Pennies, of course, are not very much money but were a common way for adults to refer to money when talking to children. Larry's mother also mentions money when she tells Larry that a new baby costs *seventeen and six,* that is, seventeen shillings and six pence. There were 20 shillings in a pound (Irish punt) at that time.

A few vocabulary items in the story either are not common in American English or might cause some confusion. Those marked *Br/Ir.* are primarily Anglo-Irish usage:

**magpie** *(line 16)* kind of bird that collects all sorts of items from everywhere for its nest

**tucking me up** *(line 119, Br/Ir.)* putting me to bed

**codded** *(line 274, Br/Ir.)* deceived, tricked

**He wants his bottom smacked** *(line 282, Br/Ir.)* He's asking for a spanking

**dotty** *(line 292, Br/Ir.)* crazy

**winning** *(line 319, Br/Ir.)* attractive, appealing

**as touchy as blazes** *(line 355, Br/Ir.)* overly sensitive

**something up with him** *(line 387, Br/Ir.)* something wrong with him

# II. ENGAGING WITH THE TEXT

## A. First Reading: Following the Story Line

To gain a general idea of how the story develops, read all the Signpost Questions in the margin before you begin to read the story. Then concentrate on answering the questions as you read.

### My Oedipus Complex

**1.**
How is life for Larry while Father is at war?

1     Father was in the army all through the war—the first war, I mean—so, up to the age of five, I never saw much of him, and what I saw did not worry me. Sometimes I woke and there was a big figure in khaki peering down at me in the candlelight. Sometimes in the early
5     morning I heard the slamming of the front door and the clatter of nailed boots down the cobbles of the lane. These were Father's entrances and exits. Like Santa Claus he came and went mysteriously.

In fact, I rather liked his visits, though it was an uncomfortable squeeze between Mother and him when I got into the big bed in the early morning. He smoked, which gave him a pleasant musty smell, and shaved, an operation of astounding interest. Each time he left a trail of souvenirs—model tanks and Gurkha knives with handles made of bullet cases, and German helmets and cap badges and button-sticks, and all sorts of military equipment—carefully stowed away in a long box on top of the wardrobe, in case they ever came in handy. There was a bit of the magpie about Father; he expected everything to come in handy. When his back was turned, Mother let me get a chair and rummage through his treasures. She didn't seem to think so highly of them as he did.

The war was the most peaceful period of my life. The window of my attic faced southeast. My mother had curtained it, but that had small effect. I always woke with the first light and, with all the responsibilities of the previous day melted, feeling myself rather like the sun, ready to illumine and rejoice. Life never seemed so simple and clear and full of possibilities as then. I put my feet out from under the clothes—I called them Mrs. Left and Mrs. Right—and invented dramatic situations for them in which they discussed the problems of the day. At least Mrs. Right did; she was very demonstrative, but I hadn't the same control of Mrs. Left, so she mostly contented herself with nodding agreement.

They discussed what Mother and I should do during the day, what Santa Claus should give a fellow for Christmas, and what steps should be taken to brighten the home. There was that little matter of the baby, for instance. Mother and I could never agree about that. Ours was the only house in the terrace without a new baby, and Mother said we couldn't afford one till Father came back from the war because they cost seventeen and six. That showed how simple she was. The Geneys up the road had a baby, and everyone knew they couldn't afford seventeen and six. It was probably a cheap baby, and Mother wanted something really good, but I felt she was too exclusive. The Geneys' baby would have done us fine.

Having settled my plans for the day, I got up, put a chair under the attic window, and lifted the frame high enough to stick out my head. The window overlooked the front gardens of the terrace behind ours, and beyond these it looked over a deep valley to the tall, red-brick houses terraced up the opposite hillside, which were all still in shadow, while those at our side of the valley were all lit up, though with long strange shadows that made them seem unfamiliar; rigid and painted.

After that I went into Mother's room and climbed into the big bed. She woke and I began to tell her of my schemes. By this time, though I never seem to have noticed it, I was petrified in my nightshirt, and I thawed as I talked until, the last frost melted, I fell asleep beside her and woke again only when I heard her below in the kitchen, making the breakfast.

After breakfast we went into town, heard Mass at St. Augustine's and said a prayer for Father, and did the shopping. If the afternoon was fine we either went for a walk in the country or a visit to Mother's great friend in the convent, Mother St. Dominic. Mother had them all praying for Father, and every night going to bed, I asked God to send him back safe from the war to us. Little, indeed, did I know what I was praying for!

One morning, I got into the big bed, and there, sure enough, was Father in his usual Santa Claus manner, but later, instead of uniform, he put on his best blue suit, and Mother was as pleased as anything. I saw nothing to be pleased about, because, out of uniform, Father was altogether less interesting, but she only beamed, and explained that our prayers had been answered, and off we went to Mass to thank God for having brought Father safely home.

The irony of it! That very day when he came in to dinner he took off his boots and put on his slippers, donned the dirty old cap he wore about the house to save him from colds, crossed his legs, and began to talk gravely to Mother, who looked anxious. Naturally, I disliked her looking anxious, because it destroyed her good looks, so I interrupted him.

"Just a moment, Larry!" she said gently.

This was only what she said when we had boring visitors, so I attached no importance to it and went on talking.

"Do be quiet, Larry!" she said impatiently. "Don't you hear me talking to Daddy?"

This was the first time I had heard those ominous words, "talking to Daddy," and I couldn't help feeling that if this was how God answered prayers, he couldn't listen to them very attentively.

"Why are you talking to Daddy?" I asked with as great a show of indifference as I could muster.

"Because Daddy and I have business to discuss. Now, don't interrupt again!"

In the afternoon, at Mother's request, Father took me for a walk. This time we went into town instead of out to the country, and I thought at first, in my usual optimistic way, that it might be an improvement. It was nothing of the sort. Father and I had quite different notions of a walk in town. He had no proper interest in trams, ships, and horses, and the only thing that seemed to divert him was talking to fellows as old as himself. When I wanted to stop he simply went on, dragging me behind him by the hand; when he wanted to stop I had no alternative but to do the same. I noticed that it seemed to be a sign that he wanted to stop for a long time whenever he leaned against a wall. The second time I saw him do it I got wild. He seemed to be settling himself forever. I pulled him by the coat and trousers, but, unlike Mother who, if you were too persistent, got into a wax and said: "Larry, if you don't behave yourself, I'll give you a good slap," Father had an extraordinary capacity for amiable inattention. I sized him up and wondered would I cry, but he seemed to be too remote to be annoyed even by that. Really, it was like going for a walk with a mountain! He either ignored the wrenching and pummeling entirely,

**2.**
How does Larry's life change the first day that Father is home from the war for good?

105 or else glanced down with a grin of amusement from his peak. I had never met anyone so absorbed in himself as he seemed.

At teatime, "talking to Daddy" began again, complicated this time by the fact that he had an evening paper, and every few minutes he put it down and told Mother something new out of it. I felt this was foul
110 play. Man for man, I was prepared to compete with him any time for Mother's attention, but when he had it all made up for him by other people it left me no chance. Several times I tried to change the subject without success.

"You must be quiet while Daddy is reading, Larry," Mother said
115 impatiently.

It was clear that she either genuinely liked talking to Father better than talking to me, or else that he had some terrible hold on her which made her afraid to admit the truth.

120 think if I prayed hard God would send Daddy back to the war?"

She seemed to think about that for a moment.

"No, dear," she said with a smile. "I don't think he would."

"Why wouldn't he, Mummy?"

"Because there isn't a war any longer, dear."
125 "But, Mummy, couldn't God make another war, if he liked?"

"He wouldn't like to, dear. It's not God who makes wars, but bad people."

"Oh!" I said.

I was disappointed about that. I began to think that God wasn't
130 quite what he was cracked up to be.

Next morning I woke at my usual hour, feeling like a bottle of champagne. I put out my feet and invented a long conversation in which Mrs. Right talked of the trouble she had with her own father till she put him in the Home. I didn't quite know what the Home was but
135 it sounded the right place for Father. Then I got my chair and stuck my head out of the attic window. Dawn was just breaking, with a guilty air that made me feel I had caught it in the act. My head bursting with stories and schemes, I stumbled in next door, and in the half-darkness scrambled into the big bed. There was no room at Mother's
140 side, so I had to get between her and Father. For the time being I had forgotten about him, and for several minutes I sat bolt upright, racking my brains to know what I could do with him. He was taking up more than his fair share of the bed, and I couldn't get comfortable, so I gave him several kicks that made him grunt and stretch. He made
145 room all right, though. Mother waked and felt for me. I settled back comfortably in the warmth of the bed with my thumb in my mouth.

"Mummy!" I hummed, loudly and contentedly.

"Sssh! dear," she whispered. "Don't wake Daddy!"

This was a new development, which threatened to be even more
150 serious than "talking to Daddy." Life without my early-morning conferences was unthinkable.

"Why!" I asked severely.

**3.**
Will things get better the second day that father is home?

**4.**
What does Larry promise to do? Can he keep his promise? Who gets angry?

"Because poor Daddy is tired."

This seemed to me a quite inadequate reason, and I was sickened
by the sentimentality of her "poor Daddy." I never liked that sort of
gush; it always struck me as insincere.

"Oh!' I said lightly. Then in my most winning tone: "Do you know
where I want to go with you today, Mummy?"

"No, dear," she sighed.

"I want to go down the Glen and fish for thornybacks with my new
net, and then I want to go out to the Fox and Hounds, and —"

"Don't-wake-Daddy!" she hissed angrily, clapping her hands across
my mouth.

But it was too late. He was awake, or nearly so. He grunted and
reached for the matches. Then he stared incredulously at his watch.

"Like a cup of tea, dear?" asked Mother in a meek, hushed voice I
had never heard her use before. It sounded almost as though she were
afraid.

"Tea?" he exclaimed indignantly. "Do you know what the time is?"

"And after that I want to go up the Rathcooney Road," I said loudly, afraid I'd forget something in all those interruptions.

"Go to sleep at once, Larry!" she said sharply.

I began to snivel. I couldn't concentrate, the way that pair went on,
and smothering my early-morning schemes was like burying a family
from the cradle.

Father said nothing, but lit his pipe and sucked it, looking out into
the shadows without minding Mother and me. I knew he was mad.
Every time I made a remark Mother hushed me irritably. I was morti-
fied. I felt it wasn't fair; there was even something sinister about it.
Every time I had pointed out to her the waste of making two beds
when we could both sleep in one, she had told me it was healthier like
that, and now here was this man, this stranger, sleeping with her
without the least regard for her health!

He got up early and made tea, but though he brought Mother a cup
he brought none for me.

"Mummy," I shouted, "I want a cup of tea, too."

"Yes, dear," she said patiently. "You can drink from Mummy's
saucer."

That settled it. Either Father or I would have to leave the house. I
didn't want to drink from Mother's saucer; I wanted to be treated as
an equal in my own home, so, just to spite her, I drank it all and left
none for her. She took that quietly, too.

But that night when she was putting me to bed, she said gently:
"Larry, I want you to promise me something."

"What is it?" I asked.

"Not to come in and disturb poor Daddy in the morning.
Promise?"

"Poor Daddy" again. I was becoming suspicious of everything
involving that quite impossible man.

"Why?" I asked.

"Because poor Daddy is worried and tired and he doesn't sleep
well."

"Why doesn't he, Mummy?"

"Well, you know, don't you, that while he was at the war Mummy
205  got the pennies from the Post Office?"

"From Miss MacCarthy?"

"That's right. But now, you see, Miss MacCarthy hasn't any more
pennies, so Daddy must go out and find us some. You know what
would happen if he couldn't?"

210  "No," I said, "tell us."

"Well, I think we might have to go out and beg for them like the
poor old woman on Fridays. We wouldn't like that, would we?"

"No," I agreed. "We wouldn't."

"So you'll promise not to come in and wake him?"

215  "Promise."

Mind you, I meant that. I knew pennies were a serious matter, and
I was all against having to go out and beg like the old woman on
Fridays. Mother laid out all my toys in a complete ring round the bed
so that, whatever way I got out, I was bound to fall over one of them.

220  When I woke I remembered my promise all right. I got up and sat
on the floor and played—for hours, it seemed to me. Then I got my
chair and looked out the attic window for more hours. I wished it was
time for Father to wake; I wished someone would make me a cup of
tea. I didn't feel in the least like the sun; instead, I was bored and so
225  very, very cold! I simply longed for the warmth and depth of the big
featherbed.

At last I could stand it no longer. I went into the next room. As
there was still no room at Mother's side I climbed over her and she
woke with a start.

230  "Larry," she whispered, gripping my arm very tightly, "what did
you promise?"

"But I did, Mummy," I wailed, caught in the very act. "I was quiet
for ever so long."

"Oh, dear, and you're perished!" she said sadly, feeling me all over.
235  "Now, if I let you stay will you promise not to talk?"

"But I want to talk, Mummy," I wailed.

"That has nothing to do with it," she said with a firmness that was
new to me. "Daddy wants to sleep. Now, do you understand that?"

I understood it only too well. I wanted to talk, he wanted to sleep—
240  whose house was it, anyway?

"Mummy," I said with equal firmness, "I think it would be healthier for Daddy to sleep in his own bed."

That seemed to stagger her, because she said nothing for a while.

"Now, once for all," she went on, "you're to be perfectly quiet or go
245  back to your own bed. Which is it to be?"

The injustice of it got me down. I had convicted her out of her own
mouth of inconsistency and unreasonableness, and she hadn't even
attempted to reply. Full of spite, I gave Father a kick, which she didn't
notice but which made him grunt and open his eyes in alarm.

250     "What time is it?" he asked in a panic-stricken voice, not looking at Mother but the door, as if he saw someone there.

    "It's early yet," she replied soothingly. "It's only the child. Go to sleep again. . . . Now Larry," she added, getting out of bed, "you've wakened Daddy and you must go back."

255     This time, for all her quiet air, I knew she meant it, and knew that my principal rights and privileges were as good as lost unless I asserted them at once. As she lifted me, I gave a screech, enough to wake the dead, not to mind Father. He groaned.

    "That damn child! Doesn't he ever sleep?"

260     "It's only a habit, dear," she said quietly, though I could see she was vexed.

    "Well, it's time he got out of it," shouted Father, beginning to heave in the bed. He suddenly gathered all the bedclothes about him, turned to the wall, and then looked back over his shoulder with noth-

265 ing showing only two small, spiteful, dark eyes. The man looked very wicked.

    To open the bedroom door, Mother had to let me down, and I broke free and dashed for the farthest corner, screeching. Father sat bolt upright in bed.

270     "Shut up, you little puppy!" he said in a choking voice.

    I was so astonished that I stopped screeching. Never, never had anyone spoken to me in that tone before. I looked at him incredulously and saw his face convulsed with rage. It was only then that I fully realized how God had codded me, listening to my prayers for the safe

275 return of this monster.

    "Shut up, you!" I bawled, beside myself.

    "What's that you said?" shouted Father, making a wild leap out of bed.

    "Mick, Mick!" cried Mother. "Don't you see the child isn't used to

280 you?"

    "I see he's better fed than taught," snarled Father, waving his arms wildly. "He wants his bottom smacked."

    All his previous shouting was as nothing to these obscene words referring to my person. They really made my blood boil.

285     "Smack your own!" I screamed hysterically. "Smack your own! Shut up! Shut up!"

    At this he lost his patience and let fly at me. He did it with the lack of conviction you'd expect of a man under Mother's horrified eyes, and it ended up as a mere tap, but the sheer indignity of being struck

290 at all by a stranger, a total stranger who had cajoled his way back from the war into our big bed as a result of my innocent intercession, made me completely dotty. I shrieked and shrieked, and danced in my bare feet, and Father, looking awkward and hairy in nothing but a short grey army shirt, glared down at me like a mountain out for murder. I

295 think it must have been then that I realized he was jealous too. And there stood Mother in her nightdress, looking as if her heart was broken between us. I hoped she felt as she looked. It seemed to me that she deserved it all.

**5.**
What happens to make
things even worse for
Larry?

300

305

310

315

320

325

330

335

340

345

From that morning out my life was a hell. Father and I were enemies, open and avowed. We conducted a series of skirmishes against one another, he trying to steal my time with Mother and I his. When she was sitting on my bed, telling me a story, he took to looking for some pair of old boots which he alleged he had left behind him at the beginning of the war. While he talked to Mother I played loudly with my toys to show my total lack of concern. He created a terrible scene one evening when he came in from work and found me at his box, playing with his regimental badges, Gurkha knives and button-sticks. Mother got up and took the box from me.

"You mustn't play with Daddy's toys unless he lets you, Larry," she said severely. "Daddy doesn't play with yours."

For some reason Father looked at her as if she had struck him and then turned away with a scowl.

"Those are not toys," he growled, taking down the box again to see had I lifted anything. "Some of those curios are very rare and valuable."

But as time went on I saw more and more how he managed to alienate Mother and me. What made it worse was that I couldn't grasp his method or see what attraction he had for Mother. In every possible way he was less winning than I. He had a common accent and made noises at his tea. I thought for a while that it might be the newspapers she was interested in, so I made up bits of news of my own to read to her. Then I thought it might be the smoking, which I personally thought attractive, and took his pipes and went round the house dribbling into them till he caught me. I even made noises at my tea, but Mother only told me I was disgusting. It all seemed to hinge round that unhealthy habit of sleeping together, so I made a point of dropping into their bedroom and nosing round, talking to myself, so that they wouldn't know I was watching them, but they were never up to anything that I could see. In the end it beat me. It seemed to depend on being grown-up and giving people rings, and I realized I'd have to wait.

But at the same time I wanted him to see that I was only waiting, not giving up the fight. One evening when he was being particularly obnoxious, chattering away well above my head, I let him have it.

"Mummy," I said, "do you know what I'm going to do when I grow up?"

"No, dear," she replied. "What?"

"I'm going to marry you," I said quietly.

Father gave a great guffaw out of him, but he didn't take me in. I knew it must only be pretense. And Mother, in spite of everything, was pleased. I felt she was probably relieved to know that one day Father's hold on her would be broken.

"Won't that be nice?" she said with a smile.

"It'll be very nice," I said confidently. "Because we're going to have lots and lots of babies."

"That's right, dear," she said placidly. "I think we'll have one soon, and then you'll have plenty of company."

I was no end pleased about that because it showed that in spite of the way she gave in to Father she still considered my wishes. Besides, it would put the Geneys in their place.

It didn't turn out like that, though. To begin with, she was very preoccupied—I supposed about where we would get the seventeen and six—and though Father took to staying out late in the evenings it did me no particular good. She stopped taking me for walks, became as touchy as blazes, and smacked me for nothing at all. Sometimes I wished I'd never mentioned the confounded baby—I seemed to have a genius for bringing calamity on myself.

And calamity it was! Sonny arrived in the most appalling hulla-baloo—even that much he couldn't do without a fuss—and from the first moment I disliked him. He was a difficult child—so far as I was concerned he was always difficult—and demanded far too much attention. Mother was simply silly about him, and couldn't see when he was only showing off. As company he was worse than useless. He slept all day, and I had to go round the house on tiptoe to avoid wak-ing him. It wasn't any longer a question of not waking Father. The slo-gan now was "Don't-wake-Sonny!" I couldn't understand why the child wouldn't sleep at the proper time, so whenever Mother's back was turned I woke him. Sometimes to keep him awake I pinched him as well. Mother caught me at it one day and gave me a most unmerciful flaking.

One evening, when Father was coming from work, I was playing trains in the front garden. I let on not to notice him; instead, I pre-tended to be talking to myself, and said in a loud voice: "If another bloody baby comes into this house, I'm going out."

Father stopped dead and looked at me over his shoulder.

"What's that you said?" he asked sternly.

"I was only talking to myself," I replied, trying to conceal my panic. "It's private."

He turned and went in without a word. Mind you, I intended it as a solemn warning, but its effect was quite different. Father started being quite nice to me. I could understand that, of course. Mother was quite sickening about Sonny. Even at mealtimes she'd get up and gawk at him in the cradle with an idiotic smile, and tell Father to do the same. He was always polite about it, but he looked so puzzled you could see he didn't know what she was talking about. He complained of the way Sonny cried at night, but she only got cross and said that Sonny never cried except when there was something up with him—which was a flaming lie, because Sonny never had anything up with him, and only cried for attention. It was really painful to see how simple-minded she was. Father wasn't attractive, but he had a fine intelligence. He saw through Sonny, and now he knew that I saw through him as well.

One night I woke with a start. There was someone beside me in the bed. For one wild moment I felt sure it must be Mother, having come to her senses and left Father for good, but then I heard Sonny in con-vulsions in the next room, and Mother saying: "There! There! There!" and I knew it wasn't she. It was Father. He was lying beside me, wide awake, breathing hard and apparently as mad as hell.

**6.**
How does Larry and Father's relationship change? Will there be a happy ending for both of them?

After a while it came to me what he was mad about. It was his turn
now. After turning me out of the big bed, he had been turned out
himself. Mother had no consideration now for anyone but that poisonous pup, Sonny. I couldn't help feeling sorry for Father. I had been
through it all myself, and even at that age I was magnanimous. I began
to stroke him down and say: "There! There!" He wasn't exactly
responsive.

"Aren't you asleep either?" he snarled.

"Ah, come on and put your arm around us, can't you?" I said, and
he did, in a sort of way. Gingerly, I suppose, is how you'd describe it.
He was very bony but better than nothing.

At Christmas he went out of his way to buy me a really nice
model railway.

400

405

410

**FOLLOW-UP**

Discuss your answers in
pairs or small groups.

# B.   Second Reading

## Taking a Closer Look

Read the story a second time. Use the questions to gain a better understanding and to bring your experience to the story.

**1.**   Aren't most children happy with the attention of both parents?
Why was Larry happy with his father gone?

**2.**   Why did Larry enjoy the time spent with his mother more than
the time spent with his father? Did you have a similar preference when
you were small?

**3.**   With Father's return, Larry's life changed in many ways. Which
change do you think was the most difficult for him?

**4.**   How long do you think Larry waited before breaking his promise
about staying in his own room after he woke up?

**5.**   What incident made Larry decide he and Father were enemies?
Have you ever felt the same way towards a parent?

**6.**   How did Larry try to win back the affection he thought he'd lost
from Mother? Do you find his tactics amusing?

**7.**   We often say, "Every cloud has a silver lining," meaning every
bad event brings something good with it. How does this proverb apply
to "My Oedipus Complex"?

### Delving More Deeply

Find the following text in the lines indicated. Use the surrounding text and your experience to give an informed answer to the questions that follow.

**1.** *It was probably a cheap baby, and Mother wanted something really good, but I felt she was too exclusive.* (lines 39–40) Was money the real reason Mother didn't have another baby? Why did Larry think so?

**2.** *I had never met anyone so absorbed in himself as he seemed.* (lines 105–106) Did Father understand why Larry was unhappy? Do you think Father was selfish?

**3.** *Next morning I woke at my usual hour, feeling like a bottle of champagne.* (lines 131–132) How exactly did Larry feel—happy or unhappy? Full of energy or lacking in it?

**4.** *...and now here was this man, this stranger, sleeping with her without the least regard for her health!* (lines 182–183) Why did Larry think that his mother and father sleeping in the same bed was unhealthy? Do you see any humor in this?

**5.** *It seemed to me that she deserved it all.* (lines 297–298) What did Mother deserve? Why did Larry have such an unkind thought?

**6.** *In the end it beat me.* (line 329) What couldn't Larry understand?

**7.** *Sometimes I wished I'd never mentioned the confounded baby...* (lines 355–356) Why was Larry unhappy about the baby? Whose idea did he think having the baby was—his own or his parents'?

# III. STRENGTHENING SKILLS THROUGH THE TEXT

# A. Responding to the Reading

Write at least 75 words on *one* of the following topics. When you finish, choose a classmate to listen to what you have written.

**1.** Did you like this story? Why or why not?

**2.** Which character in the story do you sympathize with the most? Explain.

## B. Checking Global Comprehension: Choosing the Best Summary

Read the two summaries of "My Oedipus Complex" carefully. Then decide which one is better. Which summary gives a clearer account of the main events of the story *and* interprets the events more accurately?

### Summary 1

"My Oedipus Complex" is a short story about Larry, a young boy who felt very jealous when his father came home from the war. While his father was away at war, the little boy had all of his mother's attention and spent a lot of time talking and going places with her. After Father came home, Mother had less time for Larry because she had

also to attend to Father. Because of his jealousy, Larry cried, misbehaved, and was disrespectful towards his parents, especially his father. When a new baby was born, Larry realized that Mother's attention shifted again, this time to the new baby. Now realizing that Father shared his fate, Larry was more understanding and loving towards his father.

## Summary 2

"My Oedipus Complex," a story about a family dealing with a small boy's jealousy, takes placc in Ireland at the time of World War I. When his father was away at war, Larry was very happy living alone with Mother. When Father came home, Larry couldn't stand the competition for Mother's attention, so he set out to make Father's life as miserable as his was becoming. Mother did everything she could to ease Larry's jealousy, for which Father often became angry at her. In general, every member of the family was angry with another member. Then, the new child Sonny was born, and the difficult situation worked itself out. This is a story about love in the family.

**FOLLOW-UP**
Discuss the summaries as a class.

# C. Dramatization

In groups of three, practice dramatizing lines 184–219. The narrator will read all unquoted text; students dramatizing Mother's and Larry's parts will read quotations spoken by them in the text. (Omit short items such as *I shouted* and *she said patiently* before and after quotes for a smoother dramatization.)

# D. Text-based Focus on Vocabulary

Find the word or phrase in the story which means the same as the definition. (105–110, 2) in item 1 means you should look between lines 105 and 110 for *two* words meaning "unfair conduct." Write the word or phrase in the space provided.

## The Vocabulary of Conflict

Because the action of "My Oedipus Complex" takes the form of the conflicts that arise from jealousy, a lot of the vocabulary in this story is related to anger and discontent.

⊕ ⊕ ⊕ ⊕ ⊕ ⊕ ⊕ ⊕ ⊕ ⊕ ⊕ ⊕ ⊕ ⊕ ⊕ ⊕ ⊕ ⊕ ⊕ ⊕

1. *(105–110, 2)* unfair conduct _____

2. *(105–110, 3)* self-centered _____

3. *(176–180, 1)* humiliated or shamed greatly _____

4. *(255–260, 1; 265–270, 1)* a scream in a high, irritating voice, like the tires of a car _____

5. *(260–265, 1)* annoyed, irritated and confused _____

6. *(275–280, 1)* cried loudly _____

7. *(290–295, 1)* screamed in a shrill, high-pitched voice

_____

8. *(310–315, 1)* made low, threatening, animal-like sounds

_____

9. *(315–320, 1)* come between two friends; to cause a friend to become unfriendly _____

10. *(355–360, 1)* a misfortune; a piece of very bad luck

_____

11. *(405–410, 1)* growled while showing the teeth, like an animal

_____

## General Vocabulary: Expressions

1. *(15–20, 4)* to be useful at some time _____

_____

2. *(105–110, 2)* illegal or unfair activity _____

3. *(125–130, 4)* praised as; believed to be *(slang)* _____

_____

4. *(280–285, 4)* made me very angry _____

_____

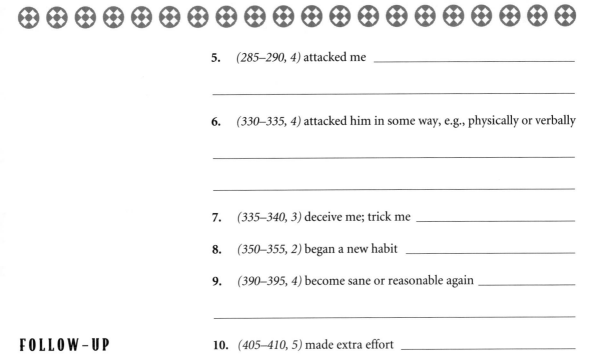

5. *(285–290, 4)* attacked me _____

_____

6. *(330–335, 4)* attacked him in some way, e.g., physically or verbally

_____

_____

7. *(335–340, 3)* deceive me; trick me _____

8. *(350–355, 2)* began a new habit _____

9. *(390–395, 4)* become sane or reasonable again _____

_____

**FOLLOW-UP**
Check your answers as
instructed by your teacher.

10. *(405–410, 5)* made extra effort _____

_____

# IV.  MOVING BEYOND THE TEXT

# A.  Discussion and Writing

Discuss the following topics as a class or in groups. Your teacher may assign a different topic to each group and ask a group leader to summarize its discussion for the class. Write on *one or more* of the topics as instructed by your teacher.

1.  Do you think jealousy is a normal part of human relations such as those between family members, friends, lovers, and co-workers?

2.  Do you think that Mother and Father were good parents? Why or why not?

3.  Could the same jealous situation occur in your country if the father were away for long periods of time and the mother and child were left alone? Why or why not?

4.  Explain the following quotation: "There is more self-love than love in jealousy" (La Rochfoucauld, *Maxims*). How does it relate to the story?

## B. Roleplay

Prepare one or more of the following roleplays orally, without writing. The first line is given to help you begin.

**1.** *[Two students: **Mother and the Priest**] Shortly after Larry's father comes home for good, Mother is talking to the priest at the church, discussing the problems she is having at home with Larry and his father. The priest advises her on how she should act to solve the problems.*

MOTHER: Father Murphy, I just don't know what to do. Larry and his father are tearing me apart.

**2.** *[Two students: Father and George] Shortly after Father comes home for good, he is talking in the local pub to his friend George from the war about his homecoming. He mentions problems with Larry, finding work, and the expected arrival of the new baby. His friend is sympathetic and gives him advice on how to solve his problems.*

FATHER: George, coming home is nothing like I expected. I've got so many problems.

**3.** *[Three students: Mother, Father, Larry] Ten years later, Mother, Father, and Larry are at home in their living room reminiscing about the time in their lives shortly after Father came home from the war. Larry is now at secondary school, Father is working at a good job, and there are several younger children in the family. They discuss what they were thinking and feeling at the time.*

FATHER: Do you remember when I first came home from the war?

# UNIT II
# Love:
# Winning
# and
# Losing

Who or what do you think the archer
represents or symbolizes?

# Lesson 6

## YOUR CHILDREN

## ARE NOT YOUR CHILDREN

### Khalil Gibran

### Lebanon / U.S.A.

# I. GETTING READY

## A. Discussion: Parents and Children

**FOLLOW-UP**
Share your list of obligations
with one or two other pairs
or the whole class.

Discuss these questions in a small group and list as many answers as
you can think of.

1.  What are the obligations of parents toward their children?

2.  What are the obligations of children toward their parents?

Read the following vocabulary list. If you are uncertain of the meanings
of any of the words, check them in a dictionary.

*archer* person who shoots arrows using a bow

*longing* desire

*dwell* live

*strive* try

*tarries* lingers; stays behind

*bows and arrows* (see picture)

*might* (noun) strength

# II. ENGAGING WITH THE TEXT

## A. First Exposure: Listening

Listen, as your teacher reads, "Your Children Are Not Your Children"
to answer this question: If "your children are not your children," then
whose children are they?

**FOLLOW-UP**
Share your answers.

Listen again to answer these questions about tone: Is the poem playful
or solemn? calm or excited?

## B. Second Exposure: Reading

Now read the poem and answer the questions which follow it.

**Your Children Are Not Your Children**

A   Your children are not your children.

B   They are the sons and daughters of Life's longing for itself.

A   They come through you but not from you,

B   And though they are with you yet they belong not to you.


A   You may give them your love but not your thought,

B   For they have their own thoughts.

A   You may house their bodies but not their souls,

B   For their souls dwell in the house of tomorrow, which you cannot
        visit, not even in your dreams.

A   You may strive to be like them, but seek not to make them like you.

B   For life goes not backward nor tarries with yesterday.


A   You are the bows from which your children as living arrows are
        sent forth.

B   The archer sees the mark upon the path of the infinite, and He bends
        you with His might that His arrows may go swift and far.

A   Let your bending in the archer's hand be for gladness;

B   For even as He loves the arrow that flies, so He loves also the bow
        that is stable.


# Questions

1.   Do parents own their children?

2.   What can parents give to their children?

3.   What can't parents give their children?

4.   What is the "house of tomorrow"?

5. In the metaphor of the archer with the arrows and bows, who are the **bows**, the **arrows**, and the **archer**?

FOLLOW-UP
Discuss your answers in small groups.

6. According to Gibran, does God give children to parents to keep or merely to take care of for a time?

# III. STRENGTHENING SKILLS THROUGH THE TEXT

## A. Choral Reading

This poem lends itself very easily to choral reading. Divide the class into two groups: the "As" and the "Bs." The As will read the lines marked **A** and the Bs will read the lines marked **B**. First, get with your groups and practice reading your parts together as a chorus. Remember that you will alternate reading and must listen carefully to the other group as they read their lines so that you can keep in rhythm.

## B. Discussion and Writing

Discuss the following topics as a class or in groups. Your teacher may assign a different topic to each group and ask a group leader to summarize its discussion for the class. Write on *one or more* of the topics as instructed by your teacher.

1. What is the message of this poem?

2. Would you like your parents to read this poem? Why or why not?

3. What is the difference between possessive love and pure love?

4. Do children belong to their parents or to God?

_____

_____

_____

_____

_____

What kinds of conflicts can there be between family members
when some of them live in urban areas and some of them live in rural areas?

# Lesson 7

## MARRIAGE

## IS A PRIVATE AFFAIR

### Chinua Achebe

### Nigeria

# I. GETTING READY

## A. Discussion: Marriage

Read the following statements. Then mark each one **A** if you agree with it and **D** if you disagree.

_____ **1.** It's important to marry a person from your own country.

_____ **2.** The parents of both the bride and the groom must agree to the marriage.

_____ **3.** People should be free to marry whomever they like.

_____ **4.** Mixed marriages (between races, ethnic groups, religions) have more problems than marriages between people from similar backgrounds.

_____ **5.** The children of mixed marriages have more problems at school and in society than other children.

_____ **6.** City people and country people think very differently about many aspects of life.

_____ **7.** I would never forgive a child of mine who married someone without my approval.

_____ **8.** It's natural for the younger generation to be less conservative socially than their parents.

_____ **9.** The younger the couple, the better the marriage.

_____ **10.** A person should put his or her parents before his or her spouse and children.

**FOLLOW-UP**
Discuss your answers in pairs or small groups.

# B. Entering the Story through Listening

Listen to the conversation between a young couple, Nnaemeka and Nene, to answer these questions about "Marriage is a Private Affair" *(lines 1–18):*

**1.** What news does Nnaemeka have for his father?

**2.** Why does he think his father will not be happy with this news?

**FOLLOW-UP**
Discuss the questions as a class.

**3.** Does Nene understand Nnaemeka's concern (according to Nnaemeka)? Why or why not?

# C. Background

Read the following information, noting the italicized words, to help you understand the story more easily and fully.

Nigeria, a country located on the western coast of Africa, has a population of more than 115 million people. There are over 250 tribes, or large extended-family groups, of which the Ibos are one of the largest and most influential.

While Lagos, the capital, is a large, bustling, cosmopolitan city with a population of about six million, most of the population of Nigeria still lives in the country. People who have recently come to live in the bigger cities usually have strong ties to their families who still live in villages, where tribal loyalties are very powerful. In this story we see how city values and tribal values can come into conflict.

A conversation in the story among the country people revolves around the possibility of consulting a *native doctor*, or native herbalist, in order to deal with problems with family members who are not conforming to the expectations of other family members. We can see that native doctors are consulted not only for physical ailments but also for psychological or social ailments. There is a strong belief in the effectiveness of certain substances gained from the plant or animal world to influence or control human *behavior* as well as to cure certain physical ailments.

# II. ENGAGING WITH THE TEXT

# A. First Reading: Following the Story Line

To gain a general idea of how the story develops, read all the Signpost Questions in the margin before you begin to read. Then concentrate on answering the questions as you read the story.

### Marriage is a Private Affair

**1.**
What problem does Nnaemeka face? What does he do about it?

1 "Have you written to your dad yet?" asked Nene one afternoon as she sat with Nnaemeka in her room at 16 Kasanga Street, Lagos.

"No. I've been thinking about it. I think it's better to tell him when I get home on leave!"

5 "But why? Your leave is such a long way off yet—six whole weeks. He should be let into our happiness now."

Nnaemeka was silent for a while, and then began very slowly as if he groped for his words: "I wish I were sure it would be happiness to him."

10 "Of course it must," replied Nene, a little surprised. "Why shouldn't it?"

"You have lived in Lagos all your life, and you know very little about people in remote parts of the country."

"That's what you always say. But I don't believe anybody will be so
15 unlike other people that they will be unhappy when their sons are engaged to marry."

"Yes. They are most unhappy if the engagement is not arranged by them. In our case it's worse—you are not even an Ibo."

This was said so seriously and so bluntly that Nene could not find
20 speech immediately. In the cosmopolitan atmosphere of the city it had always seemed to her something of a joke that a person's tribe could determine whom he married.

At last she said, "You don't really mean that he will object to your marrying me simply on that account? I had always thought you Ibos
25 were kindly-disposed to other people."

"So we are. But when it comes to marriage, well, it's not quite so simple. And this," he added, "is not peculiar to the Ibos. If your father were alive and lived in the heart of Ibibio-land he would be exactly like my father."

30 "I don't know. But anyway, as your father is so fond of you, I'm sure he will forgive you soon enough. Come on then, be a good boy and send him a nice lovely letter . . ."

"It would not be wise to break the news to him by writing. A letter will bring it upon him with a shock. I'm quite sure about that."

35 "All right, honey, suit yourself. You know your father."

As Nnaemeka walked home that evening he turned over in his mind different ways of overcoming his father's opposition, especially now that he had gone and found a girl for him. He had thought of showing his letter to Nene but decided on second thoughts not to, at
40 least for the moment. He read it again when he got home and couldn't help smiling to himself. He remembered Ugoye quite well, an Amazon of a girl who used to beat up all the boys, himself included, on the way to the stream, a complete dunce at school.

*I have found a girl who will suit you admirably—Ugoye Nweke, the*
45 *eldest daughter of our neighbor, Jacob Nweke. She has a proper Christian upbringing. When she stopped schooling some years ago her father (a man of sound judgment) sent her to live in the house of a pastor where she has received all the training a wife could need. Her Sunday School teacher has told me that she reads her Bible very fluently. I hope we*
50 *shall begin negotiations when you come home in December.*

On the second evening of his return from Lagos Nnaemeka sat with his father under a cassia tree. This was the old man's retreat where he went to read his Bible when the parching December sun had set and a fresh, reviving wind blew on the leaves.

55 "Father," began Nnaemeka suddenly, "I have come to ask for forgiveness."

"Forgiveness? For what, my son?" he asked in amazement.

"It's about this marriage question."

"Which marriage question?"

"I can't—we must—I mean it is impossible for me to marry Nweke's daughter."

"Impossible? Why?" asked his father.

"I don't love her."

"Nobody said you did. Why should you?" he asked.

"Marriage today is different…"

"Look here, my son," interrupted his father, "nothing is different. What one looks for in a wife are a good character and a Christian background."

Nnaemeka saw there was no hope along the present line of argument.

"Moreover," he said, "I am engaged to marry another girl who has all of Ugoye's good qualities, and who…"

His father did not believe his ears. "What did you say?" he asked slowly and disconcertingly.

"She is a good Christian," his son went on, "and a teacher in a Girls' School in Lagos."

"Teacher, did you say? If you consider that a qualification for a good wife I should like to point out to you, Emeka, that no Christian woman should teach. St. Paul in his letter to the Corinthians says that women should keep silence." He rose slowly from his seat and paced forwards and backwards. This was his pet subject, and he condemned vehemently those church leaders who encouraged women to teach in their schools. After he had spent his emotion on a long homily he at last came back to his son's engagement, in a seemingly milder tone.

"Whose daughter is she, anyway?"

"She is Nene Atang."

"What!" All the mildness was gone again. "Did you say Neneataga, what does that mean?"

"Nene Atang from Calabar. She is the only girl I can marry." This was a very rash reply and Nnaemeka expected the storm to burst. But it did not. His father merely walked away into his room. This was most unexpected and perplexed Nnaemeka. His father's silence was infinitely more menacing than a flood of threatening speech. That night the old man did not eat.

When he sent for Nnaemeka a day later he applied all possible ways of dissuasion. But the young man's heart was hardened, and his father eventually gave him up as lost.

"I owe it to you, my son, as a duty to show you what is right and what is wrong. Whoever put this idea into your head might as well have cut your throat. It is Satan's work." He waved his son away.

"You will change your mind, Father, when you know Nene."

"I shall never see her," was the reply. From that night the father scarcely spoke to his son. He did not, however, cease hoping that he would realize how serious was the danger he was heading for. Day and night he put him in his prayers.

**2.**

What is the reaction of his father (Okeke) when Nnaemeka tells him he wants to marry Nene?

**3.**

Will Nnaemeka follow his wishes or his father's?

Nnaemeka, for his own part, was very deeply affected by his father's grief. But he kept hoping that it would pass away. If it had occurred to him that never in the history of his people had a man married a woman who spoke a different tongue, he might have been less opti-

110 mistic. "It has never been heard," was the verdict of an old man speaking a few weeks later. In that short sentence he spoke for all of his people. This man had come with others to commiserate with Okeke when news went round about his son's behavior. By that time the son had gone back to Lagos.

115 "It has never been heard," said the old man again with a sad shake of his head.

"What did Our Lord say?" asked another gentleman. "Sons shall rise against their Fathers; it is there in the Holy Book."

"It is the beginning of the end," said another.

120 The discussion thus tending to become theological, Madubogwu, a highly practical man, brought it down once more to the ordinary level.

"Have you thought of consulting a native doctor about your son?" he asked Nnaemeka's father.

"He isn't sick," was the reply.

125 "What is he then? The boy's mind is diseased and only a good herbalist can bring him back to his right senses. The medicine he requires is *Amalile,* the same that women apply with success to recapture their husbands' straying affection."

"Madubogwu is right," said another gentleman. "This thing calls

130 for medicine."

"I shall not call in a native doctor." Nnaemeka's father was known to be obstinately ahead of his more superstitious neighbors in these matters. "I will not be another Mrs. Ochuba. If my son wants to kill himself let him do it with his own hands. It is not for me to help him."

135 "But it was her fault," said Madubogwu. "She ought to have gone to an honest herbalist. She was a clever woman, nevertheless."

"She was a wicked murderess," said Jonathan who rarely argued with his neighbors because, he often said, they were incapable of reasoning. "The medicine was prepared for her husband, it was his name

140 they called in its preparation and I am sure it would have been perfectly beneficial to him. It was wicked to put it into the herbalist's food, and say you were only trying it out."

Six months later, Nnaemeka was showing his young wife a short letter from his father:

145 *It amazes me that you could be so unfeeling as to send me your wedding picture. I would have sent it back. But on further thought I decided just to cut off your wife and send it back to you because I have nothing to do with her. How I wish that I had nothing to do with you either.*

When Nene read through this letter and looked at the mutilated

150 picture her eyes filled with tears, and she began to sob.

"Don't cry, my darling," said her husband. "He is essentially good-natured and will one day look more kindly on our marriage." But years passed and that one day did not come.

**4.**
How will this story end? Will the father, Okeke, continue to reject his son's family?

For eight years, Okeke would have nothing to do with his son,
Nnaemeka. Only three times (when Nnaemeka asked to come home
and spend his leave) did he write to him.

"I can't have you in my house," he replied on one occasion. "It can
be of no interest to me where or how you spend your leave—or your
life, for that matter."

The prejudice against Nnaemeka's marriage was not confined to
his little village. In Lagos, especially among his people who worked
there, it showed itself in a different way. Their women, when they met
at their village meeting, were not hostile to Nene. Rather, they paid
her such excessive deference as to make her feel she was not one of
them. But as time went on, Nene gradually broke through some of this
prejudice and even began to make friends among them. Slowly and
grudgingly they began to admit that she kept her home much better
than most of them.

The story eventually got to the little village in the heart of the Ibo
country that Nnaemeka and his young wife were a most happy couple.
But his father was one of the few people in the village who knew nothing about this. He always displayed so much temper whenever his
son's name was mentioned that everyone avoided it in his presence.
By a tremendous effort of will he had succeeded in pushing his son to
the back of his mind. The strain had nearly killed him but he had per-
severed, and won.

Then one day he received a letter from Nene, and in spite of himself he began to glance through it perfunctorily until all of a sudden
the expression on his face changed and he began to read more carefully.

*…Our two sons, from the day they learnt that they had a grandfather,
have insisted on being taken to him. I find it impossible to tell them that
you will not see them. I implore you to allow Nnaemeka to bring them
home for a short time during his leave next month. I shall remain here
in Lagos…*

The old man at once felt the resolution he had built up over so
many years falling in. He was telling himself that he must not give in.
He tried to steel his heart against all emotional appeals. It was a re-
enactment of that other struggle. He leaned against a window and
looked out. The sky was overcast with heavy black clouds and a high
wind began to blow filling the air with dust and dry leaves. It was one
of those rare occasions when even Nature takes a hand in a human
fight. Very soon it began to rain, the first rain in the year. It came
down in large sharp drops and was accompanied by the lightning and
thunder which mark a change of season. Okeke was trying hard not to
think of his two grandsons. But he knew he was now fighting a losing
battle. He tried to hum a favorite hymn but the pattering of large rain
drops on the roof broke up the tune. His mind immediately returned
to the children. How could he shut his door against them? By a curious mental process he imagined them standing, sad and forsaken,
under the harsh angry weather—shut out from his house.

That night he hardly slept, from remorse—and a vague fear that he
might die without making it up to them.

## B. Second Reading

### Taking a Closer Look

Read the story a second time. Use the questions to gain a better understanding and to bring your experience to the story.

1. Which of the following do you think Okeke objected to most strongly concerning his son's choice of a wife?

    a. Nene was from a different tribe.
    b. She was educated.
    c. Nnaemeka had chosen her himself.

2. How did other villagers respond to Nnaemeka's disobedience? Do you find their responses typical of the older generation? In what way were Ibos in the city more tolerant?

3. At the end of the story, is Okeke more or less obstinate? Do you think he will agree to see his grandchildren or not?

4. What is the theme of the story?

    a. Sons should not go against their father's wishes.
    b. Love will always overcome family conflicts.
    c. Being right is not always the most important thing.

### Delving More Deeply

Find the following text in the lines indicated. Use the surrounding text and your experience to give an informed answer.

1. …*Nnaemeka expected the storm to burst.* (line 90) What do you think this metaphor about a storm refers to?

2. The author continues this metaphor of the storm in line 93. Which word relates to the possible result of a storm? What might this word mean in this context?

3. *It has never been heard…* (line 110) What does "it" refer to? Where and when was this said?

4. *Sons shall rise against their Fathers; it is there in the Holy Book.* (lines 117–118) What book is Okeke talking about? In what sense will sons rise against their fathers?

5. *I shall not call in a native doctor.* (line 131) Why does Okeke feel this way?

**6. *It was a re-enactment of that other struggle.*** (lines 187–188)
What was the "other struggle?"

**FOLLOW-UP**
Discuss your answers in
small groups.

**7.** Why do you think the author ends the story with a description of a rainstorm? *(lines 189–end)*

# III. STRENGTHENING SKILLS THROUGH THE TEXT

## A. Responding to the Reading

Write at least 75 words on *one* of the following topics. When you finish, choose a classmate to listen to what you have written.

**1.** Did you like this story? Why or why not?

**2.** Write a letter to one of the characters in the story, expressing your feelings and opinions about his or her behavior in the story.

_____

_____

_____

_____

_____

_____

_____

_____

_____

_____

_____

_____

_____

_____

_____

# B.   Global Comprehension Check: Collaborative Summary

In groups of three or four, write an 80-word summary of "Marriage is a Private Affair." Choose one group member to write the summary, but work together in composing it. Choose points for the summary carefully to cover the basic events of the story. Be sure to express the theme in your summary, but do not include opinion. Write complete sentences in a cohesive paragraph (not a list), but do not exceed 80 words. Begin as indicated below:

**"Marriage is a Private Affair" by Chinua Achebe is a story about**

_____

_____

_____

_____

_____

_____

_____

_____

**FOLLOW-UP**

Exchange summaries with other groups. What ideas did others include that your group didn't? What did you include in your summary that others did not? Did your group miss any important ideas?

_____

_____

_____

_____

_____

**ALTERNATIVE FOLLOW-UP**

Each group can read its summary aloud to the class, and then the class can vote for the best one.

_____

_____

# C. Text-Based Focus on Vocabulary

Use the given line numbers to check the context in the story to help you understand the meanings of the numbered word or phrases below. Then circle the letter of the choice which is closest in meaning.

## The Vocabulary of Conflict and Reconciliation

The following vocabulary is used as the author explores the conflict between Okeke and his son and daughter-in-law.

1. *condemned vehemently* (lines 81–82)

   a. talked about jokingly
   b. criticized angrily
   c. greatly approved of

2. *[his] heart was hardened* (line 96)

   a. mind was made up
   b. heart was broken
   c. spirits were low

3. *gave him up as lost* (line 97)

   a. stopped looking for him
   b. stopped shouting at him
   c. stopped trying to change him

4. *commiserate with* (line 112)

   a. sympathize with
   b. criticize gently
   c. insult strongly

5. *paid her such excessive deference* (lines 163–164)

   a. treated with great hostility
   b. treated with too much respect
   c. mistreated verbally

6. *steel his heart against* (line 187)

   a. take what was not his
   b. ignore
   c. strengthen himself against

7. ***fighting a losing battle*** *(lines 195–196)*

    **a.**  not going to win
    **b.**  fighting harder than before
    **c.**  fighting less hard

8. ***shut his door against them*** *(line 198)*

    **a.**  turn them out of his house
    **b.**  close his heart to them
    **c.**  keep his money from them

9. ***making it up to them*** *(line 202)*

    **a.**  doing something to pay for what he'd done
    **b.**  inventing an excuse for his behavior
    **c.**  forgetting the past to make a better future

# General Vocabulary

1. ***kindly-disposed to*** *(line 25)*

    **a.**  fond of
    **b.**  friendly and helpful to
    **c.**  falsely friendly towards

2. ***upbringing*** *(line 46)*

    **a.**  childhood training and education
    **b.**  attendance at church, religious education
    **c.**  training to be a good wife and mother

3. ***retreat*** *(line 52)*

    **a.**  a place to eat and entertain friends
    **b.**  a place to work without interruption
    **c.**  a place for quiet and rest

4. ***menacing*** *(line 93)*

    **a.**  comforting
    **b.**  potentially dangerous
    **c.**  hard to understand

5. ***grief*** *(line 107)*

    **a.**  deep sorrow
    **b.**  impenetrable silence
    **c.**  inexplicable anger

6. **superstitious** *(line 132)*

    **a.** unreasonable

    **b.** believing in magic

    **c.** not very well educated

7. **mutilated** *(line 149)*

    **a.** returned

    **b.** cut, torn

    **c.** unwanted

8. **implore** *(line 182)*

    **a.** insist on

    **b.** not allow

    **c.** beg

9. **resolution** *(line 185)*

    **a.** strong family bonds

    **b.** part of a house

    **c.** determined decision

**FOLLOW-UP**

Check your answers as directed by your teacher.

# Vocabulary Bee

Divide the class into teams of four or five members. Your teacher will choose words at random from the exercises and assign one to each group in turn. Each group has one minute to prepare a sentence in which the word is used correctly and which illustrates the meaning of the word in context. At the end of the minute, the teacher will call for the sentence, which must be produced immediately upon request. (Only one person is allowed to speak for the group at this point.) The teacher will judge the sentence. Each team will receive a point for each sentence the teacher judges correct. The group with the most points wins.

**Example:** TEACHER: **hostile**

    GROUP 1: Okeke was **hostile**.

(No point is given as the sentence does not illustrate the meaning of hostile even though the grammar is correct.

    GROUP 2: Okeke was **hostile** to the idea of Nnaemeka marrying a girl Okeke didn't approve of.

(One point is given for a correct, illustrative sentence.)

# IV. MOVING BEYOND THE TEXT

## A. Discussion and Writing

Discuss the following topics as a class or in groups. Your teacher may assign a different topic to each group and ask a group leader to summarize its discussion for the class. Write on one or more of the topics as instructed by your teacher.

1. Rank Nnaemeka, Nene, and Okeke from best to worst in terms of their character. 1 = best, etc. Explain your choices.

2. Would the average father in your country react the way Okeke did in this situation? Explain.

3. Do you think Okeke's heart would have been softened in the same way if the children had been girls? Why or why not?

4. From a sociological point of view, the conflict in "Marriage is a Private Affair" is one between traditional rural values (represented by Okeke) and modern urban values (represented by Nnaemeka and Nene). Are there conflicts between traditional values and modern ones in your culture? What are they? How can the conflicts be resolved?

5. Is your society divided like the one in Nigeria, if not along tribal lines, then along those of social class, race, or religion? Can a young person marry a person from another class, race, or religion with his or her parents' and society's approval? Explain.

6. Continue telling the story in your own words. Tell what happens in the year following the end of the story. Some questions you might want to address: Did Okeke finally accept Nene? Did he reconcile with his son? What did he do for his grandchildren? Will your story have a happy ending?

7. Compare the themes of "Marriage is a Private Affair" and "Your Children Are Not Your Children."

## B. Debate: Choosing a Spouse

Your teacher will select two groups of three to four students. The first group will argue the "pro" position. The second group will argue the "con" position. The rest of the class will act as judges.

**Proposition:** *Young people should be free to marry the person of their choice.*

1. **Preparation:** The "pro" group and the "con" group meet to brainstorm arguments to support their position. Each team member selects a different argument and prepares to speak for one to two minutes.

2. **The Debate:** The "pro" team goes first. Each member speaks for up to two minutes. The "con" team then has two minutes to ask *questions* of members of the pro team. (These questions are intended to point out weaknesses in their arguments.) The "con" team now has its turn. Each member speaks for up to two minutes. Then the "pro" team has two minutes to question the "con" team. The teams then take a five-minute recess during which they prepare a one-to two-minute summary of their strongest arguments and select one person to deliver this summary. The "con" team presents its summary first, the "pro" team last.

3. **The Judgment:** Classmates should vote for the winning team not according to which side they agreed with but according to which side presented and supported (with logic and examples) the strongest arguments.

# C.  Scenarios

Your teacher will divide the class into two groups. Each person in one group will receive Scenario "A." Each person in the second group will receive Scenario "B." After everyone has read and understood his scenario, each person should tell his or her group how he or she will try to accomplish the task. When everybody has had a turn, your teacher will pair up Scenario A students with Scenario B students and give you a certain amount of time to accomplish your task. When you are finished or the time is up, return to your original group and report your results. That is, each person should take a turn and tell the group what happened. Were you successful? Why or why not? What did the other person say to you?

What do you think is bothering this man and woman?

# Lesson 8

## A DEUX
### William Wood, U.S.A.

## A WINTER'S TALE
### D.H.Lawrence, England

## MUSIC I HEARD
### Conrad Aiken, U.S.A.

# I. GETTING READY

## A. Discussion: Romantic Associations

Look at the words and phrases below. Try to imagine a romantic association for each one.

**Example:** *Blessed* makes me think of a person who is loved by the person he loves; he feels fortunate, as if God has favored him.

**FOLLOW–UP**
Share your associations with a classmate or the class.

| | | | |
|---|---|---|---|
| *to pinch* | *to beg* | *a glass* | *bread* |
| *a sigh* | *beloved* | *sobs* | *the inevitable farewell* |
| *blessed* | | | |

# II. ENGAGING WITH THE TEXT

## A. First Exposure: Listening

You will listen, as your teacher reads, to three *very different* poems about love. They differ in how the poets feel about love, that is, in the *tone* each poet uses to describe love.

### Poem 1: "A Deux"

Listen to answer these questions:

✦ Is this poem playful or serious? calm or excited?

Listen again to answer these questions:

✦ What do "I" do to "you?"

✦ What do "you" do to "me?"

**FOLLOW–UP**
Share your answers.

✦ What are they doing?

## Poem 2: "A Winter's Tale"

Read the vocabulary, and then listen to answer the questions.

*verge* border, edge

*obscures* hides, makes difficult to see

*mist* thin fog

◆    Is this poem solemn or playful? joyful or tragic?

Listen again to answer these questions:

◆    Which person has bad news to deliver—the writer or the woman he is going to meet?

**FOLLOW-UP**
Share your answers.

◆    What does this news seem to be?

## Poem 3: "Music I Heard"

Listen to answer these questions:

◆    Is this poem solemn or playful? nostalgic or expectant?

Listen again to answer these questions:

◆    What things remind the poet of the person he loved?

**FOLLOW-UP**
Share your answers.

◆    What do you think happened to the person the poet loved?

# B.    Second Exposure: Reading

Read each of the poems silently to yourself. Answer the questions that follow each poem.

## A Deux

I pinch your arm,
You twist my leg,
I make you cry,
You make me beg,
I dry your eyes,
You wipe my nose,
And that's the way
The kissing goes.

## Questions

1. How old do you think the people in the poem are?

2. Do they like each other? Why do you think so?

3. Have you ever had an experience like this?

## A Winter's Tale

Yesterday the fields were only grey with scattered snow,
And now the longest grass-leaves hardly emerge;
Yet her deep footsteps mark the snow, and go
On towards the pines at the hill's verge.

I cannot see her, since the mist's pale scarf
Obscures the dark wood and the full orange sky;
But she's waiting, I know, impatient and cold, half
Sobs struggling into her frosty sigh.

Why does she come so promptly, when she must know
She's only the nearer to the inevitable farewell?
The hill is steep, on the snow my steps are slow—
Why does she come, when she knows what I have to tell?

## Questions

1. What time of year is it in the poem? How do you know?

2. Where is "she" waiting? Why can't the narrator see her?

3. How is she feeling? Explain your answer.

4. How does the narrator feel? Explain your answer.

5. Will the narrator have the courage to deliver his message?

### Music I Heard

Music I heard with you was more than music,
And bread I broke with you was more than bread;
Now that I am without you, all is desolate;
All that was once so beautiful is dead.

Your hands once touched this table and this silver,
And I have seen your fingers hold this glass.
These things do not remember you, beloved,
And yet your touch upon them will not pass.

For it was in my heart you moved among them,
And blessed them with your hands and with your eyes;
And in my heart they will remember always,—
They knew you once, O beautiful and wise.

## Questions

1. What experiences did the narrator and the "beloved" share together? Explain your answer.

2. What are "these things" in line 7?

3. How is it possible that "they [things] will remember always?"

4. Do you think the "beloved" is a man or a woman? Explain your answer.

# III. STRENGTHENING SKILLS THROUGH THE TEXT

## A.  Characterizing the Poems

Decide which words characterize each poem the best.

| | | |
|---|---|---|
| *melancholy* | *playfulness* | *liveliness* |
| *sadness* | *light-heartedness* | *pity* |
| *grief* | *fear* | *sorrow* |

**FOLLOW-UP**
Discuss your choices.

## B.  Responding to the Reading

Choose the poem that you like the best. Write 75 words on *one* of the following topics. When you finish, choose a classmate to listen to what you have written.

1. Why did you like this poem?

2. Which lines from the poem do you like the best? Why?

_____

_____

_____

_____

_____

_____

_____

_____

_____

_____

_____

# IV. MOVING BEYOND THE TEXT

## A. Writing a Poem

Write a poem of your own of at least 4 to 6 lines on some aspect of love. Decide what tone you wish your poem to have: lighthearted, sad, sorrowful, tragic, and so on.

_____

_____

_____

_____

_____

_____

_____

**FOLLOW-UP**
Share your poem with one or more classmates.

_____

_____

Who is this woman? Where does she live?
What kind of person is she? What kind of a life does she have?

# Lesson 9

## MARÍA CONCEPCIÓN

### Katherine Anne Porter

### U.S.A.

# I. GETTING READY

# A. Discussion: Love and Vengeance

The following quotations (two from Shakespeare, one from the Bible, and one from a novel) contain words such as *vengeance, revenge, blood, love, death, grave, jealousy, fire, faithless, faithful,* and *tragedies.* In small groups discuss the meanings of these words. Then read the quotations to answer the questions which follow each one.

### Quotation 1

Vengeance is in my heart, death in my hand,
Blood and revenge are hammering in my head.
    Shakespeare, *Titus Andronicus* II.iii.

◆   How strong is the feeling for revenge if it is "hammering?" Can you visualize a person feeling this vengeful? How would the person's face look?

### Quotation 2

Love is strong as death; jealousy is cruel as the grave; the coals thereof are coals of fire.
    *Song of Solomon* 8:6

◆   What can feel like fire: love, death, or jealousy?

### Quotation 3

Those who are faithless know the pleasures of love; it is the faithful who know love's tragedies.
    Oscar Wilde, *The Picture of Dorian Gray*

◆   In what way might the faithful suffer more than the faithless? Why?

### Quotation 4

Sigh no more, ladies, sigh no more,
Men were deceivers ever,
One foot in sea and one on shore;
To one thing constant never.
    Shakespeare, *Much Ado About Nothing* II.iii.

◆   Have men changed since Shakespeare's time, or do you think this stanza is still good advice to women? Why?

**FOLLOW-UP**
Discuss your answers to the questions as a class. Then discuss which quotations you like best and why. Can you guess what the story "María Concepción" might be about?

## B.  Entering the Story through Listening

Listen to these opening paragraphs from the story to choose the answers to the questions below. Place an **X** in the blank before the correct choice in parentheses.

1.  María Concepción works ( _____ hard, _____ very little).

2.  María Concepción is ( _____ happy, _____ unhappy) with her life.

3.  María Concepción ( _____ has, _____ will have) a child.

## C.  Background

Read the following information, noting the italicized words, to help you understand the story more easily and fully.

   "María Concepción" is set in a village in Mexico. The native American culture of the village is heavily influenced by the Catholic religion brought by the Spanish conquerors. For example, the church is obviously important to the villagers, but there is also a "medicine woman" who sells strange, magical ingredients to cure the villagers' illnesses as well as charms to protect them from evil. In this village culture, male infidelity is not uncommon and women are expected to be tolerant of this behavior. María Concepción is a proud, religious woman who is unable or unwilling to accept this kind of behavior in her husband, whom she has married *in* the church.

The writer has used a number of Spanish words, some older English words, and some religious vocabulary that may be unfamiliar to you.

SPANISH
*rebozo (line 16)* a long scarf worn over the head and shoulders
*hacienda (line 51)* a large house on a ranch or farm
*jacal (lines 63, 115)* a house made of stakes driven into the ground and covered with dried grass
*tortillas (line 160)* flat Mexican bread made of ground corn or wheat
*pulque (line 351)* a cloudy alcoholic drink made from agave cactus
*brasero (line 440)* charcoal burner

OLDER ENGLISH

***thou, thy, thee*** *(lines 416–420),* **shalt** *(line 452)* older, second-person
singular forms no longer commonly used in modern English of *you*
(subject), *your, you* (object), and *will,* respectively. (These forms
are possibly used by the author to correspond to the second-person
singular pronouns and verbs used in Spanish to address children
and persons one is intimately associated with.)

RELIGIOUS VOCABULARY

***cross*** *(line 211)* the symbol of Christianity: +
***communion*** *(line 212)* a sacrament of the church (an important
religious ritual)
***devil-possessed*** *(line 213)* controlled by evil powers
***shrine*** *(line 408)* a place (not a church) devoted to a holy person and
one that believers visit to worship
***repent*** *(line 458)* to regret past actions one feels were bad
***Blessed Image Himself*** *(line 544–545)* Jesus Christ

# II. ENGAGING WITH THE TEXT

## A1. Section I: First Reading

Because it is a longer story, "María Concepción" is divided into three
sections. Read the following questions *before* you begin the story.
Then read **Section I** *(lines 1–180).*

1.   What kind of person is María Concepción? What kind of life does
she have?

2.   Why is María Concepción proud of how she got married?

3.   What does María Concepción discover when she stops on her way
for some honey?

4.   How does she feel about this incident? What will she do about it?

5.   What does María Concepción think of the American anthropolo-
gist and his work?

6.   What kind of a person is Juan?

## María Concepción *(Section I )*

1    María Concepción walked carefully, keeping to the middle of the
white dusty road, where the maguey thorns and the treacherous
curved spines of organ cactus had not gathered so profusely. She
would have enjoyed resting for a moment in the dark shade by the
5    roadside, but she had no time to waste drawing cactus needles from
her feet. Juan and his chief would be waiting for their food in the
damp trenches of the buried city.

She carried about a dozen living fowls slung over her right shoulder, their feet fastened together. Half of them fell upon the flat of her
10   back, the balance dangled uneasily over her breast. They wriggled their
benumbed and swollen legs against her neck, they twisted their stupe-
fied eyes and peered into her face inquiringly. She did not see them or
think of them. Her left arm was tired with the weight of the food basket, and she was hungry after her long morning's work.

15   Her straight back outlined itself strongly under her clean bright
blue cotton rebozo. Instinctive serenity softened her black eyes,
shaped like almonds, set far apart, and tilted a bit endwise. She walked
with the free, natural, guarded ease of the primitive woman carrying
an unborn child. The shape of her body was easy, the swelling life was
20   not a distortion, but the right inevitable proportions of a woman. She
was entirely contented. Her husband was at work and she was on her
way to market to sell her fowls.

Her small house sat half-way up a shallow hill, under a clump of
pepper-trees, a wall of organ cactus enclosing it on the side nearest to
25   the road. Now she came down into the valley, divided by the narrow
spring, and crossed a bridge of loose stones near the hut where María
Rosa the beekeeper lived with her old godmother, Lupe the medicine
woman. María Concepción had no faith in the charred owl bones, the
singed rabbit fur, the cat entrails, the messes and ointments sold by
30   Lupe to the ailing of the village. She was a good Christian, and drank
simple herb teas for headache and stomachache, or bought her remedies bottled, with printed directions that she could not read, at the
drugstore near the city market, where she went almost daily. But she
often bought a jar of honey from young María Rosa, a pretty, shy child
35   only fifteen years old.

María Concepción and her husband, Juan Villegas, were each a little past their eighteenth year. She had a good reputation with the
neighbors as an energetic religious woman who could drive a bargain
to the end. It was commonly known that if she wished to buy a new
40   rebozo for herself or a shirt for Juan, she could bring out a sack of
hard silver coins for the purpose.

She had paid for the license, nearly a year ago, the potent bit of
stamped paper which permits people to be married in the church. She
had given money to the priest before she and Juan walked together up
45   to the altar the Monday after Holy Week. It had been the adventure of
the villagers to go, three Sundays one after another, to hear the banns
called by the priest for Juan de Dios Villegas and María Concepción
Manríques, who were actually getting married in the church, instead
of behind it, which was the usual custom, less expensive, and as bind-

50　ing as any other ceremony. But María Concepción was always as proud as if she owned a hacienda.

She paused on the bridge and dabbled her feet in the water, her eyes resting themselves from the sun-rays in a fixed gaze to the far-off mountains, deeply blue under their hanging drift of clouds. It came to

55　her that she would like a fresh crust of honey. The delicious aroma of bees, their slow thrilling hum, awakened a pleasant desire for a flake of sweetness in her mouth.

"If I do not eat it now, I shall mark my child," she thought, peering through the crevices in the thick hedge of cactus that sheered up

60　nakedly, like bared knife blades set protectively around the small clearing. The place was so silent she doubted if María Rosa and Lupe were at home.

The leaning jacal of dried rush-withes and corn sheaves, bound to tall saplings thrust into the earth, roofed with yellowed maguey leaves

65　flattened and overlapping like shingles, hunched drowsy and fragrant in the warmth of noonday. The hives, similarly made, were scattered towards the back of the clearing, like small mounds of clean vegetable refuse. Over each mound there hung a dusty golden shimmer of bees.

A light gay scream of laughter rose from behind the hut; a man's

70　short laugh joined in. "Ah, hahahaha!" went the voices together high and low, like a song.

"So María Rosa has a man!" María Concepción stopped short, smiling, shifted her burden slightly, and bent forward shading her eyes to see more clearly through the spaces of the hedge.

75　María Rosa ran, dodging between beehives, parting two stunted jasmine bushes as she came, lifting her knees in swift leaps, looking over her shoulder and laughing in a quivering, excited way. A heavy jar, swung to her wrist by the handle, knocked against her thighs as she ran. Her toes pushed up sudden spurts of dust, her half-raveled

80　braids showered around her shoulders in long crinkled wisps.

Juan Villegas ran after her, also laughing strangely, his teeth set, both rows gleaming behind the small soft black beard growing sparsely on his lips, his chin, leaving his brown cheeks girl-smooth. When he seized her, he clenched so hard her chemise gave way and ripped from

85　her shoulder. She stopped laughing at this, pushed him away and stood silent, trying to pull up the torn sleeve with one hand. Her pointed chin and dark red mouth moved in an uncertain way, as if she wished to laugh again; her long black lashes flickered with the quick-moving lights in her hidden eyes.

90　María Concepción did not stir nor breathe for some seconds. Her forehead was cold, and yet boiling water seemed to be pouring slowly along her spine. An unaccountable pain was in her knees, as if they were broken. She was afraid Juan and María Rosa would feel her eyes fixed upon them and would find her there, unable to move, spying

95　upon them. But they did not pass beyond the enclosure, nor even glance towards the gap in the wall opening upon the road.

Juan lifted one of María Rosa's loosened braids and slapped her neck with it playfully. She smiled softly, consentingly. Together they moved back through the hives of honey-comb. María Rosa balanced

100 her jar on one hip and swung her long full petticoats with every step. Juan flourished his wide hat back and forth, walking proudly as a game-cock.

María Concepción came out of the heavy cloud which enwrapped her head and bound her throat, and found herself walking onward,
105 keeping the road without knowing it, feeling her way delicately, her ears strumming as if all María Rosa's bees had hived in them. Her careful sense of duty kept her moving toward the buried city where Juan's chief, the American archeologist, was taking his midday rest, waiting for his food.
110 Juan and María Rosa! She burned all over now, as if a layer of tiny fig-cactus bristles, as cruel as spun glass, had crawled under her skin. She wished to sit down quietly and wait for her death, but not until she had cut the throats of her man and that girl who were laughing and kissing under the cornstalks. Once when she was a young girl she
115 had come back from market to find her jacal burned to a pile of ash and her few silver coins gone. A dark empty feeling had filled her; she kept moving about the place, not believing her eyes, expecting it all to take shape again before her. But it was gone, and though she knew an enemy had done it, she could not find out who it was, and could only
120 curse and threaten the air. Now here was a worse thing, but she knew her enemy. María Rosa, that sinful girl, shameless! She heard herself saying a harsh, true word about María Rosa, saying it aloud as if she expected someone to agree with her: "Yes, she is a whore! She has no right to live."
125 At this moment the gray untidy head of Givens appeared over the edges of the newest trench he had caused to be dug in his field of excavations. The long deep crevasses, in which a man might stand without being seen, lay crisscrossed like orderly gashes of a giant scalpel. Nearly all of the men of the community worked for Givens, helping
130 him to uncover the lost city of their ancestors. They worked all the year through and prospered, digging every day for those small clay heads and bits of pottery and fragments of painted walls for which there was no good use on earth, being all broken and encrusted with clay. They themselves could make better ones, perfectly stout and new,
135 which they took to town and peddled to foreigners for real money. But the unearthly delight of the chief in finding these worn-out things was an endless puzzle. He would fairly roar for joy at times, waving a shattered pot or a human skull above his head, shouting for his photographer to come and make a picture of this!
140 Now he emerged, and his young enthusiast's eyes welcomed María Concepción from his old-man face, covered with hard wrinkles and burned to the color of red earth. "I hope you've brought me a nice fat one." He selected a fowl from the bunch dangling nearest him as María Concepción, wordless, leaned over the trench. "Dress it for me,
145 there's a good girl. I'll broil it."

María Concepción took the fowl by the head, and silently, swiftly drew her knife across its throat, twisting the head off with the casual firmness she might use with the top of a beet.

"Good God, woman, you do have nerve," said Givens, watching
her. "I can't do that. It gives me the creeps."

"My home country is Guadalajara," explained María Concepción,
without bravado, as she picked and gutted the fowl.

She stood and regarded Givens condescendingly, that diverting
white man who had no woman of his own to cook for him, and moreover appeared not to feel any loss of dignity in preparing his own
food. He squatted now, eyes squinted, nose wrinkled to avoid the
smoke, turning the roasting fowl busily on a stick. A mysterious man,
undoubtedly rich, and Juan's chief, therefore to be respected, to be
placated.

"The tortillas are fresh and hot, señor," she murmured gently.
"With your permission I will now go to market."

"Yes, yes, run along, bring me another of these tomorrow." Givens
turned his head to look at her again. Her grand manner sometimes
reminded him of royalty in exile. He noticed her unnatural paleness.
"The sun is too hot, eh?" he asked.

"Yes, sir. Pardon me, but Juan will be here soon?"

"He ought to be here now. Leave his food. The others will eat it."

She moved away, the blue of her rebozo became a dancing spot in
the heat waves that rose from the gray-red soil. Givens liked his
Indians best when he could feel a fatherly indulgence for their primitive childish ways. He told comic stories of Juan's escapades, of how
often he had saved him, in the past five years, from going to jail, and
even from being shot, for his varied and always unexpected misdeeds.

"I am never a minute too soon to get him out of one pickle or
another," he would say. "Well, he's a good worker, and I know how to
manage him."

After Juan was married, he used to twit him, with exactly the right
shade of condescension, on his many infidelities to María Concepción.
"She'll catch you yet, and God help you!" he was fond of saying, and
Juan would laugh with immense pleasure.

# B1.  Section I: Second Reading

Read *Section I* a second time to answer the following true/false
questions. Be prepared to explain your answers.

_____ **1.** At the beginning of the story, María Concepción was
happy with her life although it was a hard one.

_____ **2.** María Concepción was respected in her community
because she was hardworking, religious, and clever.

_____ **3.** María Concepción was proud that she was able to get
married inside the church because most people of her class could not
afford to.

━━━━━━━━━━━━━━━━━━━━━━━━━━━━━━━━━━

_____ 4. María Concepción stopped at María Rosa's place that day because she suspected that her husband Juan might be there.

_____ 5. Juan was probably at María Rosa's to get honey for his wife, who liked it very much.

_____ 6. María Concepción was so overcome by Juan's infidelity that she could not go on with her work that day.

_____ 7. Her husband's adultery brought back memories of when her home had been burned and robbed, an even more painful memory.

_____ 8. María Concepción had great respect for Givens's work even though she found the man a bit strange.

**FOLLOW-UP**
Discuss your answers to the First and Second Reading questions in small groups. Then go on to Part C1, which follows.

_____ 9. María Concepción regularly brought food to Givens and his crew.

_____ 10. Givens apparently liked Juan because he was a good worker who stayed out of trouble.

# C1.  Response and Prediction

Discuss the following questions in small groups before reading Section II.

1.  Is María Concepción's reaction to Juan's infidelity with María Rosa a normal one? Do you sympathize with her?

2.  How should María Concepción handle this situation; that is, what should she do, if anything?

3.  Will María Concepción confront Juan and/or Rosa about this infidelity? What will happen if she does?

# A2.  Section II: First Reading

Read the following questions before you begin Section II. Then read **Section II** *(lines 181–390)*.

*(lines 181–247)*
1.  Whom does María Concepción blame for Juan's infidelities?

2.  What other calamities happen to María Concepción?

**3.** How does María Concepción react to these additional calamities?

*(lines 248–342)*
**4.** Why is Juan facing the firing squad?

**5.** What does Juan tell Givens about his relationship with María Concepción?

**6.** What does Givens try to warn Juan about?

**7.** Why does life seem so perfect to Juan at this time?

*(lines 343–390)*
**8.** What happens when Juan goes home?

**9.** What overcomes María Concepción as she sets out to go to market?

### María Concepción (*Section II* )

It did not occur to María Concepción to tell Juan she had found him out. During the day her anger against him died, and her anger against María Rosa grew. She kept saying to herself, "When I was a young girl like María Rosa, if a man had caught hold of me so, I would
185 have broken my jar over his head." She forgot completely that she had not resisted even so much as María Rosa, on that day that Juan had first taken hold of her. Besides she had married him afterwards in the church, and that was a very different thing.

Juan did not come home that night, but went away to war and
190 María Rosa went with him. Juan had a rifle at his shoulder and two pistols at his belt. María Rosa wore a rifle also, slung on her back along with the blankets and the cooking pots. They joined the nearest detachment of troops in the field, and María Rosa marched ahead with the battalion of experienced women of war, which went over the
195 crops like locusts, gathering provisions for the army. She cooked with them, and ate with them what was left after the men had eaten. After battles she went out on the field with the others to salvage clothing and ammunition and guns from the slain before they should begin to swell in the heat. Sometimes they would encounter the women from
200 the other army, and a second battle as grim as the first would take place.

There was no particular scandal in the village. People shrugged, grinned. It was far better that they were gone. The neighbors went around saying that María Rosa was safer in the army than she would be in the same village with María Concepción.
205 María Concepción did not weep when Juan left her; and when the baby was born, and died within four days, she did not weep. "She is mere stone," said old Lupe, who went over and offered charms to preserve the baby.

"May you rot in hell with your charms," said María Concepción.

210   If she had not gone so regularly to church, lighting candles before the saints, kneeling with her arms spread in the form of a cross for hours at a time, and receiving holy communion every month, there might have been talk of her being devil-possessed, her face was so changed and blind-looking. But this was impossible when, after all,
215   she had been married by the priest. It must be, they reasoned, that she was being punished for her pride. They decided that this was the true cause for everything: she was altogether too proud. So they pitied her.

During the year that Juan and María Rosa were gone María Concepción sold her fowls and looked after her garden and her sack of
220   hard coins grew. Lupe had no talent for bees, and the hives did not prosper. She began to blame María Rosa for running away, and to praise María Concepción for her behavior. She used to see María Concepción at the market or at church, and she always said that no one could tell by looking at her now that she was a woman who had
225   such a heavy grief.

"I pray God everything goes well with María Concepción from this out," she would say, "for she has had her share of trouble."

When some idle person repeated this to the deserted woman, she went down to Lupe's house and stood within the clearing and called to
230   the medicine woman, who sat in her doorway stirring a mess of her infallible cure for sores: "Keep your prayers to yourself, Lupe, or offer them for others who need them. I will ask God for what I want in this world."

"And will you get it, you think, María Concepción?" asked Lupe,
235   tittering cruelly and smelling the wooden mixing spoon. "Did you pray for what you have now?"

Afterward everyone noticed that María Concepción went oftener to church, and even seldomer to the village to talk with the other women as they sat along the curb, nursing their babies and eating fruit, at the
240   end of the market-day.

"She is wrong to take us for enemies," said old Soledad, who was a thinker and a peace-maker. "All women have these troubles. Well, we should suffer together."

But María Concepción lived alone. She was gaunt, as if something
245   were gnawing her away inside, her eyes were sunken, and she would not speak a word if she could help it. She worked harder than ever, and her butchering knife was scarcely ever out of her hand.

Juan and María Rosa, disgusted with military life, came home one day without asking permission of anyone. The field of war had unrolled
250   itself, a long scroll of vexations, until the end had frayed out within twenty miles of Juan's village. So he and María Rosa, now lean as a wolf, burdened with a child daily expected, set out with no farewells to the regiment and walked home.

They arrived one morning about daybreak. Juan was picked up on
255   sight by a group of military police from the small barracks on the edge

of town, and taken to prison, where the officer in charge told him with impersonal cheerfulness that he would add one to a catch of ten waiting to be shot as deserters the next morning.

María Rosa, screaming and falling on her face in the road, was taken under the armpits by two guards and helped briskly to her jacal, now sadly run down. She was received with professional importance by Lupe, who helped the baby to be born at once.

Limping with foot soreness, a layer of dust concealing his fine new clothes got mysteriously from somewhere, Juan appeared before the captain at the barracks. The captain recognized him as head digger for his good friend Givens, and dispatched a note to Givens saying: "I am holding the person of Juan Villegas awaiting your further disposition."

When Givens showed up Juan was delivered to him with the urgent request that nothing be made public about so humane and sensible an operation on the part of military authority.

Juan walked out of the rather stifling atmosphere of the drumhead court, a definite air of swagger about him. His hat, of unreasonable dimensions and embroidered with silver thread, hung over one eyebrow, secured at the back by a cord of silver dripping with bright blue tassels. His shirt was of a checkerboard pattern in green and black, his white cotton trousers were bound by a belt of yellow leather tooled in red. His feet were bare, full of stone bruises, and sadly ragged as to toenails. He removed his cigarette from the corner of his full-lipped wide mouth. He removed the splendid hat. His black dusty hair, pressed moistly to his forehead, sprang up suddenly in a cloudy thatch of his crown. He bowed to the officer, who appeared to be gazing at a vacuum. He swung his arm wide in a free circle upsoaring towards the prison window, where forlorn heads poked over the window sill, hot eyes following after the lucky departing one. Two or three of the heads nodded, and a half dozen hands were flipped at him in an effort to imitate his own casual and heady manner.

Juan kept up this insufferable pantomime until they rounded the first clump of fig-cactus. Then he seized Givens' hand and burst into oratory. "Blessed be the day your servant Juan Villegas first came under your eyes. From this day my life is yours without condition, ten thousand thanks with all my heart!"

"For God's sake stop playing the fool," said Givens irritably. "Some day I'm going to be five minutes too late."

"Well, it is nothing much to be shot, my chief—certainly you know I was not afraid—but to be shot in a drove of deserters, against a cold wall, just in the moment of my home-coming, by order of that…"

Glittering epithets tumbled over one another like explosions of a rocket. All the scandalous analogies from the animal and vegetable worlds were applied in a vivid, unique and personal way to the life, loves, and family history of the officer who had just set him free. When he had quite cursed himself dry, and his nerves were soothed, he added: "With your permission, my chief!"

"What will María Concepción say to all this?" asked Givens. "You are very informal, Juan, for a man who was married in the church."

Juan put on his hat.

"Oh, María Concepción! That's nothing. Look, my chief, to be married in the church is a great misfortune for a man. After that he is not himself any more. How can that woman complain when I do not drink even at fiestas enough to be really drunk? I do not beat her; never, never. We were always at peace. I say to her, Come here, and she comes straight. I say, Go there, and she goes quickly. Yet sometimes I looked at her and thought, Now I am married to that woman in the church, and I felt a sinking inside, as if something were lying heavy on my stomach. With María Rosa it is all different. She is not silent; she talks. When she talks too much, I slap her and say, Silence, thou simpleton! and she weeps. She is just a girl with whom I do as I please. You know how she used to keep those clean little bees in their hives? She is like their honey to me. I swear it. I would not harm María Concepción because I am married to her in the church; but also, my chief, I will not leave María Rosa, because she pleases me more than any other woman."

"Let me tell you, Juan, things haven't been going as well as you think. You be careful. Some day María Concepción will just take your head off with that carving knife of hers. You keep that in mind."

Juan's expression was the proper blend of masculine triumph and sentimental melancholy. It was pleasant to see himself in the rôle of hero to two such desirable women. He had just escaped from the threat of a disagreeable end. His clothes were new and handsome, and they had cost him just nothing. María Rosa had collected them for him here and there after battles. He was walking in the early sunshine, smelling the good smells of ripening cactus-figs, peaches, and melons, of pungent berries dangling from the pepper-trees, and the smoke of his cigarette under his nose. He was on his way to civilian life with his patient chief. His situation was ineffably perfect, and he swallowed it whole.

"My chief," he addressed Givens handsomely, as one man of the world to another, "women are good things, but not at this moment. With your permission, I will now go to the village and eat. My God, *how* I shall eat! Tomorrow morning very early I will come to the buried city and work like seven men. Let us forget María Concepción and María Rosa. Each one in her place. I will manage them when the time comes."

News of Juan's adventure soon got abroad, and Juan found many friends about him during the morning. They frankly commended his way of leaving the army. It was in itself the act of a hero. The new hero ate a great deal and drank somewhat, the occasion being better than a feast-day. It was almost noon before he returned to visit María Rosa.

He found her sitting on a clean straw mat, rubbing fat on her three-hour-old son. Before this felicitous vision Juan's emotions so twisted him that he returned to the village and invited every man in the "Death and Resurrection" pulque shop to drink with him.

Having thus taken leave of his balance, he started back to María Rosa, and found himself unaccountably in his own house, attempting to beat María Concepción by way of reëstablishing himself in his legal household.

María Concepción, knowing all the events of that unhappy day, was not in a yielding mood, and refused to be beaten. She did not scream nor implore; she stood her ground and resisted; she even struck at him. Juan, amazed, hardly knowing what he did, stepped back and gazed at her inquiringly through a leisurely whirling film which seemed to have lodged behind his eyes. Certainly he had not even thought of touching her. Oh, well, no harm done. He gave up, turned away, half-asleep on his feet. He dropped amiably in a shadowed corner and began to snore.

María Concepción, seeing that he was quiet, began to bind the legs of her fowls. It was market-day and she was late. She fumbled and tangled the bits of cord in her haste, and set off across the plowed fields instead of taking the accustomed road. She ran with a crazy panic in her head, her stumbling legs. Now and then she would stop and look about her, trying to place herself, then go on a few steps, until she realized that she was not going towards the market.

At once she came to her senses completely, recognized the thing that troubled her so terribly, was certain of what she wanted. She sat down quietly under a sheltering thorny bush and gave herself over to her long devouring sorrow. The thing which had for so long squeezed her whole body into a tight dumb knot of suffering suddenly broke with shocking violence. She jerked with the involuntary recoil of one who receives a blow, and the sweat poured from her skin as if the wounds of her whole life were shedding their salt ichor. Drawing her rebozo over her head, she bowed her forehead on her updrawn knees, and sat there in deadly silence and immobility. From time to time she lifted her head where the sweat formed steadily and poured down her face, drenching the front of her chemise, and her mouth had the shape of crying, but there were no tears and no sound. All her being was a dark confused memory of grief burning in her at night, of deadly baffled anger eating at her by day, until her very tongue tasted bitter, and her feet were as heavy as if she were mired in the muddy roads during the time of rains.

After a great while she stood up and threw the rebozo off her face, and set out walking again.

# B2. Section II: Second Reading

Read Section II a second time to answer the following true/false questions. Be prepared to explain your answers.

_____ **1.** The local villagers were not shocked when Juan and María Rosa left together for the war.

_____ **2.** María Concepción appreciated Lupe's sympathy when her baby died.

_____ **3.** The villagers began to think that María Concepción was possessed by the devil.

_____ **4.** María Concepción became increasingly solitary and isolated from the other villagers.

_____ **5.** Juan deserted from the army.

_____ **6.** Juan was not afraid to face the firing squad.

_____ **7.** After his narrow escape from the firing squad, Juan was ready to leave María Rosa and return to María Concepción, his legal wife.

_____ **8.** Juan was drunk when he visited María Concepción.

**FOLLOW-UP**
Discuss your answers to the First and Second Reading in small groups. Then go on to Part C2, which follows.

_____ **9.** When María Concepción left home that day, she was planning to go to market.

_____ **10.** When María Concepción continued walking after her violent attack of grief and sorrow, the market was no longer her immediate destination.

# C2. Response and Prediction

Discuss the following questions in small groups before reading Section III.

**1.** Is it right of María Concepción to blame María Rosa for Juan's infidelity?

**2.** Do you agree with the villagers' criticisms of María Concepción?

**3.** Where is María Concepción going at the end of Section II? Is Juan in danger?

# A3. Section III: First Reading

Read the following questions before you begin Section III. Then read _Section III_ (lines 391–end).

**1.** What has María Concepción done that Juan feels he must comfort her so?

**2.** Are Juan and María Concepción surprised when the gendarmes come to their house?

**3.** What emotions does María Concepción feel when she sees María Rosa's corpse?

**4.** In recounting the events of the day, who tells the whole truth? Why?

**5.** Do the gendarmes believe the accounts they hear? Why don't they arrest María Concepción?

**6.** Does the story end on a happy or a sad note? How so?

### María Concepción *(Section III)*

Juan awakened slowly, with long yawns and grumblings, alternated with short relapses into sleep full of visions and clamors. A blur of orange light seared his eyeballs when he tried to unseal his lids. There came from somewhere a low voice weeping without tears, saying
395     meaningless phrases over and over. He began to listen. He tugged at the leash of his stupor, he strained to grasp those words which terrified him even though he could not quite hear them. Then he came awake with frightening suddenness, sitting up and staring at the long sharpened streak of light piercing the corn-husk walls from the level
400     disappearing sun.

María Concepción stood in the doorway, looming colossally tall to his betrayed eyes. She was talking quickly, and calling his name. Then he saw her clearly.

"God's name!" said Juan, frozen to the marrow, "here I am facing
405     my death!" for the long knife she wore habitually at her belt was in her hand. But instead, she threw it away, clear from her, and got down on her knees, crawling toward him as he had seen her crawl many times toward the shrine at Guadalupe Villa. He watched her approach with such horror that the hair of his head seemed to be lifting itself away
410     from him. Falling forward upon her face, she huddled over him, lips moving in a ghostly whisper. Her words became clear, and Juan understood them all.

For a second he could not move nor speak. Then he took her head between both his hands, and supported her in this way, saying swiftly,
415     anxiously reassuring, almost in a babble:

"Oh, thou poor creature! Oh, madwoman! Oh, my María Concepción, unfortunate! Listen.... Don't be afraid. Listen to me! I will hide thee away, I thy own man will protect thee! Quiet! Not a sound!"
420     Trying to collect himself, he held her and cursed under his breath for a few moments in the gathering darkness. María Concepción bent over, face almost on the ground, her feet folded under her, as if she would hide behind him. For the first time in his life Juan was aware of danger. This was danger. María Concepción would be dragged away

425 between two gendarmes, with him following helpless and unarmed, to
spend the rest of her days in Belén Prison, maybe. Danger! The night
swarmed with threats. He stood up and dragged her up with him. She
was silent and perfectly rigid, holding to him with resistless strength,
her hands stiffened on his arms.

430 "Get me the knife," he told her in a whisper. She obeyed, her feet
slipping along the hard earth floor, her shoulders straight, her arms
close to her side. He lighted a candle. María Concepción held the knife
out to him. It was stained and dark even to the handle with drying
blood.

435 He frowned at her harshly, noting the same stains on her chemise
and hands.

"Take off thy clothes and wash thy hands," he ordered. He washed
the knife carefully, and threw the water wide of the doorway. She
watched him and did likewise with the bowl in which she had bathed.

440 "Light the brasero and cook food for me," he told her in the same
preemptory tone. He took her garments and went out. When he
returned, she was wearing an old soiled dress, and was fanning the fire
in the charcoal burner. Seating himself cross-legged near her, he stared
at her as at a creature unknown to him, who bewildered him utterly,

445 for whom there was no possible explanation. She did not turn her
head, but kept silent and still, except for the movements of her strong
hands fanning the blaze which cast sparks and small jets of white
smoke, flaring and dying rhythmically with the motion of the fan,
lighting her face and darkening it by turns.

450 Juan's voice barely disturbed the silence: "Listen to me carefully,
and tell me the truth, and when the gendarmes come here for us, thou
shalt have nothing to fear. But there will be something for us to settle
between us afterward."

The light from the charcoal burner shone in her eyes; a yellow

455 phosphorescence glimmered behind the dark iris.

"For me everything is settled now," she answered, in a tone so ten-
der, so grave, so heavy with suffering, that Juan felt his vitals contract.
He wished to repent openly, not as a man, but as a very small child.
He could not fathom her, nor himself, nor the mysterious fortunes of

460 life grown so instantly confused where all had seemed so gay and simple. He felt too that she had become invaluable, a woman without
equal among a million women, and he could not tell why. He drew an
enormous sigh that rattled in his chest.

"Yes, yes, it is all settled. I shall not go away again. We must stay

465 here together."

Whispering, he questioned her and she answered whispering, and
he instructed her over and over until she had her lesson by heart. The
hostile darkness of the night encroached upon them, flowing over the
narrow threshold, invading their hearts. It brought with it sighs and

470 murmurs, the pad of secretive feet in the near-by road, the sharp stac-
cato whimper of wind through the cactus leaves. All these familiar,
once friendly cadences were now invested with sinister terrors; a
dread, formless and uncontrollable, took hold of them both.

"Light another candle," said Juan, loudly, in too resolute, too sharp
a tone. "Let us eat now."

475

They sat facing each other and ate from the same dish, after their
old habit. Neither tasted what they ate. With food half-way to his
mouth, Juan listened. The sound of voices rose, spread, widened at the
turn of the road along the cactus wall. A spray of lantern light shot
through the hedge, a single voice slashed the blackness, ripped the
fragile layer of silence suspended above the hut.

480

"Juan Villegas!"

"Pass, friends!" Juan roared back cheerfully.

They stood in the doorway, simple cautious gendarmes from the
village, mixed-bloods themselves with Indian sympathies, well known
to all the community. They flashed their lanterns almost apologetically
upon the pleasant, harmless scene of a man eating supper with his
wife.

485

"Pardon, brother," said the leader. "Someone has killed the woman
María Rosa, and we must question her neighbors and friends." He
paused and added with an attempt at severity, "Naturally!"

490

"Naturally," agreed Juan. "You know that I was a good friend of
María Rosa. This is bad news."

They all went away together, the men walking in a group, María
Concepción following a few steps in the rear, near Juan. No one
spoke.

495

The two points of candlelight at María Rosa's head fluttered uneasily;
the shadows shifted and dodged on the stained darkened walls. To
María Concepción everything in the smothering enclosing room
shared an evil restlessness. The watchful faces of those called as wit-
nesses, the faces of old friends, were made alien by the look of speculation in their eyes. The ridges of the rose-colored rebozo thrown over
the body varied continually, as though the thing it covered was not
perfectly in repose. Her eyes swerved over the body in the open painted coffin, from the candle tips at the head to the feet, jutting up thinly,
the small scarred soles protruding, freshly washed, a mass of crooked,
half-healed wounds, thorn-pricks and cuts of sharp stones. Her gaze
went back to the candle flame, to Juan's eyes warning her, to the gendarmes talking among themselves. Her eyes would not be controlled.

500

505

With a leap that shook her her gaze settled upon the face of María
Rosa. Instantly her blood ran smoothly again: there was nothing to
fear. Even the restless light could not give a look of life to that fixed
countenance. She was dead. María Concépcion felt her muscles give
way softly; her heart began beating steadily without effort. She knew
no more rancor against that pitiable thing, lying indifferently in its
blue coffin under the fine silk rebozo. The mouth drooped sharply at
the corners in a grimace of weeping arrested half-way. The brows were
distressed; the dead flesh could not cast off the shape of its last terror.
It was all finished. María Rosa had eaten too much honey and had had
too much love. Now she must sit in hell, crying over her sins and her
hard death forever and ever.

510

515

520

Old Lupe's cackling voice arose. She had spent the morning helping María Rosa, and it had been hard work. The child had spat blood the moment it was born, a bad sign. She thought then that back luck would come to the house. Well, about sunset she was in the yard at the back of the house grinding tomatoes and peppers. She had left mother and babe asleep. She heard a strange noise in the house, a choking and smothering calling, like someone wailing in sleep. Well, such a thing is only natural. But there followed a light, quick, thudding sound—

"Like the blows of a fist?" interrupted an officer.

"No, not at all like such a thing."

"How do you know?"

"I am well acquainted with that sound, friends," retorted Lupe. "This was something else."

She was at a loss to describe it exactly. A moment later, there came the sound of pebbles rolling and slipping under feet; then she knew someone had been there and was running away.

"Why did you wait so long before going to see?"

"I am old and hard in the joints," said Lupe. "I cannot run after people. I walked as fast as I could to the cactus hedge, for it is only by this way that anyone can enter. There was no one in the road, sir, no one. Three cows, with a dog driving them; nothing else. When I got to María Rosa, she was lying all tangled up, and from her neck to her middle she was full of knife-holes. It was a sight to move the Blessed Image Himself! Her eyes were—"

"Never mind. Who came oftenest to her house before she went away? Did you know her enemies?"

Lupe's face congealed, closed. Her spongy skin drew into a network of secretive wrinkles. She turned withdrawn and expressionless eyes upon the gendarmes.

"I am an old woman. I do not see well. I cannot hurry on my feet. I know no enemy of María Rosa. I did not see anyone leave the clearing."

"You did not hear splashing in the spring near the bridge?"

"No, sir."

"Why, then, do our dogs follow a scent there and lose it?"

"God only knows, my friend. I am an old wo—"

"Yes. How did the footfalls sound?"

"Like the tread of an evil spirit!" Lupe broke forth in a swelling oracular tone that startled them. The Indians stirred uneasily, glanced at the dead, then at Lupe. They half expected her to produce the evil spirit among them at once.

The gendarme began to lose his temper.

"No, poor unfortunate; I mean, were they heavy or light? The footsteps of a man or of a woman? Was the person shod or barefoot?"

A glance at the listening circle assured Lupe of their thrilled attention. She enjoyed the dangerous importance of her situation. She could have ruined that María Concepción with a word, but it was even sweeter to make fools of these gendarmes who went about spying on honest people. She raised her voice again. What she had not seen she could not describe, thank God! No one could harm her because her knees were stiff and she could not run even to seize a murderer. As for knowing the difference between footfalls, shod or bare, man or woman, nay, between devil and human, who ever heard of such madness?

"My eyes are not ears, gentlemen," she ended grandly, "but upon my heart I swear those footsteps fell as the tread of the spirit of evil!"

"Imbecile!" yapped the leader in a shrill voice. "Take her away, one of you! Now, Juan Villegas, tell me—"

Juan told his story patiently, several times over. He had returned to his wife that day. She had gone to market as usual. He had helped her prepare her fowls. She had returned about mid-afternoon, they had talked, she had cooked, they had eaten, nothing was amiss. Then the gendarmes came with the news about María Rosa. That was all. Yes, María Rosa had run away with him, but there had been no bad blood between his wife and María Rosa. Everybody knew that his wife was a quiet woman.

María Concepción heard her own voice answering without a break. It was true at first she was troubled when her husband went away, but after that she had not worried about him. It was the way of men, she believed. She was a church-married woman and knew her place. Well, he had come home at last. She had gone to market, but had come back early, because now she had her man to cook for. That was all.

Other voices broke in. A toothless old man said: "She is a woman of good reputation among us, and María Rosa was not." A smiling young mother, Anita, baby at breast, said: "If no one thinks so, how can you accuse her? It was the loss of her child and not of her husband that changed her so." Another: "María Rosa had a strange life, apart from us. How do we know who might have come from another place to do her evil?" And old Soledad spoke up boldly: "When I saw María Concepción in the market today, I said, 'Good luck to you, María Concepción, this is a happy day for you!'" and she gave María Concepción a long easy stare, and the smile of a born wise-woman.

María Concepción suddenly felt herself guarded, surrounded, upborne by her faithful friends. They were around her, speaking for her, defending her, the forces of life were ranged invincibly with her against the beaten dead. María Rosa had thrown away her share of strength in them, she lay forfeited among them. María Concepción looked from one to the other of the circling, intent faces. Their eyes gave back reassurance, understanding, a secret and mighty sympathy.

The gendarmes were at a loss. They, too, felt that sheltering wall cast impenetrably around her. They were certain she had done it, and yet they could not accuse her. Nobody could be accused; there was not a shred of true evidence. They shrugged their shoulders and snapped their fingers and shuffled their feet. Well, then, good night to everybody. Many pardons for having intruded. Good health!

A small bundle lying against the wall at the head of the coffin squirmed like an eel. A wail, a mere sliver of sound, issued. María Concepción took the son of María Rosa in her arms.

"He is mine," she said clearly, "I will take him with me."

No one assented in words, but an approving nod, a bare breath of complete agreement, stirred among them as they made way for her.

María Concepción, carrying the child, followed Juan from the clearing. The hut was left with its lighted candles and a crowd of old women who would sit up all night, drinking coffee and smoking and telling ghost stories.

Juan's exaltation had burned out. There was not an ember of excitement left in him. He was tired. The perilous adventure was over. María Rosa had vanished, to come no more forever. Their days of marching, of eating, of quarreling and making love between battles, were all over. Tomorrow he would go back to dull and endless labor, he must descend into the trenches of the buried city as María Rosa must go into her grave. He felt his veins fill up with bitterness, with black unendurable melancholy. Oh, Jesus! what bad luck overtakes a man!

Well, there was no way out of it now. For the moment, he craved only to sleep. He was so drowsy he could scarcely guide his feet. The occasional light touch of the woman at his elbow was as unreal, as ghostly as the brushing of a leaf against his face. He did not know why he had fought to save her, and now he forgot her. There was nothing in him except a vast blind hurt like a covered wound.

He entered the jacal, and without waiting to light a candle, threw off his clothing, sitting just within the door. He moved with lagging, half-awake hands, to strip his body of its heavy finery. With a long groaning sigh of relief he fell straight back on the floor, almost instantly asleep, his arms flung up and outward.

María Concepción, a small clay jar in her hand, approached the gentle little mother goat tethered to a sapling, which gave and yielded as she pulled at the rope's end after the farthest reaches of grass about her. The kid, tied up a few feet away, rose bleating, its feathery fleece shivering in the fresh wind. Sitting on her heels, holding his tether, she allowed him to suckle a few moments. Afterward—all her movements very deliberate and even—she drew a supply of milk for the child.

She sat against the wall of her house, near the doorway. The child, fed and asleep, was cradled in the hollow of her crossed legs. The silence overfilled the world, the skies flowed down evenly to the rim of the valley, the stealthy moon crept slantwise to the shelter of the mountains. She felt soft and warm all over; she dreamed that the newly born child was her own, and she was resting deliciously.

María Concepción could hear Juan's breathing. The sound vapored from the low doorway, calmly; the house seemed to be resting after a burdensome day. She breathed, too, very slowly and quietly, each inspiration saturating her with repose. The child's light, faint breath was a mere shadowy moth of sound in the silver air. The night, the earth under her, seemed to swell and recede together with a limitless, unhurried, benign breathing. She drooped and closed her eyes, feeling the slow rise and fall within her own body. She did not know what it was, but it eased her all through. Even as she was falling asleep, head bowed over the child, she was still aware of a strange, wakeful happiness.

# B3. Section III: Second Reading

Read Section III a second time to answer the following true/false questions. Be prepared to explain your answers.

_____ **1.** Juan thought María Concepción was going to kill him but learned she had killed María Rosa.

_____ **2.** María Concepción and Juan together destroyed the evidence of the murder she had committed.

_____ **3.** Juan felt responsible for what his wife had done and vowed his fidelity to her in the future.

_____ **4.** Juan and María Concepción appeared to go on with life as usual while he coached her as to the stories they should tell to protect her.

_____ **5.** María Concepción would probably have incriminated herself without Juan's help.

_____ **6.** Juan and María Concepción were eating heartily when the gendarmes arrived because the events of the day had left them no time to eat.

_____ **7.** María Concepción's fear at seeing the corpse during the investigation sprang from the possibility of being caught and arrested.

_____ **8.** Lupe was probably acting honestly when she told the gendarmes that it was probably an evil spirit that had killed her daughter.

_____ **9.** The villagers were more interested in protecting María Concepción than in bringing María Rosa's killer to justice.

_____ **10.** The gendarmes finally gave up their investigation because they realized that nobody knew anything about the murder.

_____ **11.** The villagers were not surprised when María Concepción took María Rosa's baby.

## FOLLOW–UP

Discuss your answers to the First and Second Reading in small groups. Then go on to Part C3, which follows.

_____ **12.** Even though Juan had done what he had to in order to protect María Concepción, he was unhappy about María Rosa's death.

_____ **13.** María Rosa's baby will probably be a source of unhappiness and a constant reminder to María Concepción of her husband's adultery.

# C3. Response

Before you go on to the next activity, discuss these questions in small groups or as a class.

1.  Of the three main characters in the story (María Concepción, Juan, and María Rosa), which one do you like the most? the least? Why?

2.  Is María Concepción basically a story about love, revenge, pride, morality, or a combination of these? Explain your choice(s).

3.  In this story, the villagers protect María Concepción from the law even though she has committed murder. Is their reaction normal? Do you consider the villagers immoral? Why did they protect her?

## Delving More Deeply

Find the following text in the lines indicated. Use the surrounding text and your experience to give an informed answer.

1.  *...boiling water seemed to be pouring slowly along her spine. An unaccountable pain was in her knees, as if they were broken. (lines 91–93)* Two similes here (*seemed* and *as if*) describe the pain that María Concepción felt. Is the pain really physical pain? What do you think caused the pain?

2.  *...her ears strumming as if all María Rosa's bees had hived in them. (lines 105–106)* This simile (*as if*) expresses María Concepción's reaction to what she saw. What emotions does this simile suggest María Concepción was feeling?

3.  *...twisting the head off with the casual firmness she might use with the top of a beet. (lines 147–148)* What do you think is in María Concepción's mind as she slaughters the chickens so coolly and unemotionally?

4.  *Juan kept up this insufferable pantomime until they rounded the first clump of fig-cactus. (lines 287–288)* Why does the author call Juan's actions a "pantomime"? To whom are they "insufferable"? Why? Why do you think Juan acted the way he did? Do you find Juan's behavior normal under the circumstances?

5. *"Let me tell you, Juan, things haven't been going as well as you think."* (lines 322–323) What is Givens referring to? What hasn't been going well?

6. *After a great while she stood up and threw the rebozo off her face, and set out walking again.* (lines 389–390) Where has María Concepción decided to go? Why do you think this decision took her so long to make?

7. *…with such horror that the hair of his head seemed to be lifting itself away from him.* (lines 408–410) What was the "horror" that Juan felt?

8. Juan: *"But there will be something for us to settle between us afterward."* María Concepción: *"For me everything is   settled now."* (lines 452–456) Juan and María Concepción are both talking about settling something, i.e. making an agreement or deciding something. What is the "something" that Juan is referring to? Is María Concepción talking about the same thing? If not, what is he talking about? What is she talking about?

9. *"Yes, yes, it is all settled."* (line 464) Is Juan using settled in his original sense or with María Concepción's meaning now? In saying this, what is he promising?

10. *María Rosa had thrown away her share of strength in them, she lay forfeited among them.* (lines 607–608) What do we learn about the morals of this community? How do the people see María Rosa?

# III. STRENGTHENING SKILLS THROUGH THE TEXT

# A.   Responding to the Reading

Write 75 words on *one* of the following topics. When you finish, choose a classmate to listen to what you have written.

1.   Did you like this story? Why or why not?

2.   Which character do you sympathize with the most? (In other words, which character do you understand, have compassion for, or agree with the most?) Why?

_____

_____

_____

_____

_____

_____

_____

_____

_____

_____

_____

_____

_____

_____

# B.  Checking Global Comprehension: Ordering the Events

Read the following sentences, which summarize the main events of
the story. Order them from 1st to 16th to give an accurate summary.
Number 1 is done for you.

_____ **a.**  Juan vowed that he would not be unfaithful to María
Concepción again.

_____ **b.**  Juan returned home after celebrating the birth of the
son he'd fathered with María Rosa.

_____ **c.**  Dr. Givens rescued Juan once again by arranging his
release from the military prison.

_____ **d.** María Concepción discovered Juan dallying at María Rosa's.

___**1**___ **e.** María Concepción and Juan Villegas were married in the church.

_____ **f.** María Concepción made it clear to Lupe that her prayers were not wanted and to the villagers that their concern was not needed.

_____ **g.** Juan fell asleep missing someone he had loved.

_____ **h.** The gendarmes led Juan and María Concepción to the scene of the crime.

_____ **i.** Juan helped María Concepción make up a story to defend herself against the questions of the gendarmes.

_____ **j.** Juan and María Rosa went off to war together.

_____ **k.** María Concepción killed María Rosa.

_____ **l.** María Concepción lost her baby shortly after birth.

_____**m.** María Concepción took María Rosa's child to look after as her own.

_____ **n.** Lupe had the chance to incriminate María Concepción, but she didn't.

_____ **o.** The gendarmes finally gave up because they knew they had no proof to accuse María Concepción of the crime.

_____ **p.** Juan and María told the gendarmes the stories they had made up to protect María Concepción.

# D. Text-Based Focus on Vocabulary

## FOLLOW-UP

Share your words with a partner. Read the sentence in which you found the word to your partner. Ask your partner to tell you what he or she thinks the word means. Explain the word if necessary. Then tell your partner why you *like* this word.

## Vocabulary: Student's Choice

Skim the story to find some of the new vocabulary that you like and which you learned from reading "María Concepción." These could be words and expressions that are useful, that you found exciting, strong, touching, or amusing, or that you just liked. Select your ten favorite new words. Circle them in the text. Number them from 1 to 10.

## Similes

"María Concepción" is full of similes like items 1 and 2 from page 31 of Lesson 3. The story is particularly rich in similes using "as if" plus the subjunctive verb. The subjunctive verb helps us recognize that the comparison is "unreal," i.e., that this is an imaginative comparison. The following are some simple examples (not from the story) to help you understand this construction.

She looks *as if* she *were* a queen. (She isn't a queen, but has the appearance of a queen.)

He talked to me *as if* he *were* my father. (He wasn't my father, but he acted that way.)

He talked *as if* he *had won* a million dollars. (He hadn't won a million dollars. He only acted that way.)

Now go back to the text of *María Concepción* and find 5 additional similes using "as if" and the subjunctive verb. Circle them in the text and put asterisks (*) next to them so that you can find them quickly.

Example: *...her feet were as heavy as if she were mired in the muddy roads during the time of rains.* (lines 487–488)

What it means: While she was sitting and thinking about what Juan and María Rosa had done to her, her feet began to feel heavy, the way they had in the past when she had been stuck and unable to continue walking in the muddy roads when it rained a lot. We can imagine her emotional condition from this imaginary comparison to a previous, real physical condition (even though her feet are not really stuck in mud at this point). She feels paralyzed, unable to move to carry out what she wants to do, perhaps.

## FOLLOW-UP

Share your "as if" similes with your classmates. Tell them which line(s) you are reading from. Explain what the simile means in the context of the story.

# IV. MOVING BEYOND THE TEXT

# A. Discussion and Writing

Discuss the following topics as a class or in groups. Your teacher may assign a different topic to each group and ask a group leader to summarize its discussion for the class. Write on one or more of the topics as instructed by your teacher.

1. Why didn't María Concepción kill her husband **as well as** or **instead of** María Rosa? Do you see María Rosa as guiltier than Juan in this instance? Is society more tolerant of a man's infidelity than of a woman's? Explain.

2. Do men tend to be less faithful in love than women? Do you think Juan will be faithful to María Concepción from this time on? Though Juan was not faithful to María Concepción, he protected her when he realized she had murdered María Rosa. Why?

3. Choose one of the four quotations from **Getting Ready.** Explain it in your own words; then mention events from "María Concepción" that illustrate the quotation.

# B.  Responding through Drawing and Poetry

"María Concepción" seems like an opera in its dramatic scope. Crimes of passion fascinate us because we all recognize the powerful feelings that jealousy and pride can arouse in us. When someone is actually driven to murder out of these urges, we can be moved not only to horror, but to pity as well. One way to express these feelings is through poetry. Another is through drawing. Choose a way to express your feelings about this story. Display your work for others to see.

1. Draw María Concepción's face when she sees Juan and María Rosa flirting and courting in the field.

2. Draw the scene when María Concepción enters her home and Juan awakens to see her with the knife in her hand.

3. Write a free-form poem about love and jealousy. One way to do this is to begin each line with the first letter of a word, such as **love.** For example, begin the first line of your poem with a word which begins with "L," the second line with a word which begins with "O," etc.

4. (In a mixed language class) Share a poem or song about love and/or jealousy in your native language with the class. Perform it in your language and then translate it for the class.

**5.** Make a collage. From the newspaper and/or magazines, find words (perhaps headlines about crimes of passion) and pictures to arrange together to express your feelings about love and jealousy.

**6.** Whole class: Each person draws a picture of what "jealousy" looks like. (Maybe it looks like an animal or a demon or someone you know.) All the students post their pictures on the wall. Then the students walk around and write on the pictures about the thoughts and feelings that the pictures arouse in them.

What do you think will happen in this story?

# UNIT III

# Misunderstandings:

# Between

# People, Generations

# and Cultures

Does the cat want to go out or stay in?
Would you want to go out or stay in?

# Lesson 10

## ON A NIGHT OF SNOW

Elizabeth Coatsworth

U.S.A.

# I. GETTING READY

## A. Discussion: Incentives

In this two-stanza poem, the mistress speaks to her cat, trying to convince it to stay inside, away from the winter night. What dangers of a winter night might she mention in her argument? What incentives to stay in might she offer the cat? Work with a partner and write your ideas below. Then read the following vocabulary to prepare you to listen.

| Dangers waiting outside | Incentives to stay in |
|---|---|
| _____ | _____ |
| _____ | _____ |
| _____ | _____ |
| _____ | _____ |
| _____ | _____ |
| _____ | _____ |

**FOLLOW-UP**
Share your ideas with the class.

*sleet:* frozen rain, often covering trees like glass

*intoning strange lore:* singing strange songs or stories

*the meadow grasses* **hang hoar:** are covered with frost, a powdery white coating of ice.

*portents:* indications, signs; omens

# II. ENGAGING WITH THE TEXT

## A. First Exposure: Listening

**FOLLOW-UP**
Listen again if necessary. Discuss your answer.

Listen to the poem as your teacher reads it to decide if the cat is convinced by its mistress's arguments to stay in or not.

# B.   Second Exposure: Reading

Read the poem quietly with a partner. One of you will read the part of
the mistress *(Stanza 1)* and the other will read the part of the cat
*(Stanza 2)*. Then answer the true-false questions together.

**On a Night of Snow**

STANZA 1   A      Cat, if you go outdoors you must walk in the snow.

B      You will come back with little white shoes on your feet,

Little white slippers of snow that have heels of sleet.

Stay by the fire, my Cat. Lie still, do not go.

See how the flames are leaping and hissing low.

I will bring you a saucer of milk like a marguerite,

So white and so smooth, so spherical and so sweet.

Stay with me, Cat. Outdoors the wild winds blow.


STANZA 2   C      Outdoors the wild winds blow, Mistress, and dark is the night.

D      Strange voices cry in the trees, intoning strange lore,

And more than cats move, lit by our eyes' green light,

On silent feet where the meadow grasses hang hoar—

Mistress, there are portents abroad of magic and might,

And things that are yet to be done. Open the door!


# Questions

_____ **1.**   The mistress is worried that the cat will get lost if it
goes out.

_____ **2.**    The cat doesn't realize that it's cold and uncomfortable outside.

_____ **3.**   The mistress wants the cat to stay with her because she
is lonely.

_____ **4.**   The cat expects to encounter other cats in the meadow.

_____ 5.   The cat sees more advantages than disadvantages in going out.

_____ 6.   The woman and the cat both know it's cold and windy out, but they each have a different point of view about it.

# III. STRENGTHENING SKILLS THROUGH THE TEXT

## A.   Rhyme

With a partner, look at the *rhyme* of the poem. The stanzas differ in rhyme, but the lines of each stanza end with one of two sounds. Complete the rhyme scheme by marking each line with **a, b, c,** or **d** as begun for you.

## B. Dramatic Reading

In pairs, prepare a dramatic reading of the poem with one person taking the part of the cat and the other taking the part of the mistress. Pairs can take turns performing their dramatic readings. Keep the rhyme scheme by pronouncing words that rhyme in the same way. The class can choose two winning pairs: the pair with the best pronunciation and the pair with the best expressive reading.

# IV.  MOVING BEYOND THE TEXT

## A.   Discussion and Writing

Discuss the following topics as a class or in groups. Your teacher may assign a different topic to each group and ask a group leader to summarize its discussion for the class. Write on one or more of the topics as instructed by your teacher.

**1.**   If a father and his daughter discuss whether or not she should buy a car with money she has earned from a summer job, each will probably have a different point of view. What might the father's point of view be? Why? What might the daughter's point of view be? Why?

**2.** The following groups usually have different points of view about many issues. List as many more groups as you can. Then choose one and discuss the topics they might disagree about.

*fathers and sons*

*husbands and wives*

*supervisors and workers*

_____

_____

_____

_____

_____

_____

_____

_____

_____

_____

_____

Does this restaurant serve fancy food?

# Lesson 11

## A BEACON IN THE NIGHT

### Morris Lurie

### Australia

# I.   GETTING READY

## A.   Discussion: Occupations and Prestige

Discuss the following questions in small groups:

**1.** What are the five most prestigious occupations or professions in your country? Rank them. Give the number 1 to the most prestigious occupation, the number 2 to the next most prestigious, etc.

1.  _____

2.  _____

3.  _____

4.  _____

5.  _____

**2.** "What do you want to be when you grow up?" is a favorite question for adults to ask children in the United States. Do adults ask children this question in your country? What do children usually answer? When you were a young child, what did you want to be when you grew up?

**3.** Who or what decides what a person's occupation or profession will be in your country? Parents? Government? The person himself? An examination system? Who or what *should* decide?

**FOLLOW-UP**
Share your answers with the class.

**4.** What occupation(s) or profession(s) would you want your children to go into? Would you insist that your children follow your choices?

## B.   Background

Read the following information, noting the italicized words, to help you understand the story more easily and fully.

"A Beacon in the Night" is set in Australia. The characters are part of an immigrant Jewish community that originally came from the **old country,** which is the way immigrants often refer to the European countries they left behind. The narrator is a 15-year-old boy whose working-class father wants him to have a better life than he, the father, has. The father holds up Yossel Shepps, the son of other working class parents, as an example, an inspiration for his sons.

**Shikse** *(Yiddish word)* means a non-Jewish girl or young woman. It is a term that is usually used negatively.

**Bar mitzvah** *(from Hebrew)* is a religious ceremony in which a 13-year-old boy is recognized as an adult.

Another reference is **Casanova,** which means a man who romantically pursues many women.

# II. ENGAGING WITH THE TEXT

## A. First Exposure: Listening

Read the guiding questions which go with each section you will listen to. Then listen to the section on the tape to answer the questions; discuss the answers to each section before continuing to the next section.

**Section 1** *(lines 1–53)*
◆ What kind of a person is Yossel Shepps? Why do the narrator and his family go to the Café Zion?

**Section 2** *(lines 54–125)*
◆ How does the narrator's father treat Yossel? What evidence is there that Yossel's parents make sacrifices to keep him in medical school?

**Section 3** *(lines 126–160)*
◆ What happens to Yossel? What happens to Mr. Shepps?

**Section 4** *(lines 161–228)*
◆ What does Mr. Shepps find out about Yossel? What is Yossel's explanation?

## B. Second Exposure: First Reading

Use the questions which follow the story to gain a better understanding and to bring your experience to the story.

## A Beacon in the Night

Allow me to present for your edification and respectful awe that
sterling figure, that man, that—well, here comes Yossel Shepps. Not
much to look at, I admit—five five when he stands up straight, big
clumsy hands and feet, cheeks like emery boards, a droopy left eyelid,
a funny way of not quite looking at you when he looks at you. But
make no mistake. Yossel is a beacon. Yossel is a signpost in this murky
world. Yossel is a light so straight and true your heart takes one look
and wants to fly up and sing. He's only twenty-two, and look, the kid's
practically a doctor.

So?

I know, I know, Jewish medical students are a dime a dozen, but
tell me this. How many of them speed straight from lectures to help
out their poor struggling parents? How many of them cram till four in
the morning and then leap up, fresh and eager, to serve up Sunday
lunch

Yossel does. Yossel is a miracle. According to my father, Yossel is a
golden wonder, a blessing, a saint. He is a shining example such as
rarely comes along, and each Sunday, when we troop into the Café
Zion for lunch, he allows us to bask in Yossel's light. Hoping madly
something will rub off on us, his two moronic sons.

For the record, let me state that I, aged fifteen, have not completely
ruled out medicine as a career. It's a faint possibility. A lot of things
are possibilities. At the moment though, I'm mainly interested in
being a film director. Or a sports journalist. My brother, aged twelve,
doesn't know what he wants to be. But he's young.

Back to Yossel Shepps. But before I tell you about him, I'd better
tell you about the Café Zion. Maybe though, to get some sense into
this, I'd better tell you about my father first.

He's a fruiterer. It's a nice little business, except he has to get up at
five in the morning four days a week and drive off in the truck to the
market (sometimes with his pajamas on under his clothes), and he
doesn't come home till eight or nine at night. Mum serves in the shop,
and they usually come home together, so you can imagine the quality
of the meals we eat. Except for Sunday. Sunday we all relax. We have
lunch in a restaurant. But if you think that means candlelight and
sweeping violins, you don't know my dad.

My father's idea of a good time is big portions. So what if the lighting is stark and bright, there's no carpet on the floor, the chairs wob-
ble, the cutlery doesn't match? So what if the tablecloth is a little bit
stained? What's that? You found a hair on your plate? Don't eat it.

For about a year we went to a restaurant that was just like that, with
a waiter who was at least seventy and who used to groan over to the
table wearing what looked like his deceased great-grandfather's clothes
from the Old Country, and as he spilled soup all over the place he'd
tell us about his aching feet, his rotting teeth, his unmarried forty-
year-old daughter, and a strange pain in the back he'd had for eleven
years. There was a menu, but it didn't make any difference, everything
tasted the same. Monumental portions. You'd stand up at the end and
want to die. "Come again," the owner used to say to us as we dragged

50 ourselves out, and for a whole year we did, and then suddenly we
switched to the Café Zion. Which is exactly the same as the first
restaurant, except for one thing.

Yossel Shepps.

"Hello, Doctor!" cries my father, as we troop in for our weekly
55 feast. "How's it going, Doctor?" he booms across the room.
"Everything all right, Doctor?"

Doctor. Doctor. My father is enamored of the word. He can't say it
often enough. It is honey on his tongue.

We sit down. The tablecloth boasts a few new stains and is rolling
60 with old crumbs, some of which I manage to sweep to the floor. My
fork is so twisted it looks like a piece of modern sculpture. I reach for
the menu, purely for something to do. I know everything on it without even looking. The menu at the Café Zion is always the same.

"Ah!" says my father, swiveling around in his chair.
65 The Doctor has arrived.

He stands, pad in hand, smiling his curious smile, giving our table
one of his not-quite-looking-at-you looks. He clears his throat. I hear
my father getting ready to speak. I make close inspection of Yossel's
truly monumental feet.
70 "Good afternoon, Doctor," says my father.

"Good afternoon," whispers Yossel Shepps.

"Well," says my father, "how are the studies?"

"Very well," says Yossel Shepps, very quietly.

"You don't find helping in the restaurant takes too much of your
75 time, Doctor?"

"No, I manage."

"Very nice," my father beams. "Tell me, Doctor, when do you
finish?"

"In three months," says Yossel Shepps.
80 "Ah! And then you'll open a little private practice, ah, Doctor?"

"Not at first," says Yossel Shepps. "I have to do a year in the
hospital."

"Pardon me, Doctor," says my father. "I forgot. A year in the
hospital. Good experience. And then you'll open up on your own?"
85 "I think so," says Yossel Shepps.

"Very nice," says my father. "A beautiful future."

He turns then to my brother and me, and the look he bestows upon
us I'd rather not describe. We make, of course, no reply. How can we?
It'd be like putting our heads in a lion's mouth.
90 "Well, Doctor," says my father, picking up the menu. "I think I feel
like a little soup. What would you recommend?"

We order. Dr. Shepps shuffles away. He certainly is a strange looking chap, but it takes all sorts to make a world. Looks aren't everything. Dr. Shepps. Personally, I wouldn't feel too happy having him
95 peering at me if I was severely ill. Lying there, close to death, maybe
with one of those tubes going up my nose, and him giving me one of
his not-quite-looking-at-you looks.

My father, still radiant from his encounter with Yossel, looks around the room. There are about ten people here, not counting us, all looking miserable as they ingest their massive portions. Then from out of the kitchen pops Mr. Shepps, just for a second, and my father gives him a big wave.

"Hello, Mr. Shepps!" he calls. "How's everything?"

"Good, good," says Mr. Shepps, with a weak smile, quickly popping back in again.

Poor Mr. Shepps. He looks terrible. His face is gray, his cheeks are sunken, his brow is creased with lines. He looks about a hundred and ten. I catch a glimpse of him through the servery window, as he stirs a big pot. He is almost a ghost.

Mrs. Shepps is in there too, but you rarely see her. A gray little woman, haggard with work.

"They work very hard, don't they?" I say to my father.

"It's a privilege!" says my father. "They're putting a son through medical school!"

"But Yossel's always wearing new clothes," I say.

"So?" says my father. "What do you want? You want him to look like a beggar? He mixes with top people, he can't afford to look bad."

"And the car?"

Mr. Shepps has bought for his son a brand-new car, a shining two-tone blue sedan, which is parked right now just outside the front door.

"Idiot!" says my father, raising crumbs as he bangs the table. "What do you think the car is for? So Yossel can hurry back here from lectures. Not waste time on a slow bus. Don't you understand anything?"

"Sorry, dad," I mumble, and keep my head down for the rest of the meal.

The months come and go, and one day when we troop into the Café Zion, what should we note but the absence of Yossel Shepps.

"Ah!" says Mr. Shepps, who has graduated to waiter. "He's in the country."

"He passed all his exams?" my father asks.

"With honors," says Mr. Shepps. "He's in a very fine hospital. We hardly see him, he's working so hard. He comes home only two or three days a week. Exhausted! You should see him."

"It's a hard year, the first one," my father says. "And how are you? How is Mrs. Shepps?"

"Good, good," says Mr. Shepps, who looks more terrible than ever. He seems to be working twice as hard, running backwards and forwards, sweat glistening on his brow. I mention this to my father.

"Fool!" he cries. "Don't you understand anything? They're proud to be working so hard. They live for their son."

The situation doesn't make sense to me. Exhausted parents, exhausted son.

"You'll see," says my father. "In two, three years. Dr. Shepps. A beautiful future."

145  Social engagements keep us from the Café Zion for the next three weeks—a wedding and two bar mitzvahs—but on the fourth week we're back, starved for real food. In we go, but what's this? It's all different. The sign's on outside, but there's no one here. Where is Mr. Shepps? Mrs. Shepps? A strange air of gloom permeates the place.

150  Nevertheless, we sit down, at our usual table. The tablecloth, anyhow, hasn't changed. We toy with the same twisted forks. My father swivels in his chair, looking round the room.

Then from out of the kitchen comes a man we have never seen before. He looks about sixty, with sad eyes, like a dog, and a shining

155  bald head.

"Oh?" says my father, "Mr. Shepps not well?"

"You didn't hear?" says the man.

"What?" says my father.

"Oi oi," says the man, shaking his head. "He hung himself. Excuse

160  me. I'll bring a chair. I'm having terrible trouble with my feet."

We sit in stunned silence, no one saying a word, as the man brings over a chair from the next table, and sits down with a weary sigh. Who has hung himself? When? Why?

"A terrible business," says the man, shaking his head. "You haven't

165  heard a word?"

"Nothing," says my father.

"Oi oi," says the man, with more head shaking, and then he tells us, slowly, the whole story. It's all about Yossel Shepps.

"He was never a doctor," the man tells us. "They threw him out in

170  the very first year. He didn't have the brains. So what's he been doing all these years? He's got himself a shikse, and every day he pays her a little visit. In the nice car his father bought for him."

My father, I note, is fiddling with his napkin.

"So what happens?" says the man. "Last week Mr. Shepps phoned

175  up the hospital in the country—he wanted to remind his son about something—and what does he hear? They haven't got a Dr. Shepps in that hospital. Never."

The man pauses here to blow his nose in an enormous handkerchief, a good half minute required to pull the voluminous folds from

180  his trouser pocket, another half minute to stuff it back again. No one speaks. He blows. He continues.

"So Mr. Shepps waits for his son to come home. Here he comes, in his shining new car. 'Listen,' says Mr. Shepps. 'I talked to the hospital this morning. They told me they never heard of you.' His son tells him

185  the truth. How can he hide it now? 'I never wanted to be a doctor,' he says. 'You forced me. You pushed me. I couldn't tell you I was thrown out. I didn't want to break your heart.' Mr. Shepps hears this story, runs upstairs and throws a rope over a beam. Have you ever heard such a thing?" he asks my father. "In this country?"

190  He goes into another routine of head shaking, this time with some low moans and a pursing of his lips. Still no one at our table says a word.

"He was practically hanging," the man goes on, "if not for Mrs. Shepps. Oi oi. A terrible business."

195 "Where is Yossel now?" I ask.

My father shoots me a mean look, but the man answers, and my father turns back to him.

"Who knows?" he says. "He ran away. I hear he took a job somewhere. In a factory."

200 "And Mr. Shepps? Mrs.?"

"I don't know," the man says to my father. "I think they're at the moment with friends. You know a Mr. Polonski? He is buying this restaurant. A very nice man. Well," he says, standing up, "would you like to order now?"

205 We eat. The food, despite everything that's happened, is exactly the same. Large silent portions. Finally my brother speaks.

"M.D." he says, "Master of Deception."

"Quiet!" my father roars. "Jokes I don't need."

He is in a terrible mood. He doesn't say a word until we get to the
210 apple compote. Then he speaks.

"Today's children," he says, "are not worth a *fortz*."

"But he never wanted to be a doctor, dad," I say. "It was all because his father pushed him."

"So what's wrong," says my father, "if a parent wants something a
215 little better for his son? Something a little better than his own miserable life?"

"Yes, dad," I say.

By the time we've finished lunch, my father has managed to swing the whole story around. Now it has become a moral tale about chil-
220 dren's ingratitude to their parents. I sit there, not saying a word.

Actually, I'm thinking. Yossel Shepps not being a doctor doesn't surprise me all that much. He didn't really have the manner. Do real doctors ever have such enormous feet?

The thing that is remarkable is how anyone with Yossel's looks
225 could win himself a girl. A shikse. Coming home exhausted, day after day. Yossel Shepps. It's unbelievable. Who would have thought, under that exterior, lay a Casanova, a sleek lover, a boudoir snake? Yossel Shepps is a beacon in the night, a shining example to us all.


# Questions

**1.** What does Yossel look like? Do people's appearances usually match their professions, in your opinion? That is, does a lawyer usually look like a lawyer, a worker like a worker?

**2.** What criteria did the narrator's father use to choose a restaurant? Would the narrator choose the same restaurants? Would you?

**3.** Would a medical student in your country have enough free time to help out at home as much as Yossel did?

4. Was the narrator as impressed by Yossel as the narrator's father was? How did the narrator and his father react differently to Yossel's parents' situation when Yossel came home only two or three days a week? Why do you think the narrator and his father saw Yossel so differently?

5. What was Yossel's deception? How did Mr. Shepps find out about it? Were you surprised by the deception? Do you think Yossel enjoyed this deception? How do you think he felt?

6. At the end, the narrator and his father view the deception differently. How does each one see it? Which one do you agree with?

## Delving More Deeply

Find the following text in the lines indicated. Use the surrounding text and your experience to give an informed answer.

1. ***Yossel is a beacon. Yossel is a signpost in this murky world.*** *(lines 6–7)* **Beacon** literally means a guiding light, like a lighthouse. Who sees Yossel as "a beacon"—the father, the narrator, or both?

2. ***…you can imagine the quality of the meals we eat.*** *(lines 33–34)* Is the quality high or low? Why?

3. ***and the look he bestows upon us I'd rather not describe.*** *(lines 87–88)* What expression do you think the father had on his face? How do you think his sons felt?

4. ***"Have you ever heard such a thing? …In this country?"*** *(lines 188–189)* In what way might "the old country" have been different from Australia?

5. ***"He was practically hanging…if not for Mrs. Shepps."*** *(lines 193–194)* Did Mr. Shepps actually succeed at suicide? Explain.

6. ***"So what's wrong…if a parent wants something a little better for his son?"*** *(lines 214–215)* What exactly is the narrator's father expressing: concern for his children's future, discontent with his own life, personal ambition?

FOLLOW-UP
Discuss your answers to the reading questions in small groups.

7. ***"It's unbelievable."*** *(line 226)* What's unbelievable? Why is it so unbelievable?

# III. STRENGTHENING SKILLS THROUGH THE TEXT

## A. Responding to the Reading

Write at least 75 words on *one* of the following topics. When you finish, choose a classmate to listen to what you have written.

1.   Did you like this story? Why or why not?

2.   Write a letter to Mr. Shepps expressing your feelings to him.

_____

_____

_____

_____

_____

_____

_____

_____

_____

_____

_____

_____

## B. Global Comprehension Check: Summary

Write an 80-word summary of "A Beacon in the Night." Choose points for the summary carefully to cover the basic events of the story. Be sure to express the theme in your summary, but do not include opinion. Write complete sentences in a cohesive paragraph (not a list), but do not exceed 80 words. Begin as follows:

"The Beacon" by Morris Lurie is a story about

_____

_____

_____

_____

_____

_____

_____

_____

_____

_____

**FOLLOW-UP**
In groups of 4 or 5 students take turns reading each others' summaries. What ideas did others include that you didn't? What do you have in your summary that others do not? Did you miss any important ideas?

# C.    Text-based Focus on Vocabulary

Find the words or phrases in the story which mean the same as the definitions below. **(10–15, 4)** in item **1** means you should look between lines 10 and 15 for a four-word phrase meaning "very common." Write the words or phrases in the spaces provided.

1.   *(10–15, 4)* very common _____

_____

2.   *(10–15, 1)* study very hard just before an exam _____

3.   *(15–20, 3)* influence _____

_____

4.   *(55–60, 4)* pleasant to say _____

_____

5. *(85–90, 7)* doing something very dangerous _____

_____

_____

**FOLLOW-UP**
Discuss your answers
with the class.

6. *(185–190, 3)* make someone suffer _____

_____

# IV. MOVING BEYOND THE TEXT

# A. Discussion and Writing

Discuss the following topics as a class or in groups. (Your teacher may assign a different topic to each group and ask a group leader to summarize its discussion for the class.) Write on *one or more* of the topics as instructed by your teacher.

1. Is it normal for immigrants to feel that their old customs are better than those in the new country? Can immigrants keep up all their old ways in a new country?

2. Who do you feel is more responsible for the deception, Mr. Shepps or Yossel? Why?

3. If you were a friend of Mr. Shepps's, what would you say to him? If you were Yossel's friend, what advice would you give him now?

4. Have you ever seen or heard of a situation like this one? Could this story have taken place in your country? Explain.

_____

_____

_____

_____

_____

_____

_____

_____

_____

_____

_____

_____

_____

_____

_____

# B.   Taking a Stand: A Short Speech

Read the questions below. Take a position on one of the issues, and be prepared to speak for two minutes on the issue in front of class. (*Do not* write out the speech; *do* prepare a note card with the main ideas of your speech. Practice delivering your speech to a partner in class.)

**1.** Every young person should be completely free to choose the kind of education and job or profession he wishes without parental interference.

**2.** One should tell the truth *in every situation* no matter how painful that truth is to others.

# Lesson 12

## IN THE SHADOW OF WAR

### Ben Okri

### Nigeria

# I. GETTING READY

## A. Writing a Story from Characters: Pairwork

Read the descriptions below of a *setting* (the location and time of the story) and of some *characters* (the persons in the story). Using the setting and characters, imagine a story *sketch* (a brief outline) to show how the characters might interact. In 10 minutes, quickly write down your sketch with your partner.

**SETTING:** a Nigerian village during the Biafran Civil War (1967–1970)

**CHARACTERS:**

*Omovo,* a young Nigerian boy, who is waiting impatiently for his father to leave for work.

*Omovo's father,* who worries about his son being out late at night while he's at work.

*A strange veiled woman,* who passes mysteriously through the village each evening, carrying a basket on her head.

*Three uniformed soldiers,* who want information about the mysterious woman.

**SKETCH:** *(begin as follows)* **One day Omovo, waiting for his father to leave for work, was looking out the window. He saw** _____

_____

_____

_____

_____

_____

_____

_____

_____

⊡ ⊡ ⊡ ⊡ ⊡ ⊡ ⊡ ⊡ ⊡ ⊡ ⊡ ⊡ ⊡ ⊡ ⊡ ⊡ ⊡

_____

_____

_____

_____

_____

_____

## FOLLOW-UP

Exchange your sketch with
other pairs.

_____

# B.  Background

Read the following information, noting the italicized words, to help
you understand the story more easily and fully.

In the story "In the Shadow of War," Ben Okri depicts the climate
that war creates in a society. We assume he's talking about the Biafran
Civil War in Nigeria (1967–1970), but his message is universal in that
it applies to more than Nigeria. In fact, the mood he describes probably exists wherever there is war. This mood is one of tension—tension
between appearances and reality, between how a child sees other people and how adults do. In a sense, the boy in the story sees the other
characters as they really are, not in terms of how they appear in the
context of war. By the end of the story, we suspect that the young boy
has entered the adult world, i.e., that he will no longer see people as
they *are* but as they *appear*. The reader never really knows to which
side of the war, if any, the different characters belong. But as readers
we do feel the climate of mistrust and human suffering brought on
by war.

Like other stories set in Africa (e.g. "No Witchcraft for Sale" and
"Marriage is a Private Affair"), superstition and magic play a role in
"In the Shadow of War." That is, certain acts may appear as supersti-
tion and magic to an outsider, but they are normal, sacred duties to
Omovo's father, who pours a ***libation***—a little palm wine to satisfy
the gods—and who ***prays to his ancestors*** before leaving the house.
There is also reference to a ***fetish***, a household object of worship. And
Omovo may not believe in ***witches***, but his friends show that they do
when they describe a mysterious veiled woman as having no shadow

and feet that don't touch the ground when she walks. Though an *eclipse* is a normal physical phenomenon, it is often the subject of superstitions. In a lunar eclipse, the reflected light of the moon is cut off because of the earth's shadow.

Some additional vocabulary that you will want to know:

***kobo:*** Nigerian money

***kwashiorkor:*** severe malnutrition, especially in children, resulting in a potbelly and change of hair color.

***Grundig:*** brand of German radio

***calabash:*** a gourd with a hard shell that is used as a container when dry.

# II.   ENGAGING WITH THE TEXT

# A.   First Reading: Following the Story Line

To gain a general idea of how the story develops, read all the Signpost Questions in the margins before you begin to read the story. Then concentrate on answering the questions as you read.

**In the Shadow of War**

**1.**

Does Omovo finally see the person he is waiting to see?

1     That afternoon three soldiers came to the village. They scattered the goats and chickens. They went to the palm-frond bar and ordered a calabash of palm-wine. They drank amidst the flies.

      Omovo watched them from the window as he waited for his father
5  to go out. They both listened to the radio. His father had bought the old Grundig cheaply from a family that had to escape the city when the war broke out. He had covered the radio with a white cloth and made it look like a household fetish. They listened to the news of bombings and air raids in the interior of the country. His father
10  combed his hair, parted it carefully, and slapped some aftershave on his unshaven face. Then he struggled into the shabby coat that he had long outgrown.

      Omovo stared out of the window, irritated with his father. At that hour, for the past seven days, a strange woman with a black veil over
15  her head had been going past the house. She went up the village paths, crossed the Express road, and disappeared into the forest. Omovo waited for her to appear.

The main news was over. The radio announcer said an eclipse of the moon was expected that night. Omovo's father wiped the sweat off his face with his palm and said, with some bitterness:

"As if an eclipse will stop this war."

"What is an eclipse?" Omovo asked.

"That's when the world goes dark and strange things happen."

"Like what?"

His father lit a cigarette.

"The dead start to walk about and sing. So don't stay out late, eh."

Omovo nodded.

"Heclipses hate children. They eat them."

Omovo didn't believe him. His father smiled, gave Omovo his ten kobo allowance, and said:

"Turn off the radio. It's bad for a child to listen to news of war."

Omovo turned it off. His father poured a libation at the doorway and then prayed to his ancestors. When he had finished he picked up his briefcase and strutted out briskly. Omovo watched him as he threaded his way up the path to the bus-stop at the main road. When a danfo bus came, and his father went with it, Omovo turned the radio back on. He sat on the window-sill and waited for the woman. The last time he saw her she had glided past with agitated flutters of her yellow smock. The children stopped what they were doing and stared at her. They had said that she had no shadow. They had said that her feet never touched the ground. As she went past, the children began to throw things at her. She didn't flinch, didn't quicken her pace, and didn't look back.

The heat was stupefying. Noises dimmed and lost their edges. The villagers stumbled about their various tasks as if they were sleep-walking. The three soldiers drank palm-wine and played draughts beneath the sun's oppressive glare. Omovo noticed that whenever children went past the bar the soldiers called them, talked to them, and gave them some money. Omovo ran down the stairs and slowly walked past the bar. The soldiers stared at him. On his way back one of them called him.

"What's your name," he asked.

Omovo hesitated, smiled mischievously, and said:

"Heclipse."

The soldier laughed, spraying Omovo's face with spit. He had a face crowded with veins. His companions seemed uninterested. They swiped flies and concentrated on their game. Their guns were on the table. Omovo noticed that they had numbers on them. The man said:

"Did your father give you that name because you have big lips?"

His companions looked at Omovo and laughed. Omovo nodded.

"You are a good boy," the man said. He paused. Then he asked, in a different voice:

"Have you seen that woman who covers her face with a black cloth?"

"No."

2.

Will Omovo follow the woman, or will he do what the soldiers want him to ?

The man gave Omovo ten kobo and said:

"She is a spy. She helps our enemies. If you see her come and tell us at once, you hear?"

Omovo refused the money and went back upstairs. He re-positioned
70   himself on the window-sill. The soldiers occasionally looked at him.
The heat got to him and soon he fell asleep in a sitting position. The
cocks, crowing dispiritedly, woke him up. He could feel the afternoon
softening into evening. The soldiers dozed in the bar. The hourly news
came on. Omovo listened without comprehension to the day's casual-
75   ties. The announcer succumbed to the stupor, yawned, apologized,
and gave further details of the fighting.

Omovo looked up and saw that the woman had already gone past.
The men had left the bar. He saw them weaving between the eaves of
the thatch houses, stumbling through the heat-mists. The woman was
80   further up the path. Omovo ran downstairs and followed the men.
One of them had taken off his uniform top. The soldier behind had
buttocks so big they had begun to split his pants. Omovo followed
them across the Express road. When they got into the forest the men
stopped following the woman, and took a different route. They
85   seemed to know what they were doing. Omovo hurried to keep the
woman in view.

He followed her through the dense vegetation. She wore faded
wrappers and a gray shawl, with the black veil covering her face. She
had a red basket on her head. He completely forgot to determine if she
90   had a shadow, or whether her feet touched the ground.

He passed unfinished estates, with their flaking ostentatious sign-
boards and their collapsing fences. He passed an empty cement factory: blocks lay crumbled in heaps and the workers' sheds were deserted.
He passed a baobab tree, under which was the intact skeleton of a
95   large animal. A snake dropped from a branch and slithered through
the undergrowth. In the distance, over the cliff edge, he heard loud
music and people singing war slogans above the noise.

He followed the woman till they came to a rough camp on the
plain below. Shadowy figures moved about in the half-light of the
100   cave. The woman went to them. The figures surrounded her and
touched her and led her into the cave. He heard their weary voices
thanking her. When the woman reappeared she was without the basket. Children with kwashiorkor stomachs and women wearing rags led
her half-way up the hill. Then, reluctantly, touching her as if they
105   might not see her again, they went back.

He followed her till they came to a muddied river. She moved as if
an invisible force were trying to blow her away. Omovo saw capsized
canoes and trailing waterlogged clothes on the dark water. He saw
floating items of sacrifice: loaves of bread in polythene wrappings,
110   gourds of food, Coca-Cola cans. When he looked at the canoes again
they had changed into the shapes of swollen dead animals. He saw
outdated currencies on the riverbank. He noticed the terrible smell in
the air. Then he heard the sound of heavy breathing from behind him,
then someone coughing and spitting. He recognized the voice of one

**3.**
Where is the woman
going? Why?

**4.**
What will the soldiers do
to the woman? What
happens to Omovo?

of the soldiers urging the others to move faster. Omovo crouched in the shadow of a tree. The soldiers strode past. Not long afterwards he heard a scream. The men had caught up with the woman. They crowded round her.

"Where are the others?" shouted one of them.

120 The woman was silent.

"You dis witch! You want to die, eh? Where are they?"

She stayed silent. Her head was bowed. One of the soldiers coughed and spat towards the river.

"Talk! Talk!" he said, slapping her.

125 The fat soldier tore off her veil and threw it to the ground. She bent down to pick it up and stopped in the attitude of kneeling, her head still bowed. Her head was bald, and disfigured with a deep corrugation. There was a livid gash along the side of her face. The bare-chested soldier pushed her. She fell on her face and lay still. The lights changed

130 over the forest and for the first time Omovo saw that the dead animals on the river were in fact the corpses of grown men. Their bodies were tangled with river-weed and their eyes were bloated. Before he could react, he heard another scream. The woman was getting up, with the veil in her hand. She turned to the fat soldier, drew herself to her

135 fullest height, and spat in his face. Waving the veil in the air, she began to howl dementedly. The two other soldiers backed away. The fat soldier wiped his face and lifted the gun to the level of her stomach. A moment before Omovo heard the shot a violent beating of wings just above him scared him from his hiding place. He ran through the for-

140 est screaming. The soldiers tramped after him. He ran through a mist which seemed to have risen from the rocks. As he ran he saw an owl staring at him from a canopy of leaves. He tripped over the roots of a tree and blacked out when his head hit the ground.

When he woke up it was very dark. He waved his fingers in front of

145 his face and saw nothing. Mistaking the darkness for blindness, he screamed, thrashed around, and ran into a door. When he recovered from his shock he heard voices outside and the radio crackling on about the war. He found his way to the balcony, full of wonder that his sight had returned. But when he got there he was surprised to find

150 his father sitting on the sunken cane chair, drinking palm-wine with the three soldiers. Omovo rushed to his father and pointed frantically at the three men.

"You must thank them," his father said. "They brought you back from the forest."

155 Omovo, overcome with delirium, began to tell his father what he had seen. But his father, smiling apologetically at the soldiers, picked up his son and carried him off to bed.

**5.**
Will the soldiers hurt Omovo?

# B.  Second Reading: Taking a Closer Look

Read the story a second time. Use the following questions to gain a better understanding and to bring your experience to the story.

1.   What kind of news did Omovo and his father hear over the radio? Do you think Omovo had any idea of what the war was about? Do you think he knew which side his father was on?

2.   What did Omovo know about the woman he was waiting to see?

3.   Why do you think the soldiers talked to the children? Why do you think Omovo wouldn't take money from the soldiers?

4.   Why didn't Omovo see the woman when she passed?

5.   What was the woman carrying in her basket and whom was she taking it to?

6.   What did the soldiers want to know from the woman?

7.   How did the woman react when the soldiers knocked her down, and what happened to the woman in the end?

8.   Why was Omovo so shocked when he woke up, and why did his father take him immediately to bed? Do you think his father acted correctly in this situation? What do you think his father will say to him when Omovo wakes? Will he speak roughly or gently to him?

## Delving More Deeply

Find the following text in the lines indicated. Use the surrounding text and your experience to give an informed answer.

1.   *That's when the world goes dark and strange things happen.* *(line 23)* This sentence describes more than an eclipse. What else does it describe?

2.   *(lines 38–43)* Does the passage about the woman describe an incident Omovo is witnessing at that moment or an incident that he is remembering?

3.   Omovo's eyes seem to trick him as he sees the same objects successively as *capsized canoes* *(lines 107–108)*, then as *swollen dead animals* *(line 111)*, and finally as *corpses of grown men* *(line 131)*. Why didn't he recognize the corpses for what they were right off?

4.   *Omovo heard the shot…* *(line 138)* What do we know has just happened?

5.   The jungle, the setting for a big portion of the story, is almost like a character. That is, the jungle seems to act, to do things the way characters in a story do. Who or what scared Omovo from his hiding place? *(lines 138–139)* What made Omovo trip over the roots? *(lines 141–142)*

⧉ ⧉ ⧉ ⧉ ⧉ ⧉ ⧉ ⧉ ⧉ ⧉ ⧉ ⧉ ⧉ ⧉ ⧉ ⧉ ⧉

# III. STRENGTHENING SKILLS THROUGH THE TEXT

## A. Responding to the Reading

Write 75 words on *one* of the following topics. When you finish, choose a classmate to listen to what you have written.

1. Did you like this story? Why or why not?

2. Did you ever get in trouble for not obeying your parents when you were younger? What happened? How did the situation end?

_____

_____

_____

_____

_____

_____

_____

_____

_____

_____

## B. Global Comprehension Exercise: Essay Questions

Write a complete paragraph for each question below that your teacher assigns. Follow this procedure:

◆ *Thinking and Making Notes*
Use part of your time thinking and making notes before you begin to write. (Your teacher may allow you to form small groups to discuss the questions and share ideas as part of thinking and making notes.)

◆ *Getting Started*

Write a topic sentence which addresses the question asked. For example, for question 1 you might begin, ***There are three incidents that
show that Omovo's father wants to protect him from the war. First,
he...*** (Notice that this topic sentence incorporates part of the question,
often a useful tactic because it saves time.)

◆ *Developing the Answer*

Continue by supporting your topic sentence with evidence *from the
story.* In an essay exam, your teacher looks for evidence that you have
read and understood the text. Therefore, your answer should demonstrate your understanding and not your opinions (unless they are
specifically asked for). Include as many relevant details and examples
as time permits. (Do *not* include irrelevant material, that is, material
not directly related to the question.)Write with your books closed
unless your teacher instructs you otherwise.

1.   What evidence is there that Omovo's father wants to protect him
from the war? Cite three incidents.

2.   There is a lot of evidence of the destruction that war brings to a
society. Mention at least three specific examples from this story.

3.   Discuss the tension between appearance and reality in the story.
Consider the difference in how Omovo sees the characters (the soldiers, the woman) and how the characters see each other.

**FOLLOW-UP**
Your teacher may ask class
members to compare
answers before, or instead
of, handing them in.

4.   Is this basically a story about war or a story about a boy coming of
age, i.e., a boy leaving childhood and entering adulthood? Explain.

## C.   Text-based Focus on Vocabulary

Find the word or phrase in the story which means the same as the
definition. (**30–35, 1**) in item **1** means you should look between lines
30 and 35 for one word meaning "walked in a stiff, self-satisfied way."
Write the word or expression in the space provided.

### The Vocabulary of Movement

1.   *(30–35, 1)* walked in a stiff, self-satisfied way _____

2.   *(35–40, 1)* moved along smoothly _____

3.   *(40–45, 1)* move or draw back _____

4. *(44–49, 1)* moved along unsteadily _____

5. *(75–80, 1)* twisting and turning _____

6. *(115–120, 1)* lowered his body to hide _____

7. *(115–120, 1)* walked with long steps _____

8. *(140–145, 1)* walked with heavy steps _____

9. *(140–145, 1)* fell _____

10. *(145–150, 2)* moved about wildly _____

## General Vocabulary

1. *(20–25, 1)* resentfulness _____

2. *(29–34, 1)* money for expenses _____

3. *(65–70, 1)* secret agent _____

4. *(70–75, 1)* were half asleep _____

5. *(105–110, 1)* overturned _____

6. *(125–130, 1)* wrinkle, fold _____

7. *(125–130, 1)* long, deep cut or wound _____

8. *(135–140, 2)* scream like a crazy person _____

**FOLLOW-UP**
Check your answers as
instructed by your teacher.

## Review/Application

Someone in the class will choose one verb of motion from **C** and act it out. The rest of the class will try to guess which verb is being demonstrated. The person who guesses correctly will then choose another verb to demonstrate, and so on.

# IV. MOVING BEYOND THE TEXT

## A. Discussion and Writing

Discuss the following topics as a class or in groups. Your teacher may assign a different topic to each group and ask a group leader to summarize its discussion for the class. Write on *one or more* of the topics as instructed by your teacher.

**1.** The title "In the Shadow of War" and the "eclipse" mentioned in the story both bring to mind images of shadows. What does it mean to live "in the shadow of war"? How is that similar to what Omovo's father says about the effects of an eclipse?

**2.** What do you think the author is trying to say about war in this story, i.e., what do you think is the message, or the theme, of the story?

**3.** Is war inevitable, or can it be avoided? Are there other ways to solve conflicts?

**4.** How do you think children like Omovo are affected by war even if they don't personally suffer injury or hunger?

**5.** Are there "good people" and "bad people" in the story? If so, who are they? How can we separate the good and the bad people in this kind of a conflict?

**6.** Some people argue that sometimes it's necessary to do "bad" things, such as use violence when it is necessary, to achieve a desirable result or end. Other people say that the end never justifies the means. Take *one* side of this issue and support it.

_____

_____

_____

_____

_____

_____

_____

_____

_____

_____

_____

_____

_____

_____

_____

## B.    Making Connections

There are always wars happening somewhere in the world. As a class, list every place in the world where there is currently a war or military activity. Then for the next few days skim the world news section of your newspaper for articles related to these activities. Everybody should bring at least one article on current war activities to class and briefly summarize it for the class. Then discuss as a class what the causes of these wars seem to be. Try to be objective and analytical. Then discuss what the effects of war on a country are—economic, political, family, social, psychological, etc.

Why does the old man sit beneath the horse?
Does he stay here long?

# Lesson 13

## A HORSE AND TWO GOATS

### R.K.Narayan

### India

# █ █ █ █ █ █ █ █ █ █ █ █ █ █ █ █ █ █ █ █

# I. GETTING READY

## A. Entering the Story through Listening

Listen to two early passages from "A Horse and Two Goats" as your teacher reads, and answer the questions which follow each passage. Discuss Passage 1 before going on to Passage 2.

**Passage I.** *(lines 201–221)* The first passage describes the encounter of Muni, an Indian peasant, with an American tourist.

1. Why did the tourist stop in Muni's village?

2. What in the village caught the tourist's interest?

3. What was Muni's reaction to the tourist? Why didn't Muni do anything?

**Passage II.** *(lines 222–232, up to "yes, no.")*

1. What misunderstandings are there between Muni and the tourist?

## B. Discussion

After listening, discuss these questions.

1. Have you experienced a misunderstanding with a foreigner? If so, was the misunderstanding due to language? Culture? Something else?

2. Do you think the tourist and Muni will reach an understanding and get along? Or are their differences too great?

3. What do you know about the Hindu religion? Can you name any of the gods, or deities?

## C. Background

Read the following information, noting the italicized words, to help you understand the story more easily and fully.

The humor of "A Horse and Two Goats" lies in the fact that the reader understands what is happening better than either of the two main characters. *Why* Muni talks on and on is perhaps more important than *what* he actually says, which deals with Hindu religion, literature, and folklore. Read his long monologues for their comic effect rather than for a deep understanding of his culture. By familiarizing yourself with the following vocabulary, however, you will be able to appreciate the humor in the juxtaposition of Muni's very elevated topics with the tourist's rather common conversation.

RELIGIOUS VOCABULARY
**Brahma, Vishnu** *(line 422)*, and **Siva** *(line 224)*: a trinity of Hindu gods—the creator, preserver, and destroyer, respectively.
**avatar** *(line 432)*: manifestation of a god in earthly form, sometimes a human and sometimes an animal.
**Krishna** *(line 473)*: an avatar of Vishnu

GENERAL VOCABULARY
**rupee** *(line 33)*: Indian currency
**caste** *(line 154)*: a hereditary social group composed of people of the same rank, economic position, and often occupation.
**khaki** *(line 264)*: yellowish-brown material for uniforms
**Brahmin** *(line 367)*: the highest Hindu caste
**Ramayana** *(line 464)*, **Mahabharata** *(line 471)*: the two most important pieces of Indian literature.

(generally not used outside of the Indian context)
**swarga** *(line 80)*: heaven
**bhang** *(line 127)*: hemp, marijuana
**namaste** *(line 229)*: traditional Hindu expression used in greeting and parting.
**Bhagwan** *(line 274)*: lord
**Parangi** *(line 371)*: foreign; here, Parangi language is English.
**Kali Yuga** *(line 391)*: the last of four stages of human time, an age of trouble and strife.
**lakh** *(line 516)*: literally, 100,000; figuratively, a very large amount

# II. ENGAGING WITH THE TEXT

## A. First Reading: Following the Story Line

Because it is a longer story, "A Horse and Three Goats" is divided into three sections for the first reading. Use the reading questions to help you predict and follow the main events of Section I.

**Section I** *(lines 1–221)*

1.  What is the village Kritam like?

2.  What is Muni's economic and social status?

**3.** How successful is Muni at getting groceries from the shopman without paying?

**4.** Why does Muni spend the day at the statue instead of at home? What happens to make him regret sitting there?

### A Horse and Two Goats *(Section I)*

Of the seven hundred thousand villages dotting the map of India, in which the majority of India's five hundred million live, flourish, and die, Kritam was probably the tiniest, indicated on the district survey map by a microscopic dot, the map being meant more for the revenue official out to collect tax than for the guidance of the motorist, who in any case could not hope to reach it since it sprawled far from the highway at the end of a rough track furrowed up by the iron-hooped wheels of bullock carts. But its size did not prevent its giving itself the grandiose name Kritam, which meant in Tamil "coronet" or "crown" on the brow of this subcontinent. The village consisted of fewer than thirty houses, only one of them built with brick and cement. Painted a brilliant yellow and blue all over with gorgeous carvings of gods and gargoyles on its balustrade, it was known as the Big House. The other houses, distributed in four streets, were generally of bamboo thatch, straw, mud, and other unspecified material. Muni's was the last house in the fourth street, beyond which stretched the fields. In his prosperous days Muni had owned a flock of forty sheep and goats and sallied forth every morning driving the flock to the highway a couple of miles away. There he would sit on the pedestal of a clay statue of a horse while his cattle grazed around. He carried a crook at the end of a bamboo pole and he snapped foliage from the avenue trees to feed his flock; he also gathered faggots and dry sticks, bundled them, and carried them home for fuel at sunset.

His wife lit the domestic fire at dawn, boiled water in a mud pot, threw into it a handful of millet flour, added salt, and gave him his first nourishment for the day. When he started out, she would put in his hand a packed lunch, once again the same millet cooked into a little ball, which he could swallow with a raw onion at midday. She was old, but he was older and needed all the attention she could give him in order to be kept alive.

His fortunes had declined gradually, unnoticed. From a flock of forty which he drove into a pen at night, his stock had now come down to two goats, which were not worth the rent of a half rupee a month the Big House charged for the use of the pen in their backyard. And so the two goats were tethered to the trunk of a drumstick tree which grew in front of his hut and from which occasionally Muni could shake down drumsticks. This morning he got six. He carried them in with a sense of triumph. Although no one could say precisely who owned the tree, it was his because he lived in its shadow.

She said, "If you were content with the drumstick leaves alone, I could boil and salt some for you."

"Oh, I am tired of eating those leaves. I have a craving to chew the drumstick out of sauce, I tell you."

"You have only four teeth in your jaw, but your craving is for big things. All right, get the stuff for the sauce, and I will prepare it for you. After all, next year you may not be alive to ask for anything. But first get me all the stuff, including a measure of rice or millet, and I will satisfy your unholy craving. Our store is empty today. Dhall, chili, curry leaves, mustard, coriander, gingelley oil, and one large potato. Go out and get all this." He repeated the list after her in order not to miss any item and walked off to the shop in the third street.

He sat on an upturned packing case below the platform of the shop. The shopman paid no attention to him. Muni kept clearing his throat, coughing, and sneezing until the shopman could not stand it any more and demanded, "What ails you? You will fly off that seat into the gutter if you sneeze so hard, young man." Muni laughed inordinately, in order to please the shopman, at being called "young man." The shopman softened and said, "You have enough of the imp inside to keep a second wife busy, but for the fact the old lady is still alive." Muni laughed appropriately again at this joke. It completely won the shopman over; he liked his sense of humor to be appreciated. Muni engaged his attention in local gossip for a few minutes, which always ended with a reference to the postman's wife, who had eloped to the city some months before.

The shopman felt most pleased to hear the worst of the postman, who had cheated him. Being an itinerant postman, he returned home to Kritam only once in ten days and every time managed to slip away again without passing the shop in the third street. By thus humoring the shopman, Muni could always ask for one or two items of food, promising repayment later. Some days the shopman was in a good mood and gave in, and sometimes he would lose his temper suddenly and bark at Muni for daring to ask for credit. This was such a day, and Muni could not progress beyond two items listed as essential components. The shopman was also displaying a remarkable memory for old facts and figures and took out an oblong ledger to support his observations. Muni felt impelled to rise and flee. But his self-respect kept him in his seat and made him listen to the worst things about himself. The shopman concluded, "If you could find five rupees and a quarter, you will have paid off an ancient debt and then could apply for admission to swarga. How much have you got now?"

"I will pay you everything on the first of the next month."

"As always, and whom do you expect to rob by then?"

Muni felt caught and mumbled, "My daughter has sent word that she will be sending me money."

"Have you a daughter?" sneered the shopman. "And she is sending you money! For what purpose, may I know?"

"Birthday, fiftieth birthday," said Muni quietly.

"Birthday! How old are you?"

Muni repeated weakly, not being sure of it himself, "Fifty." He always calculated his age from the time of the great famine when he stood as high as the parapet around the village well, but who could calculate such things accurately nowadays with so many famines occurring? The shopman felt encouraged when other customers stood around to watch and comment. Muni thought helplessly, My poverty

95  is exposed to everybody. But what can I do?

"More likely you are seventy," said the shopman. "You also forget that you mentioned a birthday five weeks ago when you wanted castor oil for your holy bath."

"Bath! Who can dream of a bath when you have to scratch the

100  tank-bed for a bowl of water? We would all be parched and dead but for the Big House, where they let us take a pot of water from their well." After saying this Muni unobtrusively rose and moved off.

He told his wife, "That scoundrel would not give me anything. So go out and sell the drumsticks for what they are worth."

105  He flung himself down in a corner to recoup from the fatigue of his visit to the shop. His wife said, "You are getting no sauce today, nor anything else. I can't find anything to give you to eat. Fast till the evening, it'll do you good. Take the goats and be gone now," she cried and added, "Don't come back before the sun is down." He knew that

110  if he obeyed her she would somehow conjure up some food for him in the evening. Only he must be careful not to argue and irritate her. Her temper was undependable in the morning but improved by evening time. She was sure to go out and work—grind corn in the Big House, sweep or scrub somewhere, and earn enough to buy foodstuff and

115  keep a dinner ready for him in the evening.

Unleashing the goats from the drumstick tree, Muni started out, driving them ahead and uttering weird cries from time to time in order to urge them on. He passed through the village with his head bowed in thought. He did not want to look at anyone or be accosted.

120  A couple of cronies lounging in the temple corridor hailed him, but he ignored their call. They had known him in the days of affluence when he lorded over a flock of fleecy sheep, not the miserable gawky goats that he had today. Of course he also used to have a few goats for those who fancied them, but real wealth lay in sheep; they bred fast and peo-

125  ple came and bought the fleece in the shearing season; and then that famous butcher from the town came over on the weekly market days bringing him betel leaves, tobacco, and often enough some bhang, which they smoked in a hut in the coconut grove, undisturbed by wives and well-wishers. After a smoke one felt light and elated and

130  inclined to forgive everyone including that brother-in-law of his who had once tried to set fire to his home. But all this seemed like the memories of a previous birth. Some pestilence afflicted his cattle (he could of course guess who had laid his animals under a curse), and even the friendly butcher would not touch one at half the price…and

135  now here he was left with the two scraggy creatures. He wished some-one would rid him of their company, too. The shopman had said that he was seventy. At seventy, one only waited to be summoned by God. When he was dead what would his wife do? They had lived in each other's company since they were children. He was told on their day of

140  wedding that he was ten years old and she was eight. During the wed-ding ceremony they had had to recite their respective ages and names.

He had thrashed her only a few times in their career, and later she had the upper hand. Progeny, none. Perhaps a large progeny would have brought him the blessing of the gods. Fertility brought merit. People

145  with fourteen sons were always so prosperous and at peace with the world and themselves. He recollected the thrill he had felt when he mentioned a daughter to that shopman; although it was not believed, what if he did not have a daughter?—his cousin in the next village had many daughters, and any one of them was as good as his; he was fond

150  of them all and would buy them sweets if he could afford it. Still, everyone in the village whispered behind their backs that Muni and his wife were a barren couple. He avoided looking at anyone; they all professed to be so high up, and everyone else in the village had more money than he. "I am the poorest fellow in our caste and no wonder

155  that they spurn me, but I won't look at them either," and so he passed on with his eyes downcast along the edge of the street, and people left him also very much alone, commenting only to the extent, "Ah, there he goes with his two goats; if he slits their throats, he may have more peace of mind." "What has he to worry about anyway? They live on

160  nothing and have none to worry about." Thus people commented when he passed through the village. Only on the outskirts did he lift his head and look up. He urged and bullied the goats until they meandered along to the foot of the horse statue on the edge of the village. He sat on its pedestal for the rest of the day. The advantage of this was

165  that he could watch the highway and see the lorries and buses pass through to the hills, and it gave him a sense of belonging to a larger world. The pedestal of the statue was broad enough for him to move around as the sun traveled up and westward; or he could also crouch under the belly of the horse, for shade.

170      The horse was nearly life-size, molded out of clay, baked, burnt, and brightly colored, and reared its head proudly, prancing its forelegs in the air and flourishing its tail in a loop; beside the horse stood a warrior with scythe-like mustachios, bulging eyes, and aquiline nose. The old image-makers believed in indicating a man of strength by

175  bulging out his eyes and sharpening his mustache tips, and also decorated the man's chest with beads which looked today like blobs of mud through the ravages of sun and wind and rain (when it came), but Muni would insist that he had known the beads to sparkle like the nine gems at one time in his life. The horse itself was said to have been

180  as white as a dhobi-washed sheet, and had had on its back a cover of pure brocade of red and black lace, matching the multicolored sash around the waist of the warrior. But none in the village remembered the splendor as no one noticed its existence. Even Muni, who spent all his waking hours at its foot, never bothered to look up. It was

185  untouched even by the young vandals of the village who gashed tree trunks with knives and tried to topple off milestones and inscribed lewd designs on all walls. This statue had been closer to the population of the village at one time, when this spot bordered the village; but when the highway was laid through (or perhaps when the tank and

190  wells dried up completely here) the village moved a couple of miles inland.

Muni sat at the foot of the statue, watching his two goats graze in the arid soil among the cactus and lantana bushes. He looked at the sun; it was tilted westward no doubt, but it was not the time yet to go back home; if he went too early his wife would have no food for him. Also he must give her time to cool off her temper and feel sympathetic, and then she would scrounge and manage to get some food. He watched the mountain road for a time signal. When the green bus appeared around the bend he could leave, and his wife would feel pleased that he had let the goats feed long enough.

195

200

He noticed now a new sort of vehicle coming down at full speed. It looked like both a motor car and a bus. He used to be intrigued by the novelty of such spectacles, but of late work was going on at the source of the river on the mountain and an assortment of people and traffic went past him, and he took it all casually and described to his wife, later in the day, everything he saw. Today, while he observed the yellow vehicle coming down, he was wondering how to describe it later to his wife, when it sputtered and stopped in front of him. A red-faced foreigner, who had been driving it, got down and went round it, stooping, looking, and poking under the vehicle; then he straightened himself up, looked at the dashboard, stared in Muni's direction, and approached him. "Excuse me, is there a gas station nearby, or do I have to wait until another car comes—" He suddenly looked up at the clay horse and cried, "Marvelous," without completing his sentence. Muni felt he should get up and run away, and cursed his age. He could not readily put his limbs into action; some years ago he could outrun a cheetah, as happened once when he went to the forest to cut fuel and it was then that two of his sheep were mauled—a sign that bad times were coming. Though he tried, he could not easily extricate himself from his seat, and then there was also the problem of the goats. He could not leave them behind.

205

210

215

220

**FOLLOW–UP**
How do you think the story will develop? What will Muni and the tourist want from each other?

**Section II** *(lines 222–397)*

1.  In what ways is Muni wary, or cautious, of the foreigner?

2.  Muni and the tourist talk about completely different things. What does each one talk about? Why does each one continue talking when he is not understood?

3.  Why is Muni relieved to talk about the horse? Does he understand the tourist's real interest in the horse?

**A Horse and Two Goats** *(Section II)*

The red-faced man wore khaki clothes—evidently a policeman or a soldier. Muni said to himself, He will chase or shoot if I start running. Some dogs chase only those who run—O Siva, protect me. I don't know why this man should be after me. Meanwhile the foreigner cried, "Marvelous!" again, nodding his head. He paced around the

225

statue with his eyes fixed on it. Muni sat frozen for a while, and then fidgeted and tried to edge away. Now the other man suddenly pressed his palms together in a salute, smiled, and said, "Namaste! How do you do?"

At which Muni spoke the only English expressions he had learnt, "Yes, no." Having exhausted his English vocabulary, he started in Tamil: "My name is Muni. These two goats are mine, and no one can gainsay it—though our village is full of slanderers these days who will not hesitate to say that what belongs to a man doesn't belong to him." He rolled his eyes and shuddered at the thought of evil-minded men and women peopling his village.

The foreigner faithfully looked in the direction indicated by Muni's fingers, gazed for a while at the two goats and the rocks, and with a puzzled expression took out his silver cigarette case and lit a cigarette. Suddenly remembering the courtesies of the season, he asked, "Do you smoke?" Muni answered "Yes, no." Whereupon the red-faced man took a cigarette and gave it to Muni, who received it with surprise, having had no offer of a smoke from anyone for years now. Those days when he smoked bhang were gone with his sheep and the large-hearted butcher. Nowadays he was not able to find even matches, let alone bhang. (His wife went across and borrowed a fire at dawn from a neighbor.) He had always wanted to smoke a cigarette; only once did the shopman give him one on credit, and he remembered how good it had tasted. The other flicked the lighter open and offered a light to Muni. Muni felt so confused about how to act that he blew on it and put it out. The other, puzzled but undaunted, flourished his lighter, presented it again, and lit Muni's cigarette. Muni drew a deep puff and started coughing; it was racking, no doubt, but extremely pleasant. When his cough subsided he wiped his eyes and took stock of the situation, understanding that the other man was not an Inquisitor of any kind. Yet, in order to make sure, he remained wary. No need to run away from a man who gave him such a potent smoke. His head was reeling from the effect of one of those strong American cigarettes made with roasted tobacco. The man said, "I come from New York," took out a wallet from his hip pocket, and presented his card.

Muni shrank away from the card. Perhaps he was trying to present a warrant and arrest him. Beware of khaki, one part of his mind warned. Take all the cigarettes or bhang or whatever is offered, but don't get caught. Beware of khaki. He wished he weren't seventy as the shopman had said. At seventy one didn't run, but surrendered to whatever came. He could only ward off trouble by talk. So he went on, all in the chaste Tamil for which Kritam was famous. (Even the worst detractors could not deny that the famous poetess Avaiyar was born in this area, although no one could say whether it was in Kritam or Kuppam, the adjoining village.) Out of this heritage the Tamil language gushed through Muni in an unimpeded flow. He said, "Before God, sir, Bhagwan, who sees everything, I tell you, sir, that we know

275 nothing of the case. If the murder was committed, whoever did it will not escape. Bhagwan is all-seeing. Don't ask me about it. I know nothing." A body had been found mutilated and thrown under a tamarind tree at the border between Kritam and Kuppam a few weeks before, giving rise to much gossip and speculation. Muni added an explana-
280 tion, "Anything is possible there. People over there will stop at nothing." The foreigner nodded his head and listened courteously though he understood nothing.

"I am sure you know when this horse was made," said the red man and smiled ingratiatingly.

285 Muni reacted to the relaxed atmosphere by smiling himself, and pleaded, "Please go away, sir, I know nothing. I promise we will hold him for you if we see any bad character around, and we will bury him up to his neck in a coconut pit if he tries to escape; but our village has always had a clean record. Must definitely be the other village."

290 Now the red man implored, "Please, please, I will speak slowly, please try to understand me. Can't you understand even a simple word of English? Everyone in this country seems to know English. I have gotten along with English everywhere in this country, but you don't speak it. Have you any religious or spiritual scruples against
295 English speech?"

Muni made some indistinct sounds in his throat and shook his head. Encouraged, the other went on to explain at length, uttering each syllable with care and deliberation. Presently he sidled over and took a seat beside the old man, explaining, "You see, last August, we
300 probably had the hottest summer in history, and I was working in shirt-sleeves in my office on the fortieth floor of the Empire State Building. We had a power failure one day, you know, and there I was stuck for four hours, no elevator, no air conditioning. All the way in the train I kept thinking, and the minute I reached home in
305 Connecticut, I told my wife, Ruth, 'We will visit India this winter, it's time to look at other civilizations.' Next day she called the travel agent first thing and told him to fix it, and so here I am. Ruth came with me but is staying back at Srinagar, and I am the one doing the rounds and joining her later."

310 Muni looked reflective at the end of this long oration and said, rather feebly, "Yes, no," as a concession to the other's language, and went on in Tamil, "When I was this high"—he indicated a foot high— "I had heard my uncle say…"

No one can tell what he was planning to say, as the other interrupt-
315 ed him at this stage to ask, "Boy, what is the secret of your teeth? How old are you?"

The old man forgot what he had started to say and remarked, "Sometimes we too lose our cattle. Jackals or cheetahs may sometimes carry them off, but sometimes it is just theft from over in the next vil-
320 lage, and then we will know who has done it. Our priest at the temple can see in the camphor flame the face of the thief, and when he is caught…" He gestured with his hands a perfect mincing of meat.

The American watched his hands intently and said, "I know what you mean. Chop something? Maybe I am holding you up and you want to chop wood? Where is your axe? Hand it to me and show me what to chop. I do enjoy it, you know, just a hobby. We get a lot of driftwood along the backwater near my house, and on Sundays I do nothing but chop wood for the fireplace. I really feel different when I watch the fire in the fireplace, although it may take all the sections of the Sunday *New York Times* to get a fire started." And he smiled at this reference.

Muni felt totally confused but decided the best thing would be to make an attempt to get away from this place. He tried to edge out, saying, "Must go home," and turned to go. The other seized his shoulder and said desperately, "Is there no one, absolutely no one here, to translate for me?" He looked up and down the road, which was deserted in this hot afternoon; a sudden gust of wind churned up the dust and dead leaves on the roadside into a ghostly column and propelled it towards the mountain road. The stranger almost pinioned Muni's back to the statue and asked, "Isn't this statue yours? Why don't you sell it to me?"

The old man now understood the reference to the horse, thought for a second, and said in his own language, "I was an urchin this high when I heard my grandfather explain this horse and warrior, and my grandfather himself was this high when he heard his grandfather, whose grandfather…"

The other man interrupted him. "I don't want to seem to have stopped here for nothing. I will offer you a good price for this," he said, indicating the horse. He had concluded without the least doubt that Muni owned this mud horse. Perhaps he guessed by the way he sat on its pedestal, like other souvenir sellers in this country presiding over their wares.

Muni followed the man's eyes and pointing fingers and dimly understood the subject matter and, feeling relieved that the theme of the mutilated body had been abandoned at least for the time being, said again, enthusiastically, "I was this high when my grandfather told me about this horse and the warrior, and my grandfather was this high when he himself…" and he was getting into a deeper bog of reminiscence each time he tried to indicate the antiquity of the statue.

The Tamil that Muni spoke was stimulating even as pure sound, and the foreigner listened with fascination. "I wish I had my tape-recorder here," he said, assuming the pleasantest expression. "Your language sounds wonderful. I get a kick out of every word you utter, here"—he indicated his ears—"but you don't have to waste your breath in sales talk. I appreciate the article. You don't have to explain its points.

"I never went to a school, in those days only Brahmin went to schools, but we had to go out and work in the fields morning till night, from sowing to harvest time…and when Pongal came and we had to cut the harvest, my father allowed me to go out and play with others at the tank, and so I don't know the Parangi language you speak, even little fellows in your country probably speak the Parangi language, but here only learned men and officers know it. We had a postman in our village who could speak to you boldly in your language, but his wife ran away with someone and he does not speak to anyone at all nowadays. Who would if a wife did what she did? Women must be watched; otherwise they will sell themselves and the home." And he laughed at his own quip.

The foreigner laughed heartily, took out another cigarette, and offered it to Muni, who now smoked with ease, deciding to stay on if the fellow was going to be so good as to keep up his cigarette supply. The American now stood up on the pedestal in the attitude of a demonstrative lecturer and said, running his finger along some of the carved decorations around the horse's neck, speaking slowly and uttering his words syllable by syllable, "I could give a sales talk for this better than anyone else.… This is a marvelous combination of yellow and indigo, though faded now.… How do you people of this country achieve these flaming colors?"

Muni, now assured that the subject was still the horse and not the dead body, said, "This is our guardian, it means death to our adversaries. At the end of Kali Yuga, this world and all other worlds will be destroyed, and the Redeemer will come in the shape of a horse called Kalki; this horse will come to life and gallop and trample down all bad men." As he spoke of bad men the figures of his shopman and his brother-in-law assumed concrete forms in his mind, and he reveled for a moment in the predicament of the fellow under the horse's hoof: served him right for trying to set fire to his home.…

**FOLLOW–UP**

Will Muni understand that the foreigner wants to buy the horse? Will Muni sell it to him?

**Section III** *(lines 398–581)*

**1.** Do Muni and the tourist grow to understand each other, more or less?

**2.** Is Muni still as wary of the foreigner as he was in the beginning? How do you know?

**3.** Why does Muni think the tourist wants to buy his goats? Why doesn't he stay until they have been taken away?

**4.** Who appreciates Muni's good fortune in the end?

**A Horse and Two Goats** *(Section III)*

While he was brooding on this pleasant vision, the foreigner utilized the pause to say, "I assure you that this will have the best home in the U.S.A. I'll push away the bookcase, you know I love books and am a member of five book clubs, and the choice and bonus volumes mount up to a pile really in our living room, as high as this horse itself. But they'll have to go. Ruth may disapprove, but I will convince her. The TV may have to be shifted, too. We can't have everything in the living room. Ruth will probably say what about when we have a party? I'm going to keep him right in the middle of the room. I don't see how that can interfere with the party—we'll stand around him and have our drinks.

Muni continued his description of the end of the world. "Our pundit discoursed at the temple once how the oceans are going to close over the earth in a huge wave and swallow us—this horse will grow bigger than the biggest wave and carry on its back only the good people and kick into the floods the evil ones—plenty of them about—" he said reflectively. "Do you know when it is going to happen?" he asked.

The foreigner now understood by the tone of the other that a question was being asked and said, "How am I transporting it? I can push the seat back and make room in the rear. That van can take in an elephant"—waving precisely at the back of the seat.

Muni was still hovering on visions of avatars and said again, "I never missed our pundit's discourses at the temple in those days during every bright half of the month, although he'd go on all night, and he told us that Vishnu is the highest god. Whenever evil men trouble us, he comes down to save us. He has come many times. The first time he incarnated as a great fish, and lifted the scriptures on his back when the flood and sea waves…"

"I am not a millionaire, but a modest businessman. My trade is coffee."

Amidst all this wilderness of obscure sound Muni caught the word "coffee" and said, "If you want to drink 'kapi,' drive further up, in the next town, they have Friday market and there they open 'kapi-otels'— so I learn from passers-by. Don't think I wander about. I go nowhere and look for nothing." His thoughts went back to the avatars. "The first avatar was in the shape of a little fish in a bowl of water, but every hour it grew bigger and bigger and became in the end a huge whale which the seas could not contain, and on the back of the whale the holy books were supported, saved, and carried." Once he had launched on the first avatar, it was inevitable that he should go on to the next, a wild boar on whose tusk the earth was lifted when a vicious conqueror of the earth carried it off and hid it at the bottom of the sea. After describing this avatar Muni concluded, "God will always save us whenever we are troubled by evil beings. When we were young we staged at full moon the story of the avatars. That's how I know the stories; we played them all night until the sun rose, and sometimes the European collector would come to watch, bringing his own chair. I had a good voice and so they always taught me songs and gave me the women's roles. I was always Goddess Lakshmi, and they dressed me in a brocade sari, loaned from the Big House…"

The foreigner said, "I repeat I am not a millionaire. Ours is a modest business; after all, we can't afford to buy more than sixty minutes of TV time in a month, which works out to two minutes a day, that's all, although in the course of time we'll maybe sponsor a one-hour show regularly if our sales graph continues to go up…"

Muni was intoxicated by the memory of his theatrical days and was about to explain how he had painted his face and worn a wig and diamond earrings when the visitor, feeling that he had spent too much time already, said, "Tell me, will you accept a hundred rupees or not for the horse? I'd love to take the whiskered soldier also but no space for him this year. I'll have to cancel my air ticket and take a boat home, I suppose. Ruth can go by air if she likes, but I will go with the horse and keep him in my cabin all the way if necessary." And he smiled at the picture of himself voyaging across the seas hugging this horse. He added, "I will have to pad it with straw so that it doesn't break…"

"When we played *Ramayana*, they dressed me as Sita," added Muni. "A teacher came and taught us the songs for the drama and we gave him fifty rupees. He incarnated himself as Rama, and he alone could destroy Ravana, the demon with ten heads who shook all the worlds; do you know the story of *Ramayana*?"

"I have my station wagon as you see. I can push the seat back and take the horse in if you will just lend me a hand with it."

"Do you know *Mahabharata*? Krishna was the eighth avatar of Vishnu, incarnated to help the Five Brothers regain their kingdom. When Krishna was a baby he danced on the thousand-hooded giant serpent and trampled it to death; and then he suckled the breasts of the demoness and left them flat as a disc, though when she came to him her bosoms were large, like mounds of earth on the banks of a dug-up canal." He indicated two mounds with his hands.

The stranger was completely mystified by the gesture. For the first time he said, "I really wonder what you are saying because your answer is crucial. We have come to the point when we should be ready to talk business."

"When the tenth avatar comes, do you know where you and I will be?" asked the old man.

"Lend me a hand and I can lift off the horse from its pedestal after picking out the cement at the joints. We can do anything if we have a basis of understanding."

At this stage the mutual mystification was complete, and there was no need even to carry on a guessing game at the meaning of words. The old man chattered away in a spirit of balancing off the credits and debits of conversational exchange, and said in order to be on the credit sale, "Oh, honorable one, I hope God has blessed you with numerous progeny. I say this because you seem to be a good man, willing to stay beside an old man and talk to him, while all day I have none to talk to except when somebody stops by to ask for a piece of tobacco. But I seldom have it, tobacco is not what it used to be at one time, and I have given up chewing. I cannot afford it nowadays." Noting the other's interest in his speech, Muni felt encouraged to ask, "How many children have you?" with appropriate gestures with his hands.

Realizing that a question was being asked, the red man replied, "I said a hundred," which encouraged Muni to go into details. "How many of your children are boys and how many girls? Where are they? Is your daughter married? Is it difficult to find a son-in-law in your country also?"

In answer to these questions the red man dashed his hand into his pocket and brought forth his wallet in order to take immediate advantage of the bearish trend in the market. He flourished a hundred-rupee currency note and said, "Well, this is what I meant."

The old man now realized that some financial element was entering their talk. He peered closely at the currency note, the like of which he had never seen in his life; he knew the five and ten by their colors although always in other people's hands, while his own earning at any time was in coppers and nickels. What was this man flourishing the note for? Perhaps asking for change. He laughed to himself at the notion of anyone coming to him for changing a thousand- or ten-thousand-rupee note. He said with a grin, "Ask our village headman, who is also a moneylender; he can change even a lakh of rupees in gold sovereigns if you prefer it that way; he thinks nobody knows, but dig the floor of his puja room and your head will reel at the sight of the hoard. The man disguises himself in rags just to mislead the public. Talk to the headman yourself because he goes mad at the sight of me. Someone took away his pumpkins with the creeper and he, for some reason, thinks it was me and my goats…that's why I never let my goats be seen anywhere near the farms." His eyes traveled to his goats nosing about, attempting to wrest nutrition from minute greenery peeping out from rock and dry earth.

The foreigner followed his look and decided that it would be a sound policy to show an interest in the old man's pets. He went up casually to them and stroked their backs with every show of courteous attention. Now the truth dawned on the old man. His dream of a lifetime was about to be realized. He understood that the red man was actually making an offer for the goats. He had reared them up in the hope of selling them some day and, with the capital, opening a small shop on this very spot. Sitting here, watching towards the hills, he had often dreamt how he would put up a thatched roof here, spread a gunny sack out on the ground, and display on it fried nuts, colored sweets, and green coconut for the thirsty and famished wayfarers on the highway, which was sometimes very busy. The animals were not prize ones for a cattle show, but he had spent his occasional savings to provide them some fancy diet now and then, and they did not look too bad. While he was reflecting thus, the red man shook his hand and left on his palm one hundred rupees in tens now, suddenly realizing that this was what the old man was asking. "It is all for you or you may share it if you have a partner."

The old man pointed at the station wagon and asked, "Are you carrying them off in that?"

"Yes, of course," said the other, understanding the transportation part of it.

The old man said, "This will be their first ride in a motor car. Carry them off after I get out of sight, otherwise they will never follow you, but only me even if I am traveling on the path to Yama Loka." He laughed at his own joke, brought his palms together in a salute, turned around and went off, and was soon out of sight beyond a clump of thicket.

The red man looked at the goats grazing peacefully. Perched on the pedestal of the horse, as the westerly sun touched off the ancient faded colors of the statue with a fresh splendor, he ruminated, "He must be gone to fetch some help, I suppose!" and settled down to wait. When a truck came downhill, he stopped it and got the help of a couple of men to detach the horse from its pedestal and place it in his station wagon. He gave them five rupees each, and for a further payment they siphoned off gas from the truck, and helped him to start his engine.

Muni hurried homeward with the cash securely tucked away at his waist in his dhoti. He shut the street door and stole up softly to his wife as she squatted before the lit oven wondering if by a miracle food would drop from the sky. Muni displayed his fortune for the day. She snatched the notes from him, counted them by the glow of the fire, and cried, "One hundred rupees! How did you come by it? Have you been stealing?"

"I have sold our goats to a red-faced man. He was absolutely crazy to have them, gave me all this money and carried them off in his motor car!"

Hardly had these words left his lips when they heard bleating outside. She opened the door and saw the two goats at her door. "Here they are!" she said. "What's the meaning of all this?"

He muttered a great curse and seized one of the goats by its ears and shouted. "Where is that man? Don't you know you are his? Why did you come back?" The goat only wriggled in his grip. He asked the same question of the other, too. The goat shook itself off. His wife glared at him and declared, "If you have thieved, the police will come tonight and break your bones. Don't involve me. I will go away to my parents...."

# B.  Second Reading

Reread the whole story. Use the questions to gain a better understanding and to bring your experience to the story.

1.   In trying to humor the shopman into giving him groceries on credit, was Muni completely truthful? Do you think he felt embarrassed at the shopman's refusal, or merely disappointed?

2.   What circumstances of his life did Muni seem ashamed of?

**3.** Was the statue of the horse an important monument to the villagers?

**4.** Why didn't Muni simply escape when the tourist stopped nearby?

**5.** Did Muni's fear discourage him from talking? Have you had the same reaction to fear?

**6.** Do you think the tourist was trying to take advantage of Muni in the dealings over the statue? Or was the tourist dealing fairly with Muni?

**7.** Was Muni trying to deceive the tourist when he talked of the statue, Indian religion, and the town's history? Or was he sincere? Does it seem he got carried away, i.e., that he went too far?

**8.** Was the decision to sell his goats a difficult one for Muni?

**9.** Were you surprised by the ending of the story? Why or why not?

# III. STRENGTHENING SKILLS THROUGH THE TEXT

# A. Responding to the Reading

Write at least 75 words on *one* of the following topics. When you finish, choose a classmate to listen to what you have written.

**1.** Did you like this story? Why or why not?

**2.** Have you had or have you heard of a similar kind of situation that was caused by a cross-cultural misunderstanding like the one between Muni and the tourist?

_____

_____

_____

_____

_____

_____

_____

_____

_____

_____

_____

_____

_____

_____

_____

_____

## B.　Dramatization

In groups of three, practice dramatizing the three scenes between
Muni and his wife *(lines 40–51; 103–115; 562–581)*. The narrator will
read all unquoted text; students dramatizing the parts of Muni and his
wife will read dialogue spoken by them in the text. (Omit short items
such as **she said, she cried** and **added,** etc., before and after quotes for
a smoother dramatization.)

## C.　Global Comprehension Check: Summary

Write a 100-word summary of "A Horse and Two Goats." Choose
points for the summary carefully to cover the basic events of the story.
Be sure to express the theme in your summary, but do not include
opinion. Write complete sentences in a cohesive paragraph (not a list),
but do not exceed 100 words. Begin as indicated below:

**"A Horse and Two Goats" by R. K. Narayan is a story about**_____

_____

_____

_____

_____

_____

_____

_____

_____

_____

_____

_____

_____

_____

_____

**FOLLOW-UP**
 In groups of 4 or 5 students, take turns reading each others' summaries. What ideas did others include that you didn't? What do you have in your summary that others do not? Did you miss any important ideas?

_____

_____

_____

_____

_____

# D.  Text-based Focus on Vocabulary

## General Vocabulary

Find the word or phrase from the left-hand column in the lines indicated. Think about what the word or phrase might mean in the context of the sentence, paragraph, and whole story. Then look for the word or phrase in the right-hand column that is closest in meaning, and write its letter next to the number of the word.

| | | | |
|---|---|---|---|
| 1. | *prosperous* (line 17) | a. | legs |
| 2. | *nourishment* (line 26) | b. | power |
| 3. | *ails* (line 55) | c. | enjoy |
| 4. | *calculated* (line 90) | d. | die |
| 5. | *be summoned by God* (line 137) | e. | financially successful |
| 6. | *the upper hand* (line 143) | f. | estimated |
| 7. | *barren* (line 152) | g. | confused |
| 8. | *limbs* (line 216) | h. | childless |
| 9. | *slanderers* (line 234) | i. | is wrong with |
| 10. | *get a kick out of* (line 363) | j. | food |
| 11. | *mystified* (line 478) | k. | people who tell lies about other people |

## Key Words

Skim the text for 10 key words that recall for you the important incidents and themes of "A Horse and Two Goats." Be able to explain what each of your words means and why you chose it as a key word.

**FOLLOW–UP**
Share your words, their meanings if necessary, and your reasons for choosing them with a partner or small group.

EXAMPLE:
*Goat:* I chose this word not as a new one or one that needs to be explained but because the goats figure prominently in the story. Muni has nothing more to do each day than to tend his goats. And the whole misunderstanding with the tourist ends in a very funny climax involving the two goats.

# IV. MOVING BEYOND THE TEXT

## A. Discussion and Writing

Discuss the following topics as a class or in groups. Your teacher may assign a different topic to each group and ask a group leader to summarize its discussion for the class. Write on one or more of the topics as instructed by your teacher.

1. Is the misunderstanding between Muni and the tourist basically because of social, cultural, or linguistic differences? A combination of the three? Explain.

2. Do you think the tourist took advantage of Muni or exploited him in any way? Do you think Narayan is making a comment on relations between rich and poor nations in this story? Why or why not?

3. Do you think Muni's standing in his community will sink or rise when the villagers find out about the horse? Why?

_____

_____

_____

_____

_____

_____

_____

_____

_____

_____

_____

_____

# B. Telling a Story: A Short Talk

Choose *one* of the following tasks. Be prepared to speak in front of the class for two minutes on the one you select. (Do *not* write out the story; *do* prepare a note card with the main ideas of your speech. Practice delivering your speech to a partner in class.)

1. Tell a true story about an experience you or somebody you know had that involved a cross-cultural misunderstanding.

2. Tell a popular children's story from your country that teaches some important cultural value in your culture.

# UNIT IV
# The Individual: Values and Integrity

Which item is the most beautiful?
Which is the most valuable?

# Lesson 14

## WE ALONE

### Alice Walker

### U.S.A.

# I. GETTING READY

## A. Discussion: Values

In the traditional sense, the *value* of an item is its *worth*. Gold is worth more than silver, for example; it has a higher monetary or market value, in part because it is scarcer than silver. In a sociological, more human sense, *to value* something is to regard it highly, as when we value someone's friendship. Look at these two lists of items. Rank **List A** according to the traditional sense. Rank **List B** according to your own personal values. Write **1** by the most valuable item, etc.

| List A | List B |
|---|---|
| gold | good friendships |
| feathers | good relations with family members |
| diamonds | a successful career |
| seashells | a happy marriage |
| stones | a good education |

**FOLLOW-UP**
Discuss your choices as a class.

# II. ENGAGING WITH THE TEXT

## A. Listening

**FOLLOW-UP**
Discuss the answer before continuing.

Listen to the poem as your teacher reads it. What three words stick in your mind at the end? Share them with the class. Then, listen a second time to answer this question: What would the poet have us value more, things that are scarce or things that are plentiful?

## B. Reading

Read the poem to yourself. Then discuss the questions that follow with a partner.

## We Alone

We alone can devalue gold
by not caring
if it falls or rises
in the marketplace.
5    Wherever there is gold
there is a chain, you know,
and if your chain
is gold
so much the worse
10   for you.

Feathers, shells
and sea-shaped stones
are all as rare.

This could be our revolution:
15   To love what is plentiful
as much as
what's scarce.

# Questions

1.  *We alone can devalue gold* *(line 1)* ***Devalue*** here means

    a.  bring down the market value of gold
    b.  make it less important personally
    c.  both **a.** and **b.**

2.  *there is a chain, you know,* *(line 6)* Does ***chain*** mean

    a.  an item of jewelry
    b.  an obligation that is like a prisoner's chain
    c.  both **a.** and **b.**? Explain.

3.   *are all as rare.* *(line 13)* **Rare** has a number of meanings in English. Does the poet use **rare** here to mean

   a.   scarce; thinly distributed or
   b.   exceptional; extraordinary, special?

4.   ***This could be our revolution*** *(line 14)* The writer is not speaking of a political revolution here. What kind of revolution does she want? Explain.

**FOLLOW-UP**
Discuss your answers as a class or in groups. Listen to the entire poem again before going on.

5.   Which group of people do you think the poet admires more—millionaires or artists? Why? Whom do you have more respect for—a businessman who has been very successful at making money or a gardener who has beautified his community?

# III. STRENGTHENING SKILLS THROUGH THE TEXT

# A.   Responding to the Reading

Write at least 75 words on *one* of the following topics. When you finish, choose a classmate to listen to what you have written.

1.   Do you find this poem inspiring, or impractical and naive?

2.   Does the poet give good advice to a materialistic world? Explain.

_____

_____

_____

_____

_____

_____

_____

_____

_____

_____

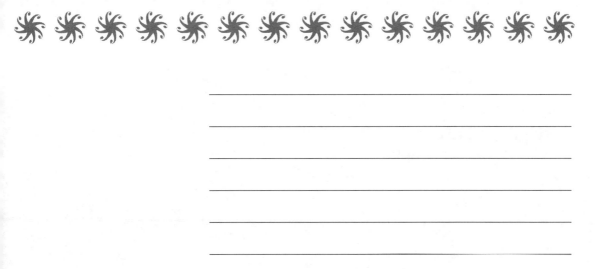

_____

_____

_____

_____

_____

_____

## B.   Poetry Reading

Listen to the poem again as your teacher reads it. Then, in groups of four, practice reading the poem. Each member of the group will read one sentence in turn. Be careful to read each sentence *as a sentence* (not as lines). If you have difficulty with pronunciation, listen to the poem again. Finally, each group can read the poem for the class.

Why has this man come to church?
Do you think he comes here often?

# Lesson 15

## THE PROBLEM OF

## OLD HARJO

John M. Oskison

U.S.A.

# I. GETTING READY

## A. Discussion: Values and Opinions on Religion

Read the following statements. Then mark each one **A** if you agree with it or **D** if you disagree.

_____ 1.   Religion is very important to most people in my country.

_____ 2.   Without religion, people would behave badly very often.

_____ 3.   It's better to have friends who have the same religion as you do.

_____ 4.   If two people from different religions wish to marry, one person should convert to the other person's religion.

_____ 5.   It's better *not* to discuss religion with people from other religions.

_____ 6.   All religions are equally good.

_____ 7.   The major religions of the world are more similar than they are different.

_____ 8.   Religion is not important. What is important is how people live their lives.

**FOLLOW-UP**
Discuss your answers in pairs or in small groups.

_____ 9.   Most people who follow a religion closely do so to be rewarded with a better afterlife, such as heaven.

## B.   Background

Read the following information, noting the italicized words, to help you understand the story more easily and fully.

Old Harjo is a Native American (a Creek Indian) living in the U.S. South some years ago. He has met Miss Evans, one of the Christian missionaries who have come to the area where Old Harjo lives to try to **convert** the Native Americans to Christianity. Old Harjo has learned from Miss Evans that he is a **sinner** in the eyes of this new religion. He is ready to **repent** his sins and wants **to be baptized** into the church so that he can **be saved**. The story is more about the conflict between two cultures—the Native American culture and the Anglo-Christian culture—than it is about religion.

*Note:* There is a reference to Mormonism in the story. The Mormons are a fairly recent sect of Christianity which for a period of time encouraged men to practice polygamy, the taking of more than one wife. Under government pressure, the Mormon church changed its *doctrine* and no longer practices polygamy.

The following words are defined here specifically as they apply to religion.

*to convert*—to change from one religion to another
*a sinner*—person who commits some act (a sin) not allowed by a religion
*to repent*—to regret or to feel sorry about one's sins
*to be baptized*—to be received into the church in a special ceremony involving water
*to be saved*—to be accepted by God after repenting one's sins
*a doctrine*—a belief or body of beliefs of a religion

# II.  ENGAGING WITH THE TEXT

# A.  First Reading: Following the Story Line

To gain a general idea of how the story develops, read all the Signpost Questions in the margins before you begin to read the story. Then concentrate on answering the questions as you read.

**1.**

What problem makes it difficult for old Harjo to be baptized and received into the church?

### The Problem of Old Harjo

1   The Spirit of the Lord had descended upon old Harjo. From the new missionary, just out from New York, he had learned that he was a sinner. The fire in the new missionary's eyes and her gracious appeal had convinced old Harjo that this was the time to repent and be saved.

5   He was very much in earnest, and he assured Miss Evans that he wanted to be baptized and received into the church at once. Miss Evans was enthusiastic and went to Mrs. Rowell with the news. It was Mrs. Rowell who had said that it was no use to try to convert the older Indians, and she, after fifteen years of work in Indian Territory mis-

10   sions, should have known. Miss Evans was pardonably proud of her conquest.

"Old Harjo converted!" exclaimed Mrs. Rowell. "Dear Miss Evans, do you know that old Harjo has two wives?" To the older woman it was as if someone had said to her "Madame, the Sultan of Turkey

15   wishes to teach one of the your mission Sabbath school classes."

"But," protested the younger woman, "he is really sincere, and—"

"Then ask him," Mrs. Rowell interrupted a bit sternly, "if he will put away one of his wives. Ask him, before he comes into the presence of the Lord, if he is willing to conform to the laws of the country in

20 which he lives, the country that guarantees his idle existence. Miss
Evans, your work is not even begun." No one who knew Mrs. Rowell
would say that she lacked sincerity and patriotism. Her own cousin
was an earnest crusader against Mormonism, and had gathered a
goodly share of that wagonload of protests that the Senate had been
25 asked to read when it was considering whether a certain statesman of
Utah should be allowed to represent his state at Washington.

In her practical, tactful way, Mrs. Rowell had kept clear of such
embarrassments. At first, she had written letters of indignant protest
to the Indian Office against the toleration of bigamy amongst the
30 tribes. A wise inspector had been sent to the mission, and this man
had pointed out that it was better to ignore certain things,
"deplorable, to be sure," than to attempt to make over the habits of
the old men. Of course, the young Indians would not be permitted to
take more than one wife each."

35 So Mrs. Rowell had discreetly limited her missionary efforts to the
young, and had exercised toward the old and bigamous only that strict
charity which even a hopeless sinner might claim.

Miss Evans, it was to be regretted, had only the vaguest notions
about "expediency"; so weak on matters of doctrine was she that the
40 news that Harjo was living with two wives didn't startle her. She was
young and possessed of but one enthusiasm—that for saving souls.

"I suppose," she ventured, "that old Harjo must put away one wife
before he can join the church?"

"There can be no question about it, Miss Evans."

45 "Then I shall have to ask him to do it." Miss Evans regretted the
necessity for forcing this sacrifice, but had no doubt that the Indian
would make it an order to accept the gift of salvation which she was
commissioned to bear to him.

Harjo lived in a "double" log cabin three miles from the mission.
50 His ten acres of corn had been gathered into its fence-rail crib; four
hogs that were to furnish his winter's bacon had been brought in from
the woods and penned conveniently near the crib; out in a corner of
the garden, a fat mound of dirt rose where the crop of turnips and
potatoes had been buried against the corrupting frost; and in the
55 hayloft of his log stable were stored many pumpkins, dried corn,
onions (suspended in bunches from the rafters) and the varied forage
that Mrs. Harjo number one and Mrs. Harjo number two had thriftily
provided. Three cows, three young heifers, two colts, and two patient,
capable mares bore the Harjo brand, a fantastic "**HH**" that the old man
60 had designed. Materially, Harjo was solvent; and if the Government
had ever come to his aid he could not recall the date.

This attempt to rehabilitate old Harjo morally, Miss Evans felt, was
not one to be made at the mission; it should be undertaken in the
Creek's own home, where the evidences of his sin should confront
65 him as she explained.

When Miss Evans rode up to the block in front of Harjo's cabin,
the old Indian came out, slowly and with a broadening smile of welcome on his face. A clean gray flannel shirt had taken the place of the
white collarless garment, with crackling stiff bosom, that he had worn

**2.**
What kind of life do Harjo
and his wives have, both
materially and spiritually?

70 to the mission meetings. Comfortable, well-patched moccasins had been substituted for creaking boots, and brown corduroys, belted in at the waist, for tight black trousers. His abundant gray hair fell down on his shoulders. In his eyes, clear and large and black, glowed the light of true hospitality. Miss Evans thought of the patriarchs as she saw him
75 lead her horse out to the stable; thus Abraham might have looked and lived.

"Harjo," began Miss Evans before following the old man to the covered passageway between the disconnected cabins, "is it true that you have two wives?" Her tone was neither stern nor accusatory. The
80 Creek had heard that question before, from scandalized missionaries and perplexed registry clerks when he went to Muscogee to enroll himself and his family in one of the many "final" records ordered to be made by the Government preparatory to dividing the Creek lands among the individual citizens.
85 For answer, Harjo called, first into the cabin that was used as a kitchen and then, in a loud, clear voice, toward the small field, where Miss Evans saw a flock of half-grown turkeys running about in the corn stubble. From the kitchen emerged a tall, thin Indian woman of fifty-five, with a red handkerchief bound severely over her head. She
90 spoke to Miss Evans and sat down in the passageway. Presently, a clear, sweet voice was heard in the field; a stout, handsome woman, about the same age as the other, climbed the rail fence and came up to the house. She, also, greeted Miss Evans briefly. Then she carried a tin basin to the well nearby, where she filled it to the brim. Setting it
95 down on the horse block, she rolled back her sleeves, tucked in the collar of her gray blouse, and plunged her face in the water. In a minute she came out of the kitchen freshened and smiling. 'Liza Harjo had been pulling dried bean stalks at one end of the field, and it was dirty work. At last old Harjo turned to Miss Evans and said, "These
100 two my wife—this one 'Liza, this one Jennie."

It was done with simple dignity. Miss Evans bowed and stammered. Three pairs of eyes were turned upon her in patient, courteous inquiry.

It was hard to state the case. The old man was so evidently proud of
105 his women, and so flattered by Miss Evans' interest in them, that he would find it hard to understand. Still, it had to be done, and Miss Evans took the plunge.

"Harjo, you want to come into our church?" The old man's face lighted.
110 "Oh, yes, I would come to Jesus, please, my friend."

"Do you know, Harjo, that the Lord commanded that one man should mate with but one woman?" The question was stated again in simpler terms, and the Indian replied, "Me know that now, my friend. Long time ago"—Harjo plainly meant the whole period previous to
115 his conversion—"me did not know. The Lord Jesus did not speak to me in that time and so I was blind. I do what blind man do."

"Harjo, you must have only one wife when you come into our church. Can't you give up one of these women?" Miss Evans glanced

**3.**

Why does Miss Evans get angry with Harjo? How does he react?

120 at the two, sitting by with smiles of polite interest on their faces, understanding nothing. They had not shared Harjo's enthusiasm either for the white man's God or his language.

"Give up my wife?" A sly smile stole over his face. He leaned closer to Miss Evans. "You tell me, my friend, which one I give up." He glanced from 'Liza to Jennie as if to weigh their attractions, and the 125 two rewarded him with their pleasantest smiles. "You tell me which one," he urged.

"Why, Harjo, how can I tell you!" Miss Evans had little sense of humor; she had taken the old man seriously.

"Then," Harjo sighed, continuing the comedy, for surely the mis- 130 sionary was jesting with him, "'Liza and Jennie must say." He talked to the Indian women for a time, and they laughed heartily. 'Liza, point- ing to the other, shook her head. At length Harjo explained, "My friend, they cannot say. Jennie, she would run a race to see which one stay, but 'Liza, she say no, she is fat and cannot run."

135 Miss Evans comprehended at last. She flushed angrily, and protest- ed, "Harjo, you are making a mock of a sacred subject; I cannot allow you to talk like this."

"But did you not speak in fun, my friend?" Harjo queried, sober- ing. "Surely you have just said what your friend, the white woman at 140 the mission (he meant Mrs. Rowell) would say, and you do not mean what you say."

"Yes, Harjo, I mean it. It is true that Mrs. Rowell raised the point first, but I agree with her. The church cannot be defiled by receiving a bigamist into its membership." Harjo saw that the young woman was 145 serious, distressingly serious. He was silent for a long time, but at last he raised his head and spoke quietly, "It is not good to talk like that if it is not in fun."

He rose and went to the stable. As he led Miss Evans' horse up to the block it was champing a mouthful of corn, the last of a generous 150 portion that Harjo had put before it. The Indian held the bridle and waited for Miss Evans to mount. She was embarrassed, humiliated, angry. It was absurd to be dismissed in this way by—"by an ignorant old bigamist!" Then the humor of it burst upon her, and its human aspect. In her anxiety concerning the spiritual welfare of the sinner 155 Harjo, she had insulted the man Harjo. She began to understand why Mrs. Rowell had said that the old Indians were hopeless.

"Harjo," she begged, coming out of the passageway, "please forgive me. I do not want you to give up one of your wives. Just tell me why you took them."

160 "I will tell you that, my friend." The old Creek looped the reins over his arm and sat down on the block. "For thirty years Jennie has lived with me as my wife. She is one of the Bear people, and she came to me when I was thirty-five and she was twenty-five. She could not come before, for her mother was old, very old, and Jennie, she stay 165 with her and feed her.

"So, when I was thirty years old I took 'Liza for my woman. She is of the Crow people. She help me make this little farm here when there was no farm for many miles around.

**4.**
What does Miss Evans suggest as a solution? Is it acceptable to Harjo?

"Well, five years 'Liza and me, we live here and work hard. But there was no child. Then the old mother of Jennie she died, and Jennie got no family left in this part of the country. So 'Liza say to me, 'Why don't you take Jennie in here?' I say, 'You don't care?' and she say, 'No, maybe we have children here then.' But we have no children— never have children. We do not like that, but God He would not let it be. So, we have lived here thirty years very happy. Only just now you make me sad."

"Harjo," cried Miss Evans, "forget what I said. Forget that you wanted to join the church." For a young mission worker with a single purpose always before her, Miss Evans was saying a strange thing. Yet she couldn't help saying it; all of her zeal seemed to have been dissipated by a simple statement of the old man.

"I cannot forget to love Jesus, and I want to be saved." Old Harjo spoke with solemn earnestness. The situation was distracting. On one side stood a convert eager for the protection of the church, asking only that he be allowed to fulfill the obligations of humanity and on the other stood the church, represented by Mrs. Rowell, that set an impossible condition on receiving old Harjo to itself. Miss Evans wanted to cry; prayer, she felt, would be entirely inadequate as a means of expression.

"Oh! Harjo," she cried out, "I don't know what to do. I must think it over and talk with Mrs. Rowell again."

But Mrs. Rowell could suggest no way out; Miss Evans' talk with her only gave the older woman another opportunity to preach the folly of wasting time on the old and "unreasonable" Indians. Certainly the church could not listen even to a hint of a compromise in this case. If Harjo wanted to be saved, there was one way and only one— unless—

"Is either of the two women old? I mean, so old that she is—an—"

"Not at all," answered Miss Evans. "They're both strong and—yes, happy. I think they will outlive Harjo."

"Can't you appeal to one of the women to go away? I dare say we could provide for her." Miss Evans, incongruously, remembered Jennie's jesting proposal to race for the right to stay with Harjo. What could the mission provide as a substitute for the little home that 'Liza had helped to create there in the edge of the woods? What other home would satisfy Jennie?

"Mrs. Rowell, are you sure that we ought to try to take one of Harjo's women from him? I'm not sure that it would in the least advance morality amongst the tribe, but I'm certain that it would make three gentle people unhappy for the rest of their lives."

"You may be right, Miss Evans." Mrs. Rowell was not seeking to create unhappiness, for enough of it inevitably came to be pictured in the little mission building. "You may be right," she repeated, "but it is a grievous misfortune that old Harjo should wish to unite with the church."

**5.**

Is there any solution for Harjo? For Miss Evans?

No one was more regular in his attendance at the mission meetings than old Harjo. Sitting well forward, he was always in plain view of Miss Evans at the organ. Before the service began, and after it was over, the old man greeted the young woman. There was never a spo-
220  ken question, but in the Creek's eyes was always a mute inquiry.

Once Miss Evans ventured to write to her old pastor in New York, and explain her trouble. This was what he wrote in reply: "I am surprised that you are troubled, for I should have expected you to rejoice, as I do, over this new and wonderful evidence of the Lord's reforming
225  power. Though the church cannot receive the old man so long as he is confessedly a bigamist and violator of his country's just laws, you should be greatly strengthened in your work through bringing him to desire salvation."

"Oh! It's easy to talk when you're free from responsibility!" cried
230  out Miss Evans. "But I woke him up to a desire for this water of salvation that he cannot take. I have seen Harjo's home, and I know how cruel and useless it would be to urge him to give up what he loves—for he does love those two women who have spent half their lives and more with him. What, what can be done?"

235  Month after month, as old Harjo continued to occupy his seat in the mission meetings, with that mute appeal in his eyes and a persistent light of hope on his face, Miss Evans repeated the question, "What can be done?" If she was sometimes tempted to say to the old man, "Stop worrying about your soul; you'll get to Heaven as surely as
240  any of us," there was always Mrs. Rowell to remind her that she was not a Mormon missionary. She could not run away from her perplexity. If she should secure a transfer to another station, she felt that Harjo would give up coming to the meetings, and in his despair become a positive influence for evil amongst his people. Mrs. Rowell would not
245  waste her energy on an obstinate old man. No, Harjo was her creation, her impossible convert, and throughout the years, until death—the great solvent which is not always a solvent—came to one of them, would continue to haunt her.

And meanwhile, what?

# B.   Second Reading: Delving More Deeply

Read the story a second time and focus on the lines indicated. Use the surrounding text and your own experience to give an informed answer to the questions.

1.   *To the older woman it was as if someone had said to her "Madame, the Sultan of Turkey wishes to teach one of your mission Sabbath school classes."* (lines 13–15) Why does the text tell us this?

2.   *"Ask him…if he is willing to conform to the laws of…the country that guarantees his idle existence."* (lines 18–20) What is Mrs. Rowell implying about Harjo and help from the government when she

talks about "the country that guarantees his idle existence"? What does this tell about Mrs. Rowell's attitudes toward the Indians?

3.   *So Mrs. Rowell had discreetly limited her missionary effort to the young, and had exercised toward the old and bigamous only that strict charity which even a hopeless sinner might claim.* (lines 35–37) How had Mrs. Rowell first tried to solve the problem of converting "bigamous" Indians? How did she finally solve it? Do you think this was a reasonable solution?

4.   *Materially, Harjo was solvent; and if the Government had ever come to his aid he could not recall the date.* (line 60–61) Was Mrs. Rowell right? (Refer to question 2.)

5.   *Miss Evans comprehended at last.* (line 135) What did Miss Evans comprehend? How did she feel?

6.   *She was embarrassed, humiliated, angry….Then the humor of it burst upon her…* (lines 151–153) What made Miss Evans feel "embarrassed, humiliated, angry"? Why did her feelings change so quickly? Have you ever had such a sudden change of feeling?

7.   *Miss Evans wanted to cry; prayer, she felt, would be entirely inadequate as a means of expression.* (lines 187–189) Why did Miss Evans want to cry? In the same situation, would Mrs. Rowell probably cry or pray?

8.   *"Is either of the two women old? I mean, so old that she is…"* (line 198) What does Mrs. Rowell mean when she asks this question? What word was she going to speak next?

9.   *…but in the Creek's eyes was always a mute inquiry.* (line 220) What was the "mute inquiry"? How do you think it made Miss Evans feel?

10.   *Stop worrying about your soul; you'll get to Heaven as surely as any of us.* (lines 239–240) Why didn't Miss Evans say this to Harjo?

# III. STRENGTHENING SKILLS THROUGH THE TEXT

# A.   Responding to the Reading

Write at least 75 words on *one* of the following topics. When you finish, choose a classmate to listen to what you have written.

1.   Did you like this story? Why or why not?

2.   Which character in the story do you sympathize with the most? Explain.

_____

_____

_____

_____

_____

_____

_____

_____

_____

_____

_____

_____

_____

_____

_____

# B.   Global Comprehension Check: Essay Questions

Write a complete paragraph for each essay question your teacher assigns. Follow the procedure explained on pages 165–166.

1.   How did Miss Evans get herself into such a difficult situation?

2.   Explain in what ways Old Harjo and his wives seem to have a good life together.

3.   How did Harjo end up with two wives?

**FOLLOW-UP**
Your teacher may ask class members to compare answers before, or instead of, handing them in.

4. Compare the two main characters, Old Harjo and Miss Evans, in terms of age, culture, religious beliefs, and their general satisfaction with life at the end of the story.

5. Discuss Old Harjo's problem. What is the problem? What is the cause of the problem? Is there a solution to his problem? Why or why not?

# C.   Dramatization

In groups of three, practice dramatizing lines 192–215. The narrator will read all unquoted text; students dramatizing Miss Evans's and Mrs. Rowell's parts will read quotations spoken by them in the text. (Omit short items such as **answered Miss Evans** and **she repeated** before and after quotes for a smoother dramatization.)

# D.   Text-based Focus on Vocabulary

## The Vocabulary of Conflict and Judgment

When people of different cultures come together, they often judge others in negative ways and try to convince the others of the superiority of their way of life. Since both ways of life cannot be superior, unresolvable conflicts often arise. The following vocabulary often applies to these types of situations.

Find the following words in their contexts. The line where the word or phrase can be found is indicated in parentheses. Study the context and guess what each word might mean on the first line. Then use your dictionary to confirm your guesses on the second line.

1.   **crusader** (line 23)  guess _____

dictionary definition _____

2.   **deplorable** (line 32) _____

_____

3.   **rehabilitate** (line 62) _____

_____

4.   **stern, accusatory** (line 79) _____

_____

5. **scandalized** (line 80) _____

_____

6. **perplexed** (line 81) _____

_____

7. **making a mock of** (line 136) _____

_____

8. **humiliated** (line 151) _____

_____

9. **ignorant** (line 152) _____

_____

10. **hopeless** (lines 37, 156) _____

_____

11. **compromise** (line 195) _____

_____

12. **obstinate** (line 245) _____

_____

# General Vocabulary

Find the word or phrase in the story which means the same as the definition. (**20–25, 1**) in item **1** means you should look between lines 20 and 25 for one word meaning "great love of one's own country." Write the word or phrase in the space provided.

1. *(20–25, 1)* great love of one's own country _____

2. *(25–30, 1)* careful to avoid offending or insulting another

_____

3. *(35–40, 1)* kindness to those in trouble _____

4. *(35–40, 1)* a need not to do the right thing _____

5. *(45–50, 1)* giving up of something to get something more

_____

6. *(60–65, 1)* in good financial condition _____

7. *(60–65, 1)* to restore to good condition _____

8. *(70–75, 1)* paternal leaders of family, tribe, or religious group

_____

9. *(105–110, 1)* made to feel important _____

10. *(130–135, 1)* joking _____

11. *(135–140, 1)* holy, belonging to God _____

12. *(150–155, 1)* related to the nonmaterial part of life

_____

13. *(220–225, 2)* silent question _____

**FOLLOW–UP**
Check your answers.

_____

14. *(235–240, 2)* silent request _____

# IV. MOVING BEYOND THE TEXT

# A. Discussion and Writing

Discuss the following topics as a class or in groups. Your teacher may assign a different topic to each group and ask a group leader to summarize its discussion for the class. Write on *one or more* of the topics as instructed by your teacher.

1. Which of the main characters do you sympathize with more—Miss Evans or Old Harjo? In other words, which one has a worse dilemma? Explain.

**2.** Choose the statement, **a, b, c,** or **d,** that you think best expresses John Oskison's theme, i.e., the message that he is conveying in "The Problem of Old Harjo." Why do you think so?

**a.** One cannot adopt something from a foreign culture without giving up something in one's own culture.

**b.** Each culture has its own validity, which must be respected by those inside and outside that culture.

**c.** In trying to help another, we need to consider whether we are really serving ourselves or the other person.

**d.** There are honest differences between cultures which cannot be reconciled no matter how well-intentioned people are.

**3.** Do you think Miss Evans's zeal was affected by what happened? How do you think her experience with Old Harjo will change her future missionary efforts?

**4.** Can a minority culture like Harjo's survive intact, i.e., without changing, inside a larger, conflicting culture?

_____

_____

_____

_____

_____

_____

_____

_____

_____

_____

_____

_____

_____

# B. Taking a Stand: A Short Speech

Read the questions below. Take a position on one of the issues, and be prepared to speak for two minutes on the issue in front of the class. (Do *not* write out the speech; *do* prepare a note card with the main ideas of your speech. Practice delivering your speech to a partner in class.)

**1.** When religion and government come into conflict, which laws should take precedence? Take a position and defend it. Consider the two examples below or others that you are familiar with.

**a.** A young man belongs to a religious group which forbids him to participate in war. The government has just drafted him into the military.

**b.** The parents of a desperately sick child believe that God alone has the power and right to cure him and will not allow him to be treated by a doctor.

**2.** Agree or disagree with this statement: *Polygamy is sometimes a justifiable conjugal arrangement.*

Are these two boys friends?
Why do you think so?

# Lesson 16

## NO WITCHCRAFT FOR SALE

### Doris Lessing

### Zimbabwe/England

# I.   GETTING READY

## A.   Entering the Story through Listening

Listen to two passages from "No Witchcraft for Sale" as your teacher reads. The passages describe the birth of Teddy, the Farquars' son, and their relationship with Gideon, their native cook who has attended a religious school at a mission. Read the questions before listening.

**Passage 1.** *(lines 1–20)*

**FOLLOW-UP**
Discuss the answers
before going on.

1.   What two things made the Farquars happy when Teddy was born?

2.   How do we know that Teddy was very special to Gideon?

**Passage 2.** *(lines 21–40)*

1.   Do you think Gideon and Mrs. Farquar had a typical boss-servant relationship? Explain.

**FOLLOW-UP**
Discuss the answers
as a class.

2.   Gideon and Mrs. Farquar were both comfortable with the clear social distinctions between masters and servants in this setting between whites and blacks. How did they justify these social differences?

## B.   Background

Read the following information, noting the italicized words, to help you understand the story more easily and fully.

"No Witchcraft for Sale" is set in Zimbabwe, southern Africa, which was colonized mainly by Dutch and English people. A few vocabulary items in the story show Dutch origin. Those used in this story are very close in sound to their English equivalents: *kraal*, a typical native African village of the region (compare to the English *corral*); *veld*, wide open land where animals graze (*field* in English); and *baas*, which you know as *boss* in English.

Besides these words from Dutch, there are two words used to refer to black Africans that are not normally used outside of the region. Whites in the story refer to the blacks as *kaffirs* and to small black children as *piccanins* and *pickaninny*. Both words have been used in American English as well and have a pejorative, i.e., very negative, sense and should be avoided.)

The word *witchcraft* in the title here refers to native knowledge that may seem magical to outsiders.

The characters in "No Witchcraft for Sale" are both whites and blacks, who not only have different cultural backgrounds but whose

everyday lives and circumstances are very different from each other. This part of Africa had been colonized mainly by British and South Africans. These white colonizers (or settlers depending on your point of view) prospered, but the native black population had very little, if any, economic or political power. Relations between colonizers and their colonized populations are often complex. Each group usually becomes somewhat dependent on the other, but one group has the upper hand and exploits the other. Nevertheless, there may be occasions where individuals from each group may have some genuine affection for each other, but since these individuals are never equals, their relations can never be as open and honest as they would be if they were equals. Recognizing that the conflict in the story arises from this kind of situation will help you to read better and perhaps to judge the characters more fairly.

# II. ENGAGING WITH THE TEXT

# A. First Reading: Following the Story Line

To gain a general idea of how the story develops, read all the Signpost Questions in the margins before you begin to read the story. Then concentrate on answering the questions as you read.

## 1.

How does Teddy and Gideon's relationship change as Teddy grows older?

### No Witchcraft for Sale

1     The Farquars had been childless for years when little Teddy was born; and they were touched by the pleasure of their servants, who brought presents of fowls and eggs and flowers to the homestead when they came to rejoice over the baby, exclaiming with delight over
5   his downy golden head and his blue eyes. They congratulated Mrs. Farquar as if she had achieved a very great thing, and she felt that she had—her smile for the lingering, admiring natives was warm and grateful.
    Later, when Teddy had his first haircut, Gideon the cook picked up
10  the soft gold tufts from the ground, and held them reverently in his hand. Then he smiled at the little boy and said: "Little Yellow Head." That became the native name for the child. Gideon and Teddy were great friends from the first. When Gideon had finished his work, he would lift Teddy on his shoulders to the shade of a big tree, and play
15  with him there, forming curious little toys from twigs and leaves and grass, or shaping animals from wetted soil. When Teddy learned to walk it was often Gideon who crouched before him, clucking encouragement, finally catching him when he fell, tossing him up in the air till they both became breathless with laughter. Mrs. Farquar was fond
20  of the old cook because of his love for her child.
    There was no second baby; and one day Gideon said: "Ah, missus, missus, the Lord above sent this one; Little Yellow Head is the most

good thing we have in our house." Because of that "we" Mrs. Farquar
felt a warm impulse towards her cook; and at the end of the month
25 she raised his wages. He had been with her now for several years; he
was one of the few natives who had his wife and children in the compound and never wanted to go home to his kraal, which was some
hundreds of miles away. Sometimes a small piccanin who had been
born the same time as Teddy, could be seen peering from the edge of
30 the bush, staring in awe at the little white boy with his miraculous fair
hair and Northern blue eyes. The two little children would gaze at
each other with a wide, interested gaze, and once Teddy put out his
hand curiously to touch the black child's cheeks and hair.

Gideon, who was watching, shook his head wonderingly, and said:
35 "Ah, missus, these are both children, and one will grow up to be a
baas, and one will be a servant;" and Mrs. Farquar smiled and said
sadly, "Yes, Gideon, I was thinking the same." She sighed. "It is God's
will," said Gideon, who was mission boy. The Farquars were very religious people; and this shared feeling about God bound servant and
40 masters even closer together.

Teddy was about six years old when he was given a scooter, and
discovered the intoxications of speed. All day he would fly around the
homestead, in and out of flowerbeds, scattering squawking chickens
and irritated dogs, finishing with a wide dizzying arc into the kitchen
45 door. There he would cry: "Gideon, look at me!" And Gideon would
laugh and say: "Very clever, Little Yellow Head." Gideon's youngest
son, who was now a herdsboy, came especially up from the compound
to see the scooter. He was afraid to come near it, but Teddy showed
off in front of him. "Piccanin," shouted Teddy, "get out of my way!"
50 And he raced in circles around the black child until he was frightened,
and fled back to the bush.

"Why did you frighten him?" asked Gideon, gravely reproachful.

Teddy said defiantly: "He's only a black boy," and laughed. Then,
when Gideon turned away from him without speaking, his face fell.
55 Very soon he slipped into the house and found an orange and brought
it to Gideon, saying: "This is for you." He could not bring himself to
say he was sorry; but he could not bear to lose Gideon's affection
either. Gideon took the orange unwillingly and sighed. "Soon you will
be going away to school, Little Yellow Head," he said wonderingly,
60 "and then you will be grown up." He shook his head gently and said,
"And that is how our lives go." He seemed to be putting a distance
between himself and Teddy, not because of resentment, but in the way
a person accepts something inevitable. The baby had lain in his arms
and smiled up into his face: the tiny boy had swung from his shoul-
65 ders and played with him by the hour. Now Gideon would not let his
flesh touch the flesh of the white child. He was kind, but there was a
grave formality in his voice that made Teddy pout and sulk away.
Also, it made him into a man: with Gideon he was polite, and carried
himself formally, and if he came into the kitchen to ask for something,
70 it was in the way a white man uses towards a servant, expecting to be
obeyed.

**2.**

How does Teddy's disaster
with the snake end?

But on the day that Teddy came staggering into the kitchen with his fists to his eyes, shrieking with pain, Gideon dropped the pot full of hot soup that he was holding, rushed to the child, and forced aside

75    his fingers. "A snake!" he exclaimed. Teddy had been on his scooter, and had come to a rest with his foot on the side of a big tub of plants. A tree-snake, hanging by its tail from the roof, had spat full into his eyes. Mrs. Farquar came running when she heard the commotion. "He'll go blind," she sobbed, holding Teddy close against her.

80    "Gideon, he'll go blind!" Already the eyes, with perhaps half an hour's sight left in them, were swollen up to the size of fists: Teddy's small white face was distorted by great purple oozing protuberances. Gideon said: "Wait a minute, missus, I'll get some medicine." He ran off into the bush.

85    Mrs. Farquar lifted the child into the house and bathed his eyes with permanganate. She had scarcely heard Gideon's words; but when she saw that her remedies had no effect at all, and remembering how she had seen natives with no sight in their eyes, because of the spitting of a snake, she began to look for the return of her cook, remembering

90    what she heard of the efficacy of native herbs. She stood by the window, holding the terrified, sobbing little boy in her arms, and peered helplessly into the bush. It was not more than a few minutes before she saw Gideon come bounding back, and in his hand he held a plant. "Do not be afraid, missus," said Gideon, "this will cure Little

95    Yellow Head's eyes." He stripped the leaves from the plant, leaving a small white fleshy root. Without even washing it, he put the root in his mouth, chewed it vigorously, and then held the spittle there while he took the child forcibly from Mrs. Farquar. He gripped Teddy down between his knees, and pressed the balls of his thumbs into the

100   swollen eyes, so that the child screamed and Mrs. Farquar cried out in protest: "Gideon, Gideon!" But Gideon took no notice. He knelt over the writhing child, pushing back the puffy lids till chinks of eyeball showed, and then he spat hard, again and again, into first one eye, and then the other. He finally lifted Teddy gently into his mother's arms,

105   and said: "His eyes will get better." But Mrs. Farquar was weeping with terror, and she could hardly thank him: it was impossible to believe that Teddy could keep his sight. In a couple of hours the swellings were gone: the eyes were inflamed and tender but Teddy could see. Mr. and Mrs. Farquar went to Gideon in the kitchen and

110   thanked him over and over again. They felt helpless because of their gratitude: it seemed they could do nothing to express it. They gave Gideon presents for his wife and children, and a big increase in wages, but these things could not pay for Teddy's now completely cured eyes. Mrs. Farquar said: "Gideon, God chose you as an instrument for His

**3.**

How does Gideon impress
his employers?

115   goodness," and Gideon said: "Yes, missus, God is very good."

Now, when such a thing happens on a farm, it cannot be long before everyone hears of it. Mr. and Mrs. Farquar told their neighbors and the story was discussed from one end of the district to the other. The bush is full of secrets. No one can live in Africa, or at least on the

120   veld, without learning very soon that there is an ancient wisdom of leaf and soil and season—and, too, perhaps most important of all, of

the darker tracts of the human mind—which is the black man's heritage. Up and down the district people were telling anecdotes, reminding each other of things that had happened to them.

125 "But I saw it myself, I tell you. It was a puff-adder bite. The kaffir's arm was swollen to the elbow, like a great shiny black bladder. He was groggy after a half a minute. He was dying. Then suddenly a kaffir walked out of the bush with his hands full of green stuff. he smeared something on the place, and next day my boy was back at work, and

130 all you could see was two small punctures in the skin."

This was the kind of tale they told. And, as always, with a certain amount of exasperation because while all of them knew that in the bush of Africa are waiting valuable drugs locked in bark, in simple-looking leaves, in roots, it was impossible to ever get the truth about

135 them from the natives themselves.

The story eventually reached town; and perhaps it was at a sun-downer party, or some such function, that a doctor, who happened to be there, challenged it. "Nonsense," he said. "These things get exaggerated in the telling. We are always checking up on this kind of story,

140 and we draw a blank every time."

Anyway, one morning there arrived a strange car at the homestead, and out stepped one of the workers from the laboratory in town, with cases full of test-tubes and chemicals.

Mr. and Mrs. Farquar were flustered and pleased and flattered.

145 They asked the scientist to lunch, and they told the story all over again, for the hundredth time. Little Teddy was there too, his blue eyes sparkling with health, to prove the truth of it. The scientist explained how humanity might benefit if this new drug could be offered for sale; and the Farquars were even more pleased: they were kind, simple peo-

150 ple, who liked to think of something good coming about because of them. But when the scientist began talking of the money that might result, their manner showed discomfort. Their feelings over the mira-cle (that was how they thought of it) were so strong and deep and reli-gious, that it was distasteful to them to think of money. The scientist,

155 seeing their faces, went back to his first point, which was the advance-ment of humanity. He was perhaps a trifle perfunctory: it was not the first time he had come salting the tail of a fabulous bush-secret.

Eventually, when the meal was over, the Farquars called Gideon into their living-room and explained to him that this baas, here, was a

160 Big Doctor from the Big City, and he had come all that way to see Gideon. At this Gideon seemed afraid; he did not understand; and Mrs. Farquar explained quickly that it was because of the wonderful thing he had done with Teddy's eyes that the Big Baas had come.

Gideon looked from Mrs. Farquar to Mr. Farquar, and then at the

165 little boy, who was showing great importance because of the occasion. At last he said grudgingly: "The Big Baas want to know what medicine I used?" He spoke incredulously, as if he could not believe that his old friends could so betray him. Mr. Farquar began explaining how a use-ful medicine could be made out of the root, and how it could be put

170 on sale, and how thousands of people, black and white, up and down the continent of Africa, could be saved by the medicine when that

spitting snake filled their eyes with poison. Gideon listened, his eyes
bent on the ground, the skin of his forehead puckering in discomfort.
When Mr. Farquar had finished he did not reply. The scientist, who all
175   this time had been leaning back in a big chair, sipping his coffee and
smiling with skeptical good-humor, chipped in and explained all over
again, in different words, about the making of drugs and the progress
of science. Also, he offered Gideon a present.

There was silence after this further explanation, and then Gideon
180   remarked indifferently that he could not remember the root. His face
was sullen and hostile, even when he looked at the Farquars, whom he
usually treated like old friends. They were beginning to feel annoyed;
and this feeling annulled the guilt that had been sprung into life by
Gideon's accusing manner. They were beginning to feel that he was
185   unreasonable. But it was at that moment that they all realized he
would never give in. The magical drug would remain where it was,
unknown and useless except for the tiny scattering of Africans who
had the knowledge, natives who might be digging a ditch for the
municipality in a ragged shirt and a pair of patched shorts, but who
190   were still born to healing, hereditary healers, being the nephews or
sons of the old witch doctors whose ugly masks and bits of bone and
all the uncouth properties of magic were the outward signs of real
power and wisdom.

The Farquars might tread on that plant fifty times a day as they
195   passed from house to garden, from cow kraal to mealie field, but they
would never know it.

But they went on persuading and arguing, with all the force of their
exasperation; and Gideon continued to say that he could not remember, or that there was no such root, or that it was the wrong season of
200   the year, or that it wasn't the root itself, but the spit from his mouth
that had cured Teddy's eyes. He said all these things one after another,
and seemed not to care that they were contradictory. He was rude and
stubborn. The Farquars could hardly recognize their gentle, lovable
old servant in this ignorant, perversely obstinate African, standing
205   there in front of them with lowered eyes, his hands twitching his
cook's apron, repeating over and over whichever one of the stupid
refusals that first entered his head.

And suddenly he appeared to give in. He lifted his head, gave a
long, blank angry look at the circle of whites, who seemed to him like
210   a circle of yelping dogs pressing around him, and said: "I will show
you the root."

They walked single file away from the homestead down a kaffir
path. It was a blazing December afternoon, with the sky full of hot
rain-clouds. Everything was hot: the sun was like a bronze tray
215   whirling overhead, there was a heat shimmer over the fields, the soil
was scorching underfoot, the dusty wind blew gritty and thick and
warm in their faces. It was a terrible day, fit only for reclining on a
verandah with iced drinks, which is where they would normally have
been at that hour.

**4.**
How do you think the
story will end? Will
Gideon give in and identify the plant for them?

220     From time to time, remembering that on the day of the snake it had taken ten minutes to find the root, someone asked: "Is it much further, Gideon?" And Gideon would answer over his shoulder, with angry politeness: "I'm looking for the root, baas." And indeed, he would frequently bend sideways and trail his hand among the grasses
225 with a gesture that was insulting in its perfunctoriness. He walked them through the bush along unknown paths for two hours, in that melting destroying heat, so that the sweat trickled coldly down them and their heads ached. They were all quite silent: the Farquars because they were angry, the scientist because he was being proved right again;
230 there was no such plant. His was a tactful silence.

    At last, six miles from the house, Gideon suddenly decided they had had enough, or perhaps his anger evaporated at that moment. He picked up, without any attempt at looking anything but casual, a handful of blue flowers from the grass, flowers that had been growing
235 plentifully all down the paths they had come.

    He handed them to the scientist without looking at him, and marched off by himself on the way home, leaving them to follow him if they chose.

    When they got back to the house, the scientist went to the kitchen
240 to thank Gideon: he was being very polite, even though there was an amused look in his eyes. Gideon was not there. Throwing the flowers casually into the back of his car, the eminent visitor departed on his way back to his laboratory.

    Gideon was back in his kitchen in time to prepare dinner, but he
245 was sulking. He spoke to Mr. Farquar like an unwilling servant. It was days before they liked each other again.

    The Farquars made inquiries about the root from the laborers. Sometimes they were answered with distrustful stares. Sometimes the natives said: "We do not know. We have never heard of the root."
250 One, the cattle boy, who had been with them a long time, and had grown to trust them a little, said: "Ask your boy in the kitchen. Now, there's a doctor for you. He's the son of a famous medicine man who used to be in these parts, and there's nothing he cannot cure." Then he added politely: "Of course, he's not as good as the white man's doc-
255 tor, we know that, but he's good for us."

    After some time, when the soreness had gone from between the Farquars and Gideon, they began to joke: "When are you going to show us the snake-root, Gideon?" And he would laugh and shake his head, saying, a little uncomfortably: "But I did show you, missus, have
260 you forgotten?"

    Much later, Teddy, as a schoolboy, would come into the kitchen and say: "You old rascal, Gideon! Do you remember that time you tricked us all by making us walk miles all over the veld for nothing? It was so far my father had to carry me!"
265     And Gideon would double up with polite laughter. After much laughing, he would suddenly straighten himself up, wipe his old eyes, and look sadly at Teddy, who was grinning mischievously at him across the kitchen: "Ah, Little Yellow Head, how you have grown! Soon you will be grown up with a farm of your own…"

## FOLLOW-UP
Discuss your answers
in small groups.

# B.  Second Reading: Taking a Closer Look

Read the story a second time. Use the questions to gain a better understanding and to bring your experience to the story.

**1.** Do you think Gideon's and the other natives' delight at Teddy's birth was genuine? Or was it the reaction they had to have as servants?

**2.** How did the incident with the scooter show Teddy's distinction between blacks and whites? Were you surprised by the change that took place in Teddy?

**3.** How did this change in Teddy affect his relationship with Gideon? Can you see both their points of view in this situation?

**4.** Do you think Teddy would really have gone blind if Gideon hadn't found and used the medicinal plant?

**5.** What caused the scientist to show up at the Farquars' one day?

**6.** Why did Gideon feel betrayed by the Farquars? Why were they annoyed with him? Whom do you sympathize with more in this situation?

**7.** Why do you think Gideon finally gave in and apparently agreed to reveal the location of the snake root?

**8.** Who was taken in (deceived) by Gideon's trick? Why did the Farquars question other natives about the snake root instead of pressuring Gideon more? Do you think Gideon was right to deceive the Farquars?

**9.** Why do you think the "storm passed" and everyone could find humor in a situation that had bothered them so much previously?

# III. STRENGTHENING SKILLS THROUGH THE TEXT

# A.  Responding to the Reading

Write at least 75 words on *one* of the following topics. When you finish, choose a classmate to listen to what you have written.

**1.** Did you like this story? Why or why not?

2. Imagine that you were a guest at the Farquars' during the events of the story. What would you say to a friend in a letter regarding your feelings about Mrs. Farquar, Gideon, and Teddy?

_____

_____

_____

_____

_____

_____

_____

_____

_____

_____

_____

_____

_____

_____

# B.  Global Comprehension Check: Pivotal Points

Each event in a story is tied to what happens before it and, in turn, will affect what happens after it. For each of the following events, briefly summarize what happens before it and causes or connects to it, and what happens after it as a result or consequence.

1. Teddy brings Gideon an orange, saying: "This is for you."

a. _____

_____

_____

b. _____

_____

_____

2. Teddy comes into the kitchen screaming with pain with his fists held to his eyes.

a. _____

_____

_____

b. _____

_____

_____

3. Gideon says: "I will show you the root."

a. _____

_____

_____

b. _____

_____

_____

**4.** The Farquars and Gideon begin to joke about the day they searched for the snake root.

**a.** _____

_____

_____

**b.** _____

_____

_____

# C.  Text-based Focus on Vocabulary

Find the word or phrase in the story which means the same as the definition. *(50–55, 3)* in item 1 means you should look between lines 50 and 55 for three words meaning "became unhappy looking." Write the word or phrase in the space provided.

## The Vocabulary of Emotions and Psychological States

The story contains a lot of vocabulary describing how people think and feel about what happens and how they show their feelings. Most of these words are associated with negative feelings.

**1.**  *(50–55, 3)* he became unhappy-looking _____

**2.**  *(60–65, 1)* anger; hostility _____

**3.**  *(110–115, 1)* thankfulness _____

**4.**  *(130–135, 1)* irritation; annoyance; anger _____

**5.**  *(140–145, 1)* felt important because of being praised

_____

**6.**  *(150–155, 1)* unpleasant, disagreeable _____

**7.**  *(165–170, 1)* unwillingly, in a resentful manner _____

**8.**  *(165–170, 1)* with disbelief or suspicion _____

9. *(165–170, 1)* deceive or trick one who trusts you _____

10. *(175–180, 1)* distrustful; unbelieving _____

11. *(180–185, 1)* without concern or care _____

12. *(180–185, 1)* bad-tempered; moody _____

13. *(200–205, 1)* stubborn; unable to be moved or changed

_____

14. *(245–250, 1)* acting angry in a quiet way; being sullen

_____

## General Vocabulary

1. *(35–40, 1)* a church established with the purpose of "saving"

people, usually a native population _____

2. *(60–65, 1)* unavoidable; sure to happen _____

3. *(90–95, 1)* ability to produce a desired effect _____

4. *(120–125, 1)* deep knowledge _____

5. *(120–125, 1)* possessions or knowledge coming from one's

ancestors _____

6. *(120–125, 1)* stories; tales _____

7. *(135–140, 1)* made to appear larger than in reality _____

8. *(150–155, 1)* a remarkable event, beyond the laws of nature

_____

9. *(185–190, 2)* quit doing something; surrender _____

10. *(190–195, 2)* native healers _____

**FOLLOW-UP**
Check your answers as
instructed by your teacher.

11. *(200–205, 1)* expressing opposite ideas _____

12. *(250-255, 2)* native healer _____

# IV. MOVING BEYOND THE TEXT

## A. Discussion and Writing

Discuss the following topics as a class or in groups. Your teacher may assign a different topic to each group and ask a group leader to summarize its discussion for the class. Write on *one or more* of the topics as instructed by your teacher.

1. Do you see Gideon as a hero in the story or as a villain? Why?

2. Is "No Witchcraft for Sale" basically a story about the effects of colonization or about personal integrity? Explain. Could this story take place someplace else, or is it tied to its colonial South African setting?

3. Is a truly honest relationship possible between two people such as Mrs. Farquar and Gideon, who are not social equals?

_____

_____

_____

_____

_____

_____

_____

_____

_____

_____

_____

_____

_____

_____

_____

# B. Roleplay Interview

*Have four students take the roles of Mrs. Farquar, Gideon, Teddy, and the scientist. They might sit together at the front of the class. Remaining students will ask questions they have about the actions and feelings of these characters.*

STUDENT: Gideon, why exactly did you agree to show the scientist where the snake root was when you had no intention of really doing so?

GIDEON: Well, you have to understand my relationship with my employers, the Farquars.

*Note: Students taking the other roles may also make comments and questions about what is said.*

Where is this woman going with the laundry basket?

# Lesson 17

## THE ELEVATOR

## Bernard Malamud

## U.S.A.

# I.   GETTING READY

## A.   Discussion: The Role of Class in Society

Read the following statements. Then mark each one **A** if you agree with it or **D** if you disagree.

_____   **1.**   All people should have the same rights regardless of how much money they have.

_____   **2.**   Generally, people with more money have better manners than poorer people do.

_____   **3.**   A person living in a foreign country has the right to publicly oppose a custom that he finds objectionable or immoral.

_____   **4.**   A true gentleman or lady treats everyone with the same courtesy.

_____   **5.**   There probably is no such thing as a classless society.

_____   **6.**   Class is defined by money, manners, and morals.

_____   **7.**   The lower classes need the upper classes.

_____   **8.**   The structure of society requires that some people hold an inferior position socially.

_____   **9.**   A person's station in life is determined by God, so people should be satisfied with their stations and not try to change them.

_____ **10.**   Social mobility—the possibility of changing classes—is a positive characteristic in a society.

**FOLLOW-UP**
Share your answers in pairs or small groups.

## B.   Background

Read the following information, noting the italicized words, to help you understand the story more easily and fully.

   Living in a foreign country often makes people very aware of different values and customs. Often these differences are interesting, and sometimes they are a little confusing or even frustrating. However, when one sees something that seems not only different but truly wrong or unjust according to the customs and beliefs of one's own culture, it is very difficult to ignore the differences and just "look the other way." "The Elevator" explores the issue of what to do in these circumstances. The story is set in Rome and contains several Italian words, as follows:

*Umbrian girl* a girl from Umbria, a region in the central part of Italy

*permesso* a word meaning "excuse me," "may I," "with your permission," etc.

*prego* a word used both to give permission and to mean "you're welcome," and "at your service."

*signora* (masc., *signore*) a polite way to address a married woman (man)

*gobbo* hunchbacked, having a deformity (a hump) on one's back

*portinaia* (masc., *portiere*) woman (man) who has charge of the entrance of a building; a concierge

*comanda* a word meaning "at your service" (literally: "command me")

*scusi* "excuse me"

# II.  ENGAGING WITH THE TEXT

## A.  First Reading: Following the Story Line

To gain a general idea of how the story develops, read all the Signpost Questions in the margins before you begin to read. Then concentrate on answering the questions as you read the story.

**1.**

What do George and Grace think is bothering their new maid, Eleonora? Do they find out for sure?

### The Elevator

1   Eleonora was an Umbrian girl whom the portiere's wife had brought up to the Agostinis' first-floor apartment after their two unhappy experiences with Italian maids, not long after they had arrived in Rome from Chicago. She was about twenty-three, thin, and

5   with bent bony shoulders which she embarrassedly characterized as gobbo—hunchbacked. But she was not unattractive and had an interesting profile, George Agostini thought. Her full face was not so interesting; like the portinaia's, also an Umbrian, it was too broad and round, and her left brown eye was slightly wider than her right. It

10   also looked sadder than her right eye.

She was an active girl, always moving in her noisy slippers at a half trot across the marble floors of the furnished two-bedroom apartment, getting things done without having to be told, and handling the two children very well. After the second girl was let go, George had

15   wished they didn't have to be bothered with a full-time live-in maid. He had suggested that maybe Grace ought to go back to sharing the signora's maid—their landlady across the hall—for three hours a day, paying her on an hourly basis, as they had when they first moved in after a rough month of apartment hunting. But when George men-

20 tioned this, Grace made a gesture of tearing her red hair, so he said nothing more. It wasn't that he didn't want her to have the girl—she certainly needed one with all the time it took to shop in six or seven stores instead of one supermarket, and she was even without a washing machine, with all the kids' things to do; but George felt he wasn't

25 comfortable with a maid always around. He didn't like people waiting on him, or watching him eat. George was heavy, and sensitive about it. He also didn't like her standing back to let him enter a room first. He didn't want her saying "Comanda" the minute he spoke her name. Furthermore he wasn't happy about the tiny maid's room the girl

30 lived in, or her sinkless bathroom, with its cramped sitzbath and no water heater. Grace, whose people had always been much better off than his, said everybody in Italy had maids and he would get used to it. George hadn't got used to the first two girls, but he did find that Eleonora bothered him less. He liked her more as a person and felt

35 sorry for her. She looked as though she had more on her back than her bent shoulders.

One afternoon about a week and a half after Eleonora had come to them, when George arrived home from the FAO office where he worked, during the long lunch break, Grace said the maid was in her

40 room crying.

"What for?" George said, worried.

"I don't know."

"Didn't you ask her?"

"Sure I did, but all I could gather was that she's had a sad life.

45 You're the linguist around here, why don't you ask her?"

"What are you so annoyed about?"

"Because I feel like a fool, frankly, not knowing what it's all about."

"Tell me what happened."

"She came out of the hall, crying, about an hour ago," Grace said.

50 "I had sent her up to the roof with a bundle of wash to do in one of the tubs up there instead of our bathtub, so she doesn't have to lug the heavy wet stuff up to the lines on the roof but can hang it out right away. Anyway, she wasn't gone five minutes before she was back crying, and that was when she answered me about her sad life. I wanted

55 to tell her I have a sad life too. We've been in Rome close to two months and I haven't even been able to see St. Peter's. When will I ever see anything?"

"Let's talk about her," George said. "Do you know what happened?"

60 "I told you I didn't. After she came back, I went down to the ground floor to talk to the portinaia—she has some smattering of English—and she told me that Eleonora had been married but had lost her husband. He died or something when she was eighteen. Then she had a baby by another guy who didn't stay around long enough to

65 see if he recognized it, and that, I suppose, is why she finds life so sad."

"Did the portinaia say whether the kid is still alive?" George asked.

"Yes. She keeps it in a convent school."

"Maybe that's what got her down," he suggested. "She thinks of her kid being away from her and then feels bad."

70

"So she starts to cry in the hall?"

"Why not in the hall? Why not anywhere so long as you feel like crying. Maybe I ought to talk to her."

Grace nodded. Her face was flushed, and George knew she was troubled.

**2.**

What problem does the maid have? Does George do anything to solve her problem?

75

He went into the corridor and knocked on the door of the maid's room. "Permesso," George said.

"Prego." Eleonora had been lying on the bed but was respectfully on her feet when George entered. He could see she had been crying. Her eyes were red and her face pale. She looked scared, and George's

80

throat went dry.

"Eleonora, I am sorry to see you like this," he said in Italian. "Is there something either my wife or I can do to help you?"

"No, Signore," she said quietly.

"What happened to you out in the hall?"

85

Her eyes glistened but she held back the tears. "Nothing. One feels like crying, so she cries. Do these things have a reason?"

"Are you satisfied with conditions here?" George asked her.

"Yes."

"If there is something we can do for you, I want you to tell us."

90

"Please don't trouble yourself about me." She lifted the bottom of her skirt, at the same time bending her head to dry her eyes on it. Her bare legs were hairy but shapely.

"No trouble at all," George said. He closed the door softly.

"Let her rest," he said to Grace.

95

"Damn! Just when I have to go out."

But in a few minutes Eleonora came out and went on with her work in the kitchen. They said nothing more and neither did she. Then at three George left for the office, and Grace put on her hat and went off to her Italian class and then to St. Peter's.

100

That night when George got home from work, Grace called him into their bedroom and said she now knew what had created all the commotion that afternoon. First the signora, after returning from an appointment with her doctor, had bounded in from across the hall, and Grace had gathered from the hot stew the old woman was in that

105

she was complaining about their maid. The portinaia then happened to come up with the six o'clock mail, and the signora laced into her for bringing an inferior type of maid into the house. Finally, when the signora had left, the portinaia told Grace that the old lady had been the one who had made Eleonora cry. She had apparently forbidden

110

the girl to use the elevator. She would listen behind the door, and as soon as she heard someone putting the key into the elevator lock, she would fling open her door, and if it was Eleonora, as she had suspected, she would cry out, "The key is not for you. The key is not for you." She would stand in front of the elevator, waving her arms to prevent

115

her from entering. "Use the stairs," she cried, "the stairs are for walking. There is no need to fly, or God would have given you wings."

"Anyway," Grace went on, "Eleonora must have been outwitting her or something, because what she would do, according to the portinaia, was go upstairs to the next floor and call the elevator from there.

120 But today the signora got suspicious and followed Eleonora up the stairs. She gave her a bad time up there. When she blew in here before, Eleonora got so scared that she ran to her room and locked the door. The signora said she would have to ask us not to give our girl the key anymore. She shook her keys at me."

125 "What did you say after that?" George asked.

"Nothing. I wasn't going to pick a fight with her even if I could speak the language. A month of hunting apartments was enough for me."

"We have a lease," said George.

130 "Leases have been broken."

"She wouldn't do it—she needs the money."

"I wouldn't bet on it," said Grace.

"It burns me up," George said. "Why shouldn't the girl use the elevator to lug the clothes up to the roof? Five floors is a long haul."

135 "Apparently none of the other girls does," Grace said. "I saw one of them carrying a basket of wash up the stairs on her head."

"They ought to join the acrobats' union."

"We have to stick to their customs."

"I'd still like to tell the old dame off."

140 "This is Rome, George, not Chicago. You came here of your own free will."

"Where's Eleonora?" George asked.

"In the kitchen."

George went into the kitchen. Eleonora was washing the children's

145 supper dishes in a pan of hot water. When George came in she looked up with fear, the fear in her left eye shining more brightly than in her right.

"I'm sorry about the business in the hall," George said with sympathy, "but why didn't you tell me about it this afternoon?"

150 "I don't want to make trouble."

"Would you like me to talk to the signora?"

"No, no."

"I want you to ride in the elevator if you want to."

"Thank you, but it doesn't matter."

155 "Then why are you crying?"

"I'm always crying, Signore. Don't bother to notice it."

"Have it your own way," George said.

He thought that ended it, but a week later as he came into the building at lunchtime he saw Eleonora getting into the elevator with a

160 laundry bundle. The portinaia had just opened the door for her with her key, but when she saw George she quickly ducked down the stairs to the basement. George got on the elevator with Eleonora. Her face was crimson.

"I see you don't mind using the elevator," he said.

165 "Ah, Signore"—she shrugged—"we must all try to improve ourselves."

**3.**
What two bad things happen to Eleonora?

"Are you no longer afraid of the signora?"

"Her girl told me the signora is sick," Eleonora said happily.

Eleonora's luck held, George learned, because the signora stayed
170 too sick to be watching the elevator, and one day after the maid rode
up in it to the roof, she met a plumber's helper working on the wash-
tubs, Fabrizio Occhiogrosso, who asked her to go out with him on her
next afternoon off. Eleonora, who had been doing little on her
Thursday and Sunday afternoons off, mostly spending her time with
175 the portinaia, readily accepted. Fabrizio, a short man with pointed
shoes, a thick trunk, hairy arms, and the swarthy face of a Spaniard,
came for her on his motorbike and away they would go together, she
sitting on the seat behind him, holding both arms around his belly.
She sat astride the seat, and when Fabrizio, after impatiently revving
180 the Vespa, roared up the narrow street, the wind fluttered her skirt
and her bare legs were exposed above the knees.

"Where do they go?" George once asked Grace.

"She says he has a room on the Via della Purificazióne."

"Do they always go to his room?"

185 "She says they sometimes ride to the Borghese Gardens or go to the
movies."

One night in early December, after the maid had mentioned that
Fabrizio was her fiancé now, George and Grace stood at their living-
room window looking down into the street as Eleonora got on the
190 motorbike and it raced off out of sight.

"I hope she knows what she's doing," he muttered in a worried
tone. "I don't much take to Fabrizio."

"So long as she doesn't get pregnant too soon. I'd hate to lose her."

George was silent for a time, then remarked, "How responsible do
195 you suppose we are for her morals?"

"Her morals?" laughed Grace. "Are you batty?"

"I never had a maid before," George said.

"This is our third."

"I mean in principle."

200 "Stop mothering the world," said Grace.

Then one Sunday after midnight Eleonora came home on the verge
of fainting. What George had thought might happen had. Fabrizio had
taken off into the night on his motorbike. When they had arrived at
his room early that evening, a girl from Perugia was sitting on his bed.
205 The portiere had let her in after she had showed him an engagement
ring and a snapshot of her and Fabrizio in a rowboat. When Eleonora
demanded to know who this one was, the plumber's helper did not
bother to explain but ran down the stairs, mounted his Vespa, and
drove away. The girl disappeared. Eleonora wandered the streets for
210 hours, then returned to Fabrizio's room. The portiere told her that he
had been back, packed his valise, and left for Perugia, the young lady
riding on the back seat.

Eleonora dragged herself home. When she got up the next morning
to make breakfast she was a skeleton of herself and the gobbo looked
215 like a hill. She said nothing and they asked nothing. What Grace wanted to know she later got from the portinaia. Eleonora no longer ran

through her chores but did everything wearily, each movement like flowing stone. Afraid she would collapse, George advised her to take a week off and go home. He would pay her salary and give her something extra for the bus.

"No, Signore," she said dully, "it is better for me to work." She said, "I have been through so much, more is not noticeable."

But then she had to notice it. One afternoon she absentmindedly picked up Grace's keys and got on the elevator with a bag of clothes to be washed. The signora, having recovered her health, was waiting for her. She flung open the door, grabbed Eleonora by the arm as she was about to close the elevator door, and dragged her out.

"Whore," she cried, "don't steal the privileges of your betters. Use the stairs."

Grace opened the apartment door to see what the shouting was about, and Eleonora, with a yowl, rushed past her. She locked herself in her room and sat there all afternoon without moving. She wept copiously. Grace, on the verge of exhaustion, could do nothing with her. When George came home from work that evening he tried to coax her out, but she shouted at him to leave her alone.

George was thoroughly fed up. "I've had enough," he said. He thought out how he would handle the signora, then told Grace he was going across the hall.

"Don't do it," she shouted, but he was already on his way.

George knocked on the signora's door. She was a woman of past sixty-five, a widow, always dressed in black. Her face was long and gray, but her eyes were bright black. Her husband had left her these two apartments across the hall from each other that he had owned outright. She lived in the smaller and rented the other, furnished, at a good rent. George knew that this was her only source of income. She had once been a schoolteacher.

"Scusi, Signora," said George. "I have come with a request."

"Prego." She asked him to sit.

George took a chair near the terrace window. "I would really appreciate it, Signora, if you will let our girl go into the elevator with the laundry when my wife sends her up to the tubs. She is not a fortunate person and we would like to make her life a little easier for her."

"I am sorry," answered the signora with dignity, "but I can't permit her to enter the elevator."

"She's a good girl and you have upset her very much."

"Good," said the signora, "I am glad. She must remember her place, even if you don't. This is Italy, not America. You must understand that we have to live with these people long after you, who come to stay for a year or two, return to your own country."

"Signora, she does no harm in the elevator. We are not asking you to ride with her. After all, the elevators are a convenience for all who live in this house and therefore ought to be open for those who work for us here."

"No," said the signora.

"Why not think it over and let me know your answer tomorrow? I assure you I wouldn't ask this if I didn't think it was important."

"I have thought it over," she said stiffly, "and I have given you the same answer I will give tomorrow."

George got up. "In that case," he said, "if you won't listen to rea-
270  son, I consider my lease with you ended. You have had your last month's rent. We will move on the first of February."

The signora looked as if she had just swallowed a fork.

"The lease is a sacred contract," she said, trembling. "It is against the law to break it."

275  "I consider that you have already broken it," George said quietly, "by creating conditions that make it very hard for my family to func-tion in this apartment. I am simply acknowledging a situation that already exists."

"If you move out, I will take a lawyer and make you pay for the
280  whole year."

"A lawyer will cost you half the rent he might collect," George answered. "And if my lawyer is better than yours, you will get nothing and owe your lawyer besides."

"Oh, you Americans," said the signora bitterly. "How well I under-
285  stand you. Your money is your dirty foot with which you kick the world. Who wants you here," she cried, "with your soaps and tooth-pastes and your dirty gangster movies!"

"I would like to remind you that my origin is Italian," George said.

"You have long ago forgotten your origin," she shouted.

290  George left the apartment and went back to his own.

"I'll bet you did it," Grace greeted him. Her face was ashen.

"I did," said George.

"I'll bet you fixed us good. Oh, you ought to be proud. How will we ever find another apartment in the dead of winter with two kids?"

295  She left George and locked herself in the children's bedroom. They were both awake and got out of bed to be with her.

George sat in the living room in the dark. I did it, he was thinking.

After a while the doorbell rang. He got up and put on the light. It was the signora and she looked unwell. She entered the living room at
300  George's invitation and sat there with great dignity.

"I am sorry I raised my voice to a guest in my house," she said. Her mouth was loose and her eyes glistened.

"I am sorry I offended you," George said.

She did not speak for a while, then said, "Let the girl use the eleva-
305  tor." The signora broke into tears.

When she had dried her eyes, she said, "You have no idea how bad things have become since the war. The girls are disrespectful. Their demands are endless, it is impossible to keep up with them. They talk back, they take every advantage. They crown themselves with privi-
310  leges. It is a struggle to keep them in their place. After all, what have we left when we lose our self-respect?" The signora wept heartbrokenly.

After she had gone, George stood at the window. Across the street a beggar played a flute.

I didn't do it well, George thought. He felt depressed.

315  On her afternoon off Eleonora rode up and down on the elevator.

**FOLLOW-UP**
Discuss your answers to the First Reading.

## B.    Second Reading

**FOLLOW-UP**
Take turns sharing your questions about the places in the text that you marked during Second Reading.

Reread "The Elevator," marking any places that are still difficult to understand or confusing to you.

# III. STRENGTHENING SKILLS THROUGH THE TEXT

## A.    Responding to the Reading

Write steadily on a separate sheet of paper for 20 minutes about your reaction to the story. Write about

**a.**    whether you liked or disliked the story and why;

**b.**    what you think of the characters in the story; and/or

**c.**    what you still find unclear in the text.

Then form a group with two or three other students. Take turns reading what you have written to the other members of the group. After each person reads, other group members should respond with comments, questions, or help in understanding unclear portions of the text.

## B.    Dramatization

In groups of three, practice dramatizing lines 249–290. The narrator will read all unquoted text; students dramatizing George's and the Signora's parts will read quotations spoken by them in the text. (Omit short items such as ***said the signora*** and ***he said*** before and after quotes for a smoother dramatization.)

## C.    Text-based Focus on Vocabulary

Find the word or phrase in the left-hand column in the lines indicated. Think of what it might mean in its context. Then choose the definition in the right-hand column that matches that meaning and write its letter next to the number of the word or phrase.

# Expressions

| | | | |
|---|---|---|---|
| 1. | *(line 31)* **better off** | a. | depend on |
| 2. | *(line 104)* **hot stew** | b. | like |
| 3. | *(line 106)* **laced into** | c. | scold, criticize |
| 4. | *(line 121)* **gave her a bad time** | d. | arrived suddenly |
| 5. | *(line 121)* **blew in** | e. | persecuted her; allowed her no peace |
| 6. | *(line 132)* **bet on** | f. | attacked (verbally) |
| 7. | *(line 133)* **burns me up** | g. | those who are socially superior |
| 8. | *(line 139)* **tell…off** | h. | bad, irritable mood |
| 9. | *(line 192)* **take…to** | i. | makes me furious |
| 10. | *(line 228)* **betters** | j. | in a better financial situation |

# Figurative Language

Find the following figurative expressions in the story in the lines indicated and answer the questions.

1. *Grace made a gesture of tearing her…hair…* *(line 20)* What was she expressing?

2. *She looked as though she had more on her back than her bent shoulders.* *(lines 35–36)* What did it appear that she had on her back?

3. *Her face was crimson.* *(lines 162–163)* What was she feeling?

4. *Stop mothering the world…* *(line 200)* How is George "mothering the world"? Do you agree with Grace?

5. *…she was a skeleton of herself and the gobbo looked like a hill.* *(lines 214–215)* What does the author mean? Paraphrase this in literal language.

**6.** **...don't steal the privileges of your betters.** *(line 228)* What does the signora mean? Do you think that Eleonora was stealing the privileges of her betters?

**7.** **It is a struggle to keep them in their place.** *(line 310)* Who is "them"? What is "their place"?

# IV. MOVING BEYOND THE TEXT

# A. Discussion and Writing

Discuss the following topics as a class or in groups. Your teacher may assign a different topic to each group and ask a group leader to summarize its discussion for the class. Write on *one or more* of the topics as instructed by your teacher.

**1.** Who do you feel was right in the conflict over the maid's use of the elevator—George or the Signora? Why?

**2.** If Eleonora, for any reason, suddenly became the landlady in this apartment building, do you think she would treat the maids more kindly than the Signora treated her? Explain.

**3.** Could this same story occur in your country? Would a person with more money feel he or she had the right to limit the privileges of a servant as the Signora did?

**4.** In the long run, has George helped Eleonora or hurt her by intervening in her troubles with the Signora? What will happen to Eleonora when George and his family leave Italy?

**5.** Are there ever any situations where people living in a foreign culture have the right or even the responsibility to interfere when they see what seems like an unjust situation, or should foreigners always just mind their own business?

**6.** Numbers 1, 8, 9, or 10 of the questions in Part I. A. (Discussion) at the beginning of the lesson would also make suitable writing topics. Choose one of them and relate your choice to "The Elevator."

_____

_____

_____

_____

_____

_____

_____

_____

_____

_____

_____

_____

_____

_____

_____

# B.   Taking a Stand: A Short Speech

Read the statements below. Take a position on *one* of the issues, and be prepared to speak for two minutes on the issue in front of class. (Do *not* write out the speech; *do* prepare a note card with the main ideas of your speech. Practice delivering your speech to a partner in class.)

**1.**   A person living in a foreign country has the right to publicly oppose a custom that he finds objectionable or immoral.

**2.**   A true gentleman or lady treats everyone with the same courtesy.

**3.**   There probably is no such thing as a classless society.

What are these boys doing? When it's time to go, will this little black boy and the white go to the same house? The same neighborhood?

# Lesson 18

## THE ANTHEAP

### Doris Lessing

### Zimbabwe/England

# I.  GETTING READY

# A.  Entering the Story through Listening

Listen to two early passages from "The Antheap" as your teacher reads, and answer the questions which follow each passage.

**Passage 1.** *(lines 221–250)*

In the first passage, we learn about the *malaria* of young Tommy Clarke, and how his mother and his father's boss, Mr. Macintosh, react and interact. *Blackwater* is a very severe case of malaria, which is carried by mosquitoes and is often treated with *quinine*. *Screens* on windows and doors keep out mosquitoes and thus help deter the disease.

1.  How did Tommy get through his first bout with malaria?

2.  Why did he come down with it again?

3.  What solution to the problem did Mrs. Clarke propose to Mr. Macintosh?

4.  Did Mr. Macintosh agree to her solution immediately? Later on?

**FOLLOW–UP**
Discuss the answers
as a class.

5.  Mrs. Clarke and Mr. Macintosh speak to each other roughly. Does this mean they don't get along? How would you characterize their relationship?

**Passage 2.** *(lines 261–297)*

In this passage, Tommy and his mother discuss, among other things, the *compound*: This is where the blacks live and where Tommy spends his days playing. His mother uses a pejorative term, *kaffirs*, when she refers to the blacks.

1.  What was Mrs. Clarke's new regime (plan, system) to keep Tommy safe from malaria?

**FOLLOW–UP**
Discuss the answers
as a class.

2.  What part of the plan did Tommy object to?

3.  Did Tommy obey his mother? What was the result?

## Questions

Discuss the following questions as a class.

1.  What do we learn about the setting of the story from these passages? About the climate?

**2.** What race are Mrs. Clarke, Mr. Macintosh, and Tommy? How do you know?

**3.** What reasons other than the possibility of malaria might Mrs. Clarke have for forbidding her son from going to the compound?

**4.** What do you know about racial relations in southern Africa in the past and today?

# B.   Background

Read the following information, noting the italicized words, to help you understand the story more easily and fully.

"The Antheap" is set in a mining community in southern Africa. The characters are both blacks and whites, who not only have different cultural backgrounds but whose everyday lives and circumstances are very different from each other. This part of Africa was colonized mainly by British and white South Africans. These colonizers (or settlers, depending on your point of view) prospered, but the native black population had very little, if any, economic or political power. They were economically exploited while being forcibly kept separate from the white population in all other spheres of life. Acts of Parliament such as the *Native Employment Act* and the *Native Passes Act*, laws passed by the white government, may be seen in this light. In a more positive light is the *Natives Juvenile Employment Act*, probably passed to protect black children from exploitation.

Some vocabulary in the story, because of the Dutch origin of many white settlers, comes from the Dutch language but has entered English in southern Africa. *Kopje* refers to rock formations in the mountains, where the story is set. A *duiker* (die' ker) is a small African antelope. The word *kaffir*, used by some whites to refer to blacks, has a pejorative connotation; it should be avoided outside the story. The natives call white people in positions of authority *baas* (boss).

Some expressions in the story seem quite British to an American ear. *Damned cheek!* is an expression of surprise at someone's boldness; "What nerve!" would be more likely in the United States. *He went purple* would be rendered "He turned red in the face" by an American; both describe extreme, sudden anger in a person.

# II. ENGAGING WITH THE TEXT

## A1. First Reading: Following the Story Line

*Note:* This longer story is divided into four parts; read it one part at a time. Do the First and Second Reading questions, and then write down two questions for each section that you would like to discuss with classmates.

Read the following questions and keep them in mind as you read Section I. Use the questions to help you predict and follow the main events of the story.

**1.**   What makes this land inhospitable? Why do people live here anyway?

**2.**   What is Mr. Macintosh's position toward the land? Toward his workers?

**3.**   Mr. Macintosh and the Clarkes do not have much in common, but they get along well. Why?

**4.**   Why does Tommy spend time in the compound where the blacks live?

**5.**   Which is a worse experience for Tommy, suffering from malaria or not being allowed to go to the compound?

**6.**   Why does Tommy form little clay figures of Betty, Freddy, and Dirk? Why do you think the death of the duiker affects him so much?

**7.**   Does Tommy become more dependent or more independent of his parents and their ideas?

**8.**   Why does Mrs. Clarke make such sudden arrangements to send Tommy away to school?

### The Antheap (*Section I*)

1   Beyond the plain rose the mountains, blue and hazy in a strong blue sky. Coming closer they were brown and gray and green, ranged heavily one beside the other, but the sky was still blue. Climbing up through the pass the plain flattened and diminished behind, and the
5   peaks rose sharp and dark gray from lower heights of heaped granite boulders, and the sky overhead was deeply blue and clear and the heat came shimmering off in waves from every surface. "Through the range, down the pass, and into the plain the other side—let's go quickly, there it will be cooler, the walking easier." So thinks the

10 traveler. So the traveler has been thinking for many centuries, walking quickly to leave the stifling mountains, to gain the cool plain where the wind moves freely. But there is no plain. Instead, the pass opens into a hollow which is closely surrounded by *kopjes:* the mountains clench themselves into a fist here, and the palm is a mile-wide reach of

15 thick bush, where the heat gathers and clings, radiating from boulders, rocking off the trees, pouring down from a sky which is not blue, but thick and low and yellow, because of the smoke that rises, and has been rising so long from this mountain-imprisoned hollow. For though it is hot and close and arid half the year, and then warm and

20 steamy and wet in the rains, there is gold here, so there are always people, and everywhere in the bush are pits and slits where the prospectors have been, or shallow holes, or even deep shafts. They say that the Bushmen were here, seeking gold, hundreds of years ago. Perhaps, it is possible. They say that trains of Arabs came from the coast, with slaves

25 and warriors, looking for gold to enrich the courts of the Queen of Sheba. No one has proved they did not.

But it is at least certain that at the turn of the century there was a big mining company which sunk half a dozen fabulously deep shafts, and found gold going ounces to the ton sometimes, but it is a capri-

30 cious and chancy piece of ground, with the reefs all broken and unpredictable, and so this company loaded its heavy equipment into lorries and off they went to look for gold somewhere else, and in a place where the reefs lay more evenly.

For a few years the hollow in the mountains was left silent, no

35 smoke rose to dim the sky, except perhaps for an occasional prospector, whose fire was a single column of wavering blue smoke, as from the cigarette of a giant, rising into the blue, hot sky.

Then all at once the hollow was filled with violence and noise and activity and hundreds of people. Mr. Macintosh had bought the rights

40 to mine this gold. They told him he was foolish, that no single man, no matter how rich, could afford to take chances in this place.

But they did not reckon with the character of Mr. Macintosh, who had already made a fortune and lost it, in Australia, and then made another in New Zealand, which he still had. He proposed to increase it

45 here. Of course, he had no intention of sinking those expensive shafts which might not reach gold and hold the dipping, chancy reefs and seams. The right course was quite clear to Mr. Macintosh, and this course he followed, though it was against every known rule of proper mining.

50 He simply hired hundreds of African laborers and set them to shovel up the soil in the center of that high, enclosed hollow in the mountains, so that there was soon a deeper hollow, then a vast pit, then a gulf like an inverted mountain. Mr. Macintosh was taking great swallows of the earth, like a gold-eating monster, with no fancy ideas

55 about digging shafts or spending money on roofing tunnels. The earth was hauled, at first, up the shelving sides of the gulf in buckets, and these were suspended by ropes made of twisted bark fiber, for why

spend money on steel ropes when this fiber was offered free to mankind on every tree? And if it got brittle and broke and the buckets went plunging into the pit, then they were not harmed by the fall, and there was plenty of fiber left on the trees. Later, when the gulf grew too deep, there were trucks on rails, and it was not unknown for these, too, to go sliding and plunging to the bottom, because in all Mr. Macintosh's dealings there was a fine, easy good-humor, which meant he was more likely to laugh at such an accident than grow angry. And if someone's head got in the way of the falling buckets or trucks, then there were plenty of black heads and hands for the hiring. And if the loose, sloping bluffs of soil fell in landslides, or if a tunnel, narrow as an ant-bear's hole, that was run off sideways from the main pit like a tentacle exploring for new reefs, caved in suddenly, swallowing half a dozen men—well, one can't make an omelette without breaking eggs. This was Mr. Macintosh's favorite motto.

The Africans who worked this mine called it "the pit of death," and they called Mr. Macintosh "The Gold Stomach." Nevertheless, they came in their hundreds to work for him, thus providing free arguments for those who said: "The native doesn't understand good treatment, he only appreciates the whip, look at Macintosh, he's never short of labor."

Mr. Macintosh's mine, raised high in the mountains, was far from the nearest police station, and he took care that there was always plenty of kaffir beer brewed in the compound, and if the police patrols came searching for criminals, these could count on Mr. Macintosh facing the police for them and assuring them that such and such a native, Registration Number Y2345678, had never worked for him. Yes, of course they could see his books.

Mr. Macintosh's books and records might appear to the simple-minded as casual and ineffective, but these were not the words used of his methods by those who worked for him, and so Mr. Macintosh kept his books himself. He employed no bookkeeper, no clerk. In fact, he employed only one white man, an engineer. For the rest, he had six overseers or boss-boys whom he paid good salaries and treated like important people.

The engineer was Mr. Clarke, and his house and Mr. Macintosh's house were on one side of the big pit, and the compound for the Africans was on the other side. Mr. Clarke earned fifty pounds a month, which was more than he would earn anywhere else. He was a silent, hardworking man, except when he got drunk, which was not often. Three or four times in the year he would be off work for a week, and then Mr. Macintosh did his work for him till he recovered, when he greeted him with the good-humored words: "Well, laddie, got that off your chest?"

Mr. Macintosh did not drink at all. His not drinking was a passionate business, for like many Scots people he ran to extremes. Never a drop of liquor could be found in his house. Also, he was religious, in a reminiscent sort of way, because of his parents, who had been very religious. He lived in a two-roomed shack, with a bare wooden table in it, three wooden chairs, a bed and a wardrobe. The cook boiled beef

and carrots and potatoes three days a week, roasted beef three days,
and cooked a chicken on Sundays.

110     Mr. Macintosh was one of the richest men in the country, he was
more than a millionaire. People used to say of him: But for heaven's
sake, he could do anything, go anywhere, what's the point of having so
much money if you live in the back of beyond with a parcel of blacks
on top of a big hole in the ground?

115     But to Mr. Macintosh it seemed quite natural to live so, and when
he went for a holiday to Cape Town, where he lived in the most
expensive hotel, he always came back again long before he was expected. He did not like holidays. He liked working.

    He wore old, oily khaki trousers, tied at the waist with an old red
120 tie, and he wore a red handkerchief loose around his neck over a white
cotton singlet. He was short and broad and strong, with a big square
head tilted back on a thick neck. His heavy brown arms and neck
sprouted thick black hair around the edges of the singlet. His eyes
were small and gray and shrewd. His mouth was thin, pressed tight in
125 the middle. He wore an old felt hat on the back of his head, and carried a stick cut from the bush, and he went strolling around the edge
of the pit, slashing the stick at bushes and grass or sometimes at lazy
Africans, and he shouted orders to his boss-boys, and watched the
swarms of workers far below him in the bottom of the pit, and then he
130 would go to his little office and make up his books, and so he spent his
day. In the evenings he sometimes asked Mr. Clarke to come over and
play cards.

    Then Mr. Clarke would say to his wife: "Annie, he wants me," and
she nodded and told her cook to make supper early.

135     Mrs. Clarke was the only white woman on the mine. She did not
mind this, being a naturally solitary person. Also, she had been pro-
foundly grateful to reach this haven of fifty pounds a month with a
man who did not mind her husband's bouts of drinking. She was a
woman of early middle age, with a thin, flat body, a thin colorless face,
140 and quiet blue eyes. Living here, in this destroying heat, year after
year, did not make her ill, it sapped her slowly, leaving her rather
numbed and silent. She spoke very little, but then she roused herself
and said what was necessary.

    For instance, when they first arrived at the mine it was to a two-
145 roomed house. She walked over to Mr. Macintosh and said: "You are
alone, but you have four rooms. There are two of us and the baby, and
we have two rooms. There's no sense in it." Mr. Macintosh gave her a
quick, hard look, his mouth tightened, and then he began to laugh.
"Well, yes, that is so," he said, laughing, and he made the change at
150 once, chuckling every time he remembered how the quiet Annie
Clarke had put him in his place.

    Similarly, about once a month Annie Clarke went to his house and
said: "Now get out of my way. I'll get things straight for you." And
when she'd finished tidying up she said: "You're nothing but a pig,
155 and that's the truth." She was referring to his habit of throwing his

clothes everywhere, or wearing them for weeks unwashed, and also to
other matters which no one else dared to refer to, even as indirectly as
this. To this he might reply, chuckling with the pleasure of teasing her:
"You're a married woman, Mrs. Clarke," and she said: "Nothing stops
160    you getting married that I can see." And she walked away very
straight, her cheeks burning with indignation.

She was very fond of him, and he of her. And Mr. Clarke liked and
admired him, and he liked Mr. Clarke. And since Mr. Clarke and Mrs.
Clarke lived amiably together in their four-roomed house, sharing bed
165    and board without ever quarreling, it was to be presumed they liked
each other too. But they seldom spoke. What was there to say?

It was to this silence, to these understood truths, that little Tommy
had to grow up and adjust himself.

Tommy Clarke was three months old when he came to the mine,
170    and day and night his ears were filled with noise, every day and every
night for years, so that he did not think of it as noise, rather, it was a
different kind of silence. The mine-stamps thudded gold, gold, gold,
gold, gold, gold, on and on, never changing, never stopping. So he did
not hear them. But there came a day when the machinery broke, and it
175    was when Tommy was three years old, and the silence was so terrible
and so empty that he went screeching to his mother: "It's stopped, it's
stopped," and he wept, shivering, in a corner until the thudding began
again. It was as if the heart of the world had gone silent. But when it
started to beat, Tommy heard it, and he knew the difference between
180    silence and sound, and his ears acquired a new sensitivity, like a conscience. He heard the shouting and the singing from the swarms of
working Africans, reckless, noisy people because of the danger they
always must live with. He heard the picks ringing on stone, the softer,
deeper thud of picks on thick earth. He heard the clang of the trucks,
185    and the roar of falling earth, and the rumbling of trolleys on rails. And
at night the owls hooted and the nightjars screamed, and the crickets
chirped. And when it stormed it seemed the sky itself was flinging
down bolts of noise against the mountains, for the thunder rolled and
crashed, and the lightning darted from peak to peak around him. It
190    was never silent, never, save for that awful moment when the big heart
stopped beating. Yet later he longed for it to stop again, just for an
hour, so that he might hear a true silence. That was when he was a little older, and the quietness of his parents was beginning to trouble
him. There they were, always so gentle, saying so little only: That's
195    how things are; or: You ask so many questions; or: You'll understand
when you grow up.

It was a false silence, much worse than that real silence had been.

He would play beside his mother in the kitchen, who never said
anything but Yes and No, and—with a patient, sighing voice, as if
200    even his voice tired her: You talk so much, Tommy!

And he was carried on his father's shoulders around the big, black
working machines, and they couldn't speak because of the din the
machines made. And Mr. Macintosh would say: Well, laddie? and give

205　him sweets from his pocket, which he always kept there, especially for Tommy. And once he saw Mr. Macintosh and his father playing cards in the evening, and they didn't talk at all, except for the words that the game needed.

So Tommy escaped to the friendly din of the compound across the great gulf, and played all day with the black children, dancing in their
210　dances, running through the bush after rabbits, or working wet clay into shapes of bird or beast. No silence there, everything noisy and cheerful, and at evening he returned to his equable, silent parents, and after the meal he lay in bed listening to the thud, thud, thud, thud, thud, thud, of the stamps. In the compound across the gulf they were
215　drinking and dancing, the drums made a quick beating against the slow thud of the stamps, and the dancers around the fires yelled, a high, undulating sound like a big wind coming fast and crooked through a gap in the mountains. That was a different world, to which he belonged as much as to this one, where people said: Finish your
220　pudding; or: It's time for bed; and very little else.

When he was five years old he got malaria and was very sick. He recovered, but in the rainy season of the next year he got it again. Both times Mr. Macintosh got into his big American car and went streaking across the thirty miles of bush to the nearest hospital for the doctor.
225　The doctor said quinine, and be careful to screen for mosquitoes. It was easy to give quinine, but Mrs. Clarke, that tired, easy-going woman, found it hard to say: Don't, and Be in by six; and Don't go near the water; and so, when Tommy was seven, he got malaria again. And now Mrs. Clarke was worried, because the doctor spoke severely,
230　mentioning blackwater.

Mr. Macintosh drove the doctor back to his hospital and then came home, and at once went to see Tommy, for he loved Tommy very deeply.

Mrs. Clarke said: "What do you expect, with all these holes every-
235　where, they're full of water all the wet season."

"Well, lassie, I can't fill in all the holes and shafts, people have been digging up here since the Queen of Sheba."

"Never mind about the Queen of Sheba. At least you could screen our house properly."
240　"I pay your husband fifty pounds a month," said Mr. Macintosh, conscious of being in the right.

"Fifty pounds and a proper house," said Annie Clarke.

Mr. Macintosh gave her that quick, narrow look, and then laughed loudly. A week later the house was encased in fine wire mesh all round
245　from roof-edge to verandah-edge, so that it looked like a new meat safe, and Mrs. Clarke went over to Mr. Macintosh's house and gave it a grand cleaning, and when she left she said: "You're nothing but a pig, you're as rich as the Oppenheimers, why don't you buy yourself some new vests at least. And you'll be getting malaria, too, the way
250　you go traipsing about at nights."

She returned to Tommy, who was seated on the verandah behind the gray-glistening wire-netting, in a big deck-chair. He was very thin and white after the fever. He was a long child, bony, and his eyes were

big and black, and his mouth full and pouting from the petulances of
the illness. He had a mass of richly-brown hair, like caramels, on his
head. His mother looked at this pale child of hers, who was yet so
brightly colored and full of vitality, and her tired will-power revived
enough to determine a new régime for him. He was never to be out
after six at night, when the mosquitoes were abroad. He was never to
be out before the sun rose.

"You can get up," she said and he got up, thankfully throwing aside
his covers.

"I'll go over to the compound," he said at once.

She hesitated, and then said: "You mustn't play there any more."

"Why not?" he asked, already fidgeting on the steps outside the
wire-netting cage.

Ah, how she hated these Whys, and Why nots! They tired her utterly. "Because I say so," she snapped.

But he persisted: "I always play there."

"You're getting too big now, and you'll be going to school soon."

Tommy sank on to the steps and remained there, looking away
over the great pit to the busy, sunlit compound. He had known this
moment was coming, of course. It was a knowledge that was part of
the silence. And yet he had not known it. He said: "Why, why, why,
why?" singing it out in a persistent wail.

"Because I say so." Then, in tired desperation: "You get sick from
the Africans, too."

At this, he switched his large black eyes from the scenery to his
mother, and she flushed a little. For they were derisively scornful. Yet
she half-believed it herself, or rather, must believe it, for all through
the wet season the bush would lie waterlogged and festering with mosquitoes, and nothing could be done about it, and one has to put the
blame on something.

She said: "Don't argue. You're not to play with them. You're too
big now to play with a lot of dirty kaffirs. When you were little it was
different, but now you're a big boy."

Tommy sat on the steps in the sweltering afternoon sun that came
thick and yellow through the haze of dust and smoke over the
mountains, and he said nothing. He made no attempt to go near the
compound, now that his growing to manhood depended on his not
playing with the black people. So he had been made to feel. Yet he did
not believe a word of it, not really.

Some days later, he was kicking a football by himself around the
back of the house when a group of black children called to him from
the bush, and he turned away as if he had not seen them. They called
again and then ran away. And Tommy wept bitterly, for now he was
alone.

He went to the edge of the big pit and lay on his stomach looking
down. The sun blazed through him so that his bones ached, and he
shook his mass of hair forward over his eyes to shield them. Below, the
great pit was so deep that the men working on the bottom of it were
like ants. The trucks that climbed up the almost vertical sides were like

matchboxes. The system of ladders and steps cut in the earth, which
the workers used to climb up and down, seemed so flimsy across the
gulf that a stone might dislodge it. Indeed, falling stones often did.
Tommy sprawled, gripping the earth tight with tense belly and flung
limbs, and stared down. They were all like ants and flies. Mr.
Macintosh, too, when he went down, which he did often, for no one
could say he was a coward. And his father, and Tommy himself, they
were all no bigger than little insects.

It was like an enormous ant-working, as brightly tinted as a fresh
antheap. The levels of earth around the mouth of the pit were reddish,
then lower down gray and gravelly, and lower still, clear yellow. Heaps
of the inert, heavy yellow soil, brought up from the bottom, lay all
around him. He stretched out his hand and took some of it. It was
unresponsive, lying lifeless and dense on his fingers, a little damp from
the rain. He clenched his fist, and loosened it, and now the mass of
yellow earth lay shaped on his palm, showing the marks of his fingers.
A shape like—what? A bit of root? A fragment of rock rotted by water?
He rolled his palms vigorously around it, and it became smooth like a
water-ground stone. Then he sat up and took more earth, and formed
a pit, and up the sides flying ladders with bits of stick, and little kips of
wetted earth for the trucks. Soon the sun dried it, and it all cracked
and fell apart. Tommy gave the model a kick and went moodily back
to the house. The sun was going down. It seemed that he had left a
golden age of freedom behind, and now there was a new country of
restrictions and time-tables.

He mother saw how he suffered, but thought: Soon he'll go to
school and find companions.

But he was only just seven, and very young to go all the way to the
city to boarding-school. She sent for school-books, and taught him to
read. Yet this was for only two or three hours in the day, and for the
rest he mooned about, as she complained, gazing away over the gulf to
the compound, from where he could hear the noise of the playing
children. He was stoical about it, or so it seemed, but underneath he
was suffering badly from this new knowledge, which was much more
vital than anything he had learned from the school-books. He knew
the word loneliness, and lying at the edge of the pit he formed the yellow clay into little figures which he called Betty and Freddy and Dirk.
Playmates. Dirk was the name of the boy he liked best among the children in the compound over the gulf.

One day his mother called him to the back door. There stood Dirk,
and he was holding between his hands a tiny duiker, the size of a thin
cat. Tommy ran forward, and was about to exclaim with Dirk over the
little animal, when he remembered his new status. He stopped, stiffened himself, and said: "How much?"

Dirk, keeping his eyes evasive, said: "One shilling, baas."

Tommy glanced at his mother and then said, proudly, his voice
high: "Damned cheek, too much."

Annie Clarke flushed. She was ashamed and flustered. She came
forward and said quickly: "It's all right, Tommy, I'll give you the
shilling." She took the coin from the pocket of her apron and gave it

to Tommy, who handed it at once to Dirk. Tommy took the little animal gently in his hands, and his tenderness for this frightened and
355    lonely creature rushed to his eyes and he turned away so that Dirk couldn't see—he would have been bitterly ashamed to show softness in front of Dirk, who was so tough and fearless.

Dirk stood back, watching, unwilling to see the last of the buck. Then he said: "It's just born, it can die."

360    Mrs. Clarke said, dismissingly: "Yes, Tommy will look after it." Dirk walked away slowly, fingering the shilling in his pocket, but looking back at where Tommy and his mother were making a nest for the little buck in a packing-case. Mrs. Clarke made a feeding-bottle with some linen stuffed into the neck of a tomato sauce bottle and filled it
365    with milk and water and sugar. Tommy knelt by the buck and tried to drip the milk into its mouth.

It lay trembling lifting its delicate head from the crumpled, huddled limbs, too weak to move, the big eyes dark and forlorn. Then the trembling became a spasm of weakness and the head collapsed with a
370    soft thud against the side of the box, and then slowly, and with a trembling effort, the neck lifted the head again. Tommy tried to push the wad of linen into the soft mouth, and the milk wetted the fur and ran down over the buck's chest, and he wanted to cry.

"But it'll die, Mother, it'll die," he shouted, angrily.

375    "You mustn't force it," said Annie Clarke, and she went away to her household duties. Tommy knelt there with the bottle, stroking the trembling little buck and suffering every time the thin neck collapsed with weakness, and tried again and again to interest it in the milk. But the buck wouldn't drink at all.

380    "Why?" shouted Tommy, in the anger of his misery. "Why won't it drink? Why? Why?"

"But it's only just born," said Mrs. Clarke. The cord was still on the creature's navel, like a shriveling, dark stick.

That night Tommy took the little buck into his room, and secretly
385    in the dark lifted it, folded in a blanket, into his bed. He could feel it trembling fitfully against his chest, and he cried into the dark because he knew it was going to die.

In the morning when he woke, the buck could not lift its head at all, and it was a weak, collapsed weight on Tommy's chest, a chilly
390    weight. The blanket in which it lay was messed with yellow stuff like a scrambled egg. Tommy washed the buck gently, and wrapped it again in new coverings, and laid it on the verandah where the sun could warm it.

Mrs. Clarke gently forced the jaws open and poured down milk
395    until the buck choked. Tommy knelt beside it all morning, suffering as he had never suffered before. The tears ran steadily down his face and he wished he could die too, and Mrs. Clarke wished very much she could catch Dirk and give him a good beating, which would be unjust, but might do something to relieve her feelings. "Besides," she said to
400    her husband, "it's nothing but cruelty, taking a tiny thing like that from its mother."

Late that afternoon the buck died, and Mr. Clarke, who had not seen his son's misery over it, casually threw the tiny, stiff corpse to the cookboy and told him to go and bury it. Tommy stood on the veran-
405 dah, his face tight and angry, and watched the cookboy shovel his little buck hastily under some bushes, and return whistling.

Then he went into the room where his mother and father were sitting and said: "Why is Dirk yellow and not dark brown like the other kaffirs?"
410 Silence. Mr. Clarke and Annie Clarke looked at each other. Then Mr. Clarke said: "They come different colors."

Tommy looked forcefully at his mother, who said: "He's a half-caste."

"What's a half-caste?"
415 "You'll understand when you grow up."

Tommy looked from his father, who was filling his pipe, his eyes lowered to the work, then at his mother, whose cheekbones held that proud, bright flush.

"I understand now," he said defiantly.
420 "Then why do you ask?" said Mrs. Clarke, with anger. Why, she was saying, do you infringe the rule of silence?

Tommy went out, and to the brink of the great pit. There he lay, wondering why he had said he understood when he did not. Though in a sense he did. He was remembering, though he had not noticed it
425 before, that among the gang of children in the compound were two yellow children. Dirk was one, and Dirk's sister another. She was a tiny child, who came toddling on the fringe of the older children's games. But Dirk's mother was black, or rather, dark-brown like the others. And Dirk was not really yellow, but light copper-colored. The
430 color of this earth, were it a little darker. Tommy's fingers were fiddling with the damp clay. He looked at the little figures he had made, Betty and Freddy. Idly, he smashed them. Then he picked up Dirk and flung him down. But he must have flung him down too carefully, for he did not break, and so he set the figure against the stalk of a weed.
435 He took a clump of clay, and as his fingers experimentally pushed and kneaded it, the shape grew into the shape of a little duiker. But not a sick duiker, which had died because it had been taken from its mother. Not at all, it was a fine strong duiker, standing with one hoof raised and its head listening, ears pricked forward.
440 Tommy knelt on the verge of the great pit, absorbed, while the duiker grew into its proper form. He became dissatisfied—it was too small. He impatiently smashed what he had done, and taking a big heap of the yellowish, dense soil, shook water on it from an old rusty railway sleeper that had collected rainwater, and made the mass soft
445 and workable. Then he began again. The duiker would be half life-size.

And so his hands worked and his mind worried along its path of questions? Why? Why? Why? And finally: If Dirk is half black, or rather half white and half dark-brown, then who is his father?

For a long time his mind hovered on the edge of the answer, but
450 did not finally reach it. But from time to time he looked across the gulf to where Mr. Macintosh was strolling, swinging his big cudgel and

he thought: There are only two white men on this mine.

The buck was now finished, and he wetted his fingers in rusty rainwater, and smoothed down the soft clay to make it glisten like the surfaces of fur, but at once it dried and dulled, and as he knelt there he thought how the sun would crack it and it would fall to pieces, and an angry dissatisfaction filled him and he hung his head and wanted very much to cry. And just as the first tears were coming he heard a soft whistle from behind him, and turned, and there was Dirk, kneeling behind a bush and looking out through the parted leaves.

"Is the buck all right?" asked Dirk.

Tommy said: "It's dead," and he kicked his foot at his model duiker so that the thick clay fell apart in lumps.

Dirk said: "Don't do that, it's nice," and he sprang forward and tried to fit the pieces together.

"It's no good, the sun'll crack it," said Tommy, and he began to cry, although he was so ashamed to cry in front of Dirk. "The buck's dead," he wept, "it's dead."

"I can get you another," said Dirk, looking at Tommy rather surprised. "I killed its mother with a stone. It's easy."

Dirk was seven, like Tommy. He was tall and strong, like Tommy. His eyes were dark and full, but his mouth was not full and soft, but long and narrow, clenched in the middle. His hair was very black and soft and long, falling uncut around his face, and his skin was a smooth, yellowish copper. Tommy stopped crying and looked at Dirk. He said: "It's cruel to kill a buck's mother with a stone." Dirk's mouth parted in surprised laughter over his big white teeth. Tommy watched him laugh, and he thought: Well, now I know who his father is.

He looked away to his home, which was two hundred yards off, exposed to the sun's glare among low bushes of hibiscus and poinsettia. He looked at Mr. Macintosh's house, which was a few hundred yards farther off. Then he looked at Dirk. He was full of anger, which he did not understand, but he did understand that he was also defiant, and this was a moment of decision. After a long time he said: "They can see us from here," and the decision was made.

They got up, but as Dirk rose he saw the little clay figure laid against a stem, and he picked it up. "This is me," he said at once. For crude as the thing was, it was unmistakably Dirk, who smiled with pleasure. "Can I have it?" he asked, and Tommy nodded, equally proud and pleased.

They went off into the bush between the two houses, and then on for perhaps half a mile. This was the deserted part of the hollow in the mountains, no one came here, all the bustle and noise was on the other side. In front of them rose a sharp peak, and low at its foot was a high anthill, draped with Christmas fern and thick with shrub.

The two boys went inside the curtains of fern and sat down. No one could see them here. Dirk carefully put the little clay figure of himself inside a hole in the roots of a tree. Then he said: "Make the buck again." Tommy took his knife and knelt beside a fallen tree, and tried to carve the buck from it. The wood was soft and rotten, and was

easily carved, and by night there was the clumsy shape of the buck coming out of the trunk. Dirk said: "Now we've both got something."

The next day the two boys made their ways separately to the antheap and played there together, and so it was every day.

505 Then one evening Mrs. Clarke said to Tommy just as he was going to bed: "I thought I told you not to play with the kaffirs?"

Tommy stood very still. Then he lifted his head and said to her, with a strong look across at his father: "Why shouldn't I play with Mr. Macintosh's son?"

510 Mrs. Clarke stopped breathing for a moment, and closed her eyes. She opened them in appeal at her husband. But Mr. Clarke was filling his pipe. Tommy waited and then said good night and went to his room.

There he undressed slowly and climbed into the narrow iron bed 515 and lay quietly, listening to the thud, thud, gold, gold, thud, thud, of the mine stamps. Over in the compound they were dancing, and the tom-toms were beating fast, like the quick beat of the buck's heart that night as it lay on his chest. They were yelling like the wind coming through gaps in a mountain and through the window he could see the 520 high, flaring light of the fires, and the black figures of the dancing people were wild and active against it.

Mrs. Clarke came quickly in. She was crying. "Tommy," she said, sitting on the edge of his bed in the dark.

"Yes?" he said, cautiously.

525 "You mustn't say that again. Not ever."

He said nothing. His mother's hand was urgently pressing his arm. "Your father might lose his job," said Mrs. Clarke, wildly. "We'd never get this money anywhere else. Never. You must understand, Tommy."

"I do understand," said Tommy, stiffly, very sorry for his mother, 530 but hating her at the same time. "Just don't say it, Tommy, don't ever say it." Then she kissed him in a way that was both fond and appealing, and went out, shutting the door. To her husband she said it was time Tommy went to school, and next day she wrote to make the arrangements.

# B1.  Second Reading: Delving More Deeply

Read Section I a second time and focus on the lines indicated. Use the surrounding text and your experience to give an informed answer to the questions below.

1.  *The Africans who worked this mine called it "the pit of death," and they called Mr. Macintosh "The Gold Stomach."* (lines 73–74) What does this tell us about Mr. Macintosh? About the workers and the economic situation in this country? Would you want to work for Mr. Macintosh?

2. **"Well, laddie, got that off your chest?"** *(lines 100–101)* Which of the following adjectives describe Mr. Macintosh's position regarding his employee, Mr. Clarke?

demanding          understanding          unforgiving          ruthless

serious          tolerant          fun-loving

3. **"You're nothing but a pig, and that's the truth." She was referring to his habit of throwing his clothes everywhere, or wearing them for weeks unwashed, and also to other matters which no one else dared to refer to, even as indirectly as this.** *(lines 154–158)* What might these "other matters" be? Does he know what she is hinting at? Do you know anybody that you like a lot but whose behavior you disapprove of?

4. **It was a false silence, much worse than that real silence had been.** *(line 197)* What is the false silence? The real silence? What does Tommy realize about his parents? Do you think his parents are just naturally silent people, or is this silence unnatural?

5. **"You're too big now to play with a lot of dirty kaffirs. When you were little it was different, but now you're a big boy."** *(lines 284–286)* Why was it okay to play with the black children before but not now? Do you think it is natural for parents to restrict their child's playmates in this way?

6. **…and Mrs. Clarke wished very much she could catch Dirk and give him a good beating, which would be unjust, but might do something to relieve her feelings.** *(lines 397–399)* Why does she want to beat Dirk? Why would it be unjust? Does Mrs. Clarke's reaction seem normal to you?

7. **Tommy watched him laugh, and he thought: Well, now I know who his father is.** *(lines 477–478)* Who is Dirk's father? Do you think it's unusual for a seven-year-old to think about such things?

8. **He was full of anger, which he did not understand, but he did understand that he was also defiant, and this was a moment of decision.** *(lines 482–484)* Why was Tommy angry? What decision did he make? Do you think his decision was wise?

9. **Mrs. Clarke stopped breathing for a moment, and closed her eyes.** *(lines 510)* What emotion did she feel? Explain.

Now write two questions of your own about Section I that you would like to discuss with your classmates.

1. _____

_____

Discuss your answers to the First and Second Reading questions in small groups. Then discuss the questions each student wrote.

2. _____

_____

## Bridge 1

Discuss these questions before going on to Section II.

◆   Do you like the story so far? Why or why not?

◆   Which character is the most interesting to you? Why?

◆   Do you think Tommy will do well at school? Will he be happy there?

# A2.   First Reading: Following the Story Line

Read the following questions and keep them in mind as you read Section II. Use the questions to help you predict and follow the events of the story.

1.   Why do Tommy and Dirk fight after Tommy offers to help Dirk?

2.   What does Dirk learn from Tommy? What does Tommy learn from teaching Dirk?

3.   What do Mr. Macintosh and Dirk have in common, in Tommy's opinion?

4.   What does Tommy realize about his friendship with Dirk?

5.   In what way do both Tommy and Dirk grow years older in just a short time?

6.   Why do you think Tommy rejects Mr. Macintosh's offer to go abroad to school and to sea?

535 And so now Tommy made the long journey by car and train into the city four times a year, and four times a year he came back for the holidays. Mr. Macintosh always drove him to the station and gave him ten shillings pocket money, and he came to fetch him in the car with his parents, and he always said: "Well, laddie, and how's school?" And

540 Tommy said: "Fine, Mr. Macintosh." And Mr. Macintosh said: "We'll make a college man of you yet."

When he said this, the flush came bright and proud on Annie Clarke's cheeks, and she looked quickly at Mr. Clarke, who was smiling and embarrassed. But Mr. Macintosh laid his hands on Tommy's

545 shoulders and said: "There's my laddie, there's my laddie," and Tommy kept his shoulders stiff and still. Afterwards, Mrs. Clarke would say, nervously: "He's fond of you, Tommy, he'll do right by you." And once she said: "It's natural, he's got no children of his own." But Tommy scowled at her and she flushed and said: "There's

550 things you don't understand yet, Tommy, and you'll regret it if you throw away your chances." Tommy turned away with an impatient movement. Yet it was not so clear at all, for it was almost as if he were a rich man's son, with all that pocket money, and the parcels of biscuits and sweets that Mr. Macintosh sent into school during the term,

555 and being fetched in the great rich car. And underneath it all he felt as if he were dragged along by the nose. He felt as if he were part of a conspiracy of some kind that no one ever spoke about. Silence. His real feelings were growing up slow and complicated and obstinate underneath that silence.

560 At school it was not at all complicated, it was the other world. There Tommy did his lessons and played with his friends and did not think of Dirk. Or rather, his thoughts of him were proper for that world. A half-caste, ignorant, living in the kaffir location—he felt ashamed that he played with Dirk in the holidays, and he told no one.

565 Even on the train coming home he would think like that of Dirk, but the nearer he reached home the more his thoughts wavered and darkened. On the first evening at home he would speak of the school, and how he was first in the class, and he played with this boy or that, or went to such fine houses in the city as a guest. The very first morning

570 he would be standing on the verandah looking at the big pit and at the compound away beyond it, and his mother watched him, smiling in nervous supplication. And then he walked down the steps, away from the pit, and into the bush to the antheap. There Dirk was waiting for him. So it was every holiday. Neither of the boys spoke at first of what

575 divided them. But, on the eve of Tommy's return to school after he had been there a year, Dirk said: "You're getting educated, but I've nothing to learn." Tommy said: "I'll bring back books and teach you." He said this in a quick voice, as if ashamed, and Dirk's eyes were accusing and angry. He gave his sarcastic laugh and said: "That's what

580 you say, white boy."

It was not pleasant, but what Tommy said was not pleasant either, like a favor wrung out of a condescending person.

The two boys were sitting on the antheap under the fine lacy curtains of Christmas fern, looking at the rocky peak soaring into the
585  smoky yellowish sky. There was the most unpleasant sort of annoyance in Tommy, and he felt ashamed of it. And on Dirk's face there
was an aggressive but ashamed look. They continued to sit there, a little apart, full of dislike for each other, and knowing that the dislike
came from the pressure of the outside world. "I said I'd teach you,
590  didn't I?" said Tommy, grandly, shying a stone at a bush so that leaves
flew off in all directions. "You white bastard," said Dirk, in a low
voice, and he let out that sudden ugly laugh, showing his white teeth.
"What did you say?" said Tommy, going pale and jumping to his feet.
"You heard," said Dirk, still laughing. He too got up. Then Tommy
595  flung himself on Dirk and they over-balanced and rolled off into the
bushes, kicking and scratching. They rolled apart and began fighting
properly, with fists. Tommy was better fed and more healthy. Dirk was
tougher. They were a match, and they stopped when they were too
tired and battered to go on. They staggered over to the antheap and
600  sat there side by side, panting, wiping the blood off their faces. At last
they lay on their backs on the rough slant of the anthill and looked up
at the sky. Every trace of dislike had vanished, and they felt easy and
quiet. When the sun went down they walked together through the
bush to a point where they could not be seen from the houses, and
605  there they said, as always: "See you tomorrow."

When Mr. Macintosh gave him the usual ten shillings, he put them
into his pocket thinking he would buy a football, but he did not. The
ten shillings stayed unspent until it was nearly the end of term, and
then he went to the shops and bought a reader and some exercise
610  books and pencils, and an arithmetic. He hid these at the bottom of
his trunk and whipped them out before his mother could see them.

He took them to the antheap next morning, but before he could
reach it he saw there was a little shed built on it, and the Christmas
fern had been draped like a veil across the roof of the shed. The bushes
615  had been cut on the top of the anthill, but left on the sides, so that the
shed looked as if it rose from the tops of the bushes. The shed was of
unbarked poles pushed into the earth, the roof was of thatch, and the
upper half of the front was left open. Inside there was a bench of poles
and a table of planks on poles. There sat Dirk, waiting hungrily, and
620  Tommy went and sat beside him, putting the books and pencils on
the table.

"This shed is fine," said Tommy, but Dirk was already looking at
the books. So he began to teach Dirk how to read. And for all that holiday they were together in the shed while Dirk pored over the books.
625  He found them more difficult than Tommy did, because they were full
of words for things Dirk did not know, like curtains or carpet, and
teaching Dirk to read the word carpet meant telling him all about car-
pets and the furnishings of a house. Often Tommy felt bored and restless and said: "Let's play," but Dirk said fiercely: "No, I want to read."
630  Tommy grew fretful, for after all he had been working in the term and
now he felt entitled to play. So there was another fight. Dirk said
Tommy was a lazy white bastard, and Tommy said Dirk was a dirty

635

half-caste. They fought as before, evenly matched and to no conclu-sion, and afterwards felt fine and friendly, and even made jokes about the fighting. It was arranged that they should work in the mornings only and leave the afternoons for play. When Tommy went back home that evening his mother saw the scratches on his face and the swollen nose, and said hopefully: "Have you and Dirk been fighting?" But Tommy said no, he had hit his face on a tree.

640

645

His parents, of course, knew about the shed in the bush, but did not speak of it to Mr. Macintosh. No one did. For Dirk's very exis-tence was something to be ignored by everyone, and none of the workers, not even the overseers, would dare to mention Dirk's name. When Mr. Macintosh asked Tommy what he had done to his face, he said he had slipped and fallen.

650

655

660

And so their eighth year and their ninth went past. Dirk could read and write and do all the sums that Tommy could do. He was always handicapped by not knowing the different way of living and soon he said, angrily, it wasn't fair, and there was another fight about it, and then Tommy began another way of teaching. He would tell how it was to go to a cinema in the city, every detail of it, how the seats were arranged in such a way, and one paid so much, and the lights were like this, and the picture on the screen worked like that. Or he would describe how at school they ate such things for breakfast and other things for lunch. Or tell how the man had come with picture slides talking about China. The two boys got out an atlas and found China, and Tommy told Dirk every word of what the lecturer had said. Or it might be Italy or some other country. And they would argue that the lecturer should have said this or that, for Dirk was always hotly scorn-ful of the white man's way of looking at things, so arrogant, he said. Soon Tommy saw things through Dirk; he saw the other life in town clear and brightly-colored and a little distorted, as Dirk did.

665

670

Soon, at school, Tommy would involuntarily think: I must remem-ber this to tell Dirk. It was impossible for him to do anything, say any-thing, without being very conscious of just how it happened, as if Dirk's black, sarcastic eye had got inside him, Tommy, and never closed. And a feeling of unwillingness grew in Tommy, because of the strain of fitting these two worlds together. He found himself swearing at niggers or kaffirs like the other boys, and more violently than they did, but immediately afterwards he would find himself thinking: I must remember this so as to tell Dirk. Because of all this thinking, and seeing everything clear all the time, he was very bright at school, and found the work easy. He was two classes ahead of his age.

675

680

That was the tenth year, and one day Tommy went to the shed in the bush and Dirk was not waiting for him. It was the first day of the holidays. All the term he had been remembering things to tell Dirk, and now Dirk was not there. A dove was sitting on the Christmas fern, cooing lazily in the hot morning, a sleepy, lonely sound. When Tommy came pushing through the bushes it flew away. The mine-stamps thudded heavily, gold, gold, and Tommy saw that the shed was empty even of books, for the case where they were usually kept was hanging open.

He went running to his mother: "Where's Dirk?" he asked.

"How should I know?" said Annie Clarke, cautiously. She really did not know.

"You do know, you do!" he cried, angrily. And then he went racing off to the big pit. Mr. Macintosh was sitting on an upturned truck on the edge, watching the hundreds of workers below him, moving like ants on the yellow bottom. "Well, laddie?" he asked, amiably, and moved over for Tommy to sit by him.

"Where's Dirk?" asked Tommy, accusingly, standing in front of him.

Mr. Macintosh tipped his old felt hat even further back and scratched at his front hair and looked at Tommy.

"Dirk's working," he said, at last.

"Where?"

Mr. Macintosh pointed at the bottom of the pit. Then he said again: "Sit down, laddie, I want to talk to you."

"I don't want to," said Tommy, and he turned away and went blundering over the veld to the shed. He sat on the bench and cried, and when dinnertime came he did not go home. All that day he sat in the shed, and when he had finished crying he remained on the bench, leaning his back against the poles of the shed, and stared into the bush. The doves cooed and cooed, kru-kruuuu, kru-kruuuuu, and a woodpecker tapped, and the mine-stamps thudded. Yet it was very quiet, a hand of silence gripped the bush, and he could hear the borers and the ants at work in the poles of the bench he sat on. He could see that although the anthill seemed dead, a mound of hard, peaked, baked earth, it was very much alive, for there was a fresh outbreak of wet, damp earth in the floor of the shed. There was a fine crust of reddish, lacey earth over the poles of the walls. The shed would have to be built again soon, because the ants and borers would have eaten it through. But what was the use of a shed without Dirk?

All that day he stayed there, and did not return until dark, and when his mother said: "What's the matter with you, why are you crying?" he said angrily, "I don't know," matching her dishonesty with his own. The next day, even before breakfast, he was off to the shed, and did not return until dark, and refused his supper although he had not eaten all day.

And the next day it was the same, but now he was bored and lonely. He took his knife from his pocket and whittled at a stick, and it became a boy, bent and straining under the weight of a heavy load, his arms clenched up to support it. He took the figure home at suppertime and ate with it on the table in front of him.

"What's that?" asked Annie Clarke, and Tommy answered: "Dirk."

He took it to his bedroom, and sat in the soft lamp-light, working away with his knife, and he had it in his hand the following morning when he met Mr. Macintosh at the brink of the pit. "What's that, laddie?" asked Mr. Macintosh, and Tommy said: "Dirk."

Mr. Macintosh's mouth went thin, and then he smiled and said: "Let me have it."

"No, it's for Dirk."

Mr. Macintosh took out his wallet and said: "I'll pay you for it."

"I don't want any money," said Tommy, angrily, and Mr.
735 Macintosh, greatly disturbed, put back his wallet. Then Tommy, hesi-
tating, said: "Yes, I do." Mr. Macintosh, his values confirmed, was
relieved, and he took out his wallet again and produced a pound note,
which seemed to him very generous. "Five pounds," said Tommy,
promptly. Mr. Macintosh first scowled, then laughed. He tipped back
740 his head and roared with laughter. "Well, laddie you'll make a businessman yet. Five pounds for a little bit of wood!"

"Make it for yourself then, if it's just a bit of wood."

Mr. Macintosh counted out five pounds and handed them over.
"What are you going to do with that money?" he asked, as he watched
745 Tommy buttoning them carefully into his shirt pocket. "Give them to
Dirk," said Tommy, triumphantly, and Mr. Macintosh's heavy old face
went purple. He watched while Tommy walked away from him, sitting
on the truck, letting the heavy cudgel swing lightly against his shoes.
He solved his immediate problem by thinking: He's a good laddie, he's
750 got a good heart.

That night Mrs. Clarke came over while he was sitting over his
roast beef and cabbage, and said: "Mr. Macintosh, I want a word with
you." He nodded at a chair, but she did not sit. "Tommy's upset," she
said delicately, "he's been used to Dirk, and now he's got no one to
755 play with."

For a moment Mr. Macintosh kept his eyes lowered, then he said:
"It's easily fixed, Annie, don't worry yourself." He spoke heartily, as it
was easy for him to do, speaking of a worker, who might be released at
his whim for other duties.

760 That bright protesting flush came on to her cheeks, in spite of herself, and she looked quickly at him, with real indignation. But he
ignored it and said: "I'll fix it in the morning, Annie."

She thanked him and went back home, suffering because she had
not said those words which had always soothed her conscience in the
765 past: You're nothing but a pig, Mr. Macintosh…

As for Tommy, he was sitting in the shed, crying his eyes out. And
then, when there were no more tears, there came such a storm of
anger and pain that he would never forget it as long as he lived. What
for? He did not know, and that was the worst of it. It was not simply
770 Mr. Macintosh, who loved him, and who thus so blackly betrayed his
own flesh and blood, nor the silences of his parents. Something deeper, felt working in the substance of life as he could hear those ants
working away with those busy jaws at the roots of the poles he sat on,
to make new material for their different forms of life. He was testing
775 those words which were used, or not used—merely suggested—all the
time, and for a ten-year-old boy it was almost too hard to bear. A
child may say of a companion one day that he hates so and so, and the
next: He is my friend. That is how a relationship is, shifting and
changing, and children are kept safe in their hates and loves by the

780 fabric of social life their parents make over their heads. And middle-aged people say: This is my friend, this is my enemy, including all the shifts and changes of feeling in one word, for the sake of an easy mind. In between these ages, at about twenty perhaps, there is a time when the young people test everything, and accept many hard and cruel
785 truths about living, and that is because they do not know how hard it is to accept them finally, and for the rest of their lives. It is easy to be truthful at twenty.

But it is not easy at ten, a little boy entirely alone, looking at words like friendship. What, then, was friendship? Dirk was his friend, that
790 he knew, but did he like Dirk? Did he love him? Sometimes not at all. He remembered how Dirk had said: "I'll get you another baby buck. I'll kill its mother with a stone." He remembered his feeling of revulsion at the cruelty. Dirk was cruel. But—and here Tommy unexpectedly laughed, and for the first time he understood Dirk's way of laughing.
795 It was really funny to say that Dirk was cruel, when his very existence was a cruelty. Yet Mr. Macintosh laughed in exactly the same way, and his skin was white, or rather, white browned over by the sun. Why was Mr. Macintosh also entitled to laugh, with that same abrupt ugliness? Perhaps somewhere in the beginnings of the rich Mr. Macintosh
800 there had been the same cruelty, and that had worked its way through the life of Mr. Macintosh until it turned into the cruelty of Dirk, the colored boy, the half-caste? If so, it was all much harder to understand.

And then Tommy thought how Dirk seemed to wait always, as if
805 he, Tommy, were bound to stand by him, as if this were a justice that was perfectly clear to Dirk; and he, Tommy, did in fact fight with Mr. Macintosh for Dirk, and he could behave in no other way. Why? Because Dirk was his friend? Yet there were times when he hated Dirk, and certainly Dirk hated him, and when they fought they could have
810 killed each other easily, and with joy.

Well, then? Well, then? What was friendship, and why were they bound so closely, and by what? Slowly the little boy, sitting alone on his antheap, came to an understanding which is proper to middle-aged people, that resignation in knowledge which is called irony. Such
815 a person may know, for instance, that he is bound most deeply to another person, although he does not like that person, in the way the word is ordinarily used, or the way he talks, or his politics, or anything else. And yet they are friends and will always be friends, and what happens to this bound couple affects each most deeply, even though they
820 may be in different continents, or may never see each other again. Or after twenty years they may meet, and there is no need to say a word, everything is understood. This is one of the ways of friendship, and just as real as amiability or being alike.

Well, then? For it is a hard and difficult knowledge for any little
825 boy to accept. But he accepted it, and knew that he and Dirk were closer than brothers and always would be so. He grew many years older in that day of painful struggle, while he listened to the mine-stamps saying gold, gold, and to the ants working away with their jaws to destroy the bench he sat on, to make food for themselves.

830  Next morning Dirk came to the shed, and Tommy, looking at him, knew that he, too, had grown years older in the months of working in the great pit. Ten years old—but he had been working with men and he was not a child.

Tommy took out the five pound notes and gave them to Dirk.

835  Dirk pushed them back. "What for?" he asked.

"I got them from him," said Tommy, and at once Dirk took them as if they were his right.

And at once, inside Tommy, came indignation, for he felt he was being taken for granted, and he said: "Why aren't you working?"

840  "He said I needn't. He means, while you are having your holidays."

"I got you free," said Tommy, boasting.

Dirk's eyes narrowed in anger. "He's my father," he said, for the first time.

845  "But he made you work," said Tommy, taunting him. And then: "Why do you work? I wouldn't. I should say no."

"So you would say no?" said Dirk in angry sarcasm.

"There's no law to make you."

"So there's no law, white boy, no law…" But Tommy had sprung at

850  him, and they were fighting again, rolling over and over, and this time they fell apart from exhaustion and lay on the ground panting for a long time.

Later Dirk said: "Why do we fight, it's silly?"

"I don't know," said Tommy, and he began to laugh, and Dirk

855  laughed too. They were to fight often in the future, but never with such bitterness, because of the way they were laughing now.

It was the following holidays before they fought again. Dirk was waiting for him in the shed.

"Did he let you go?" asked Tommy at once, putting down new

860  books on the table for Dirk.

"I just came," said Dirk. "I didn't ask."

They sat together on the bench, and at once a leg gave way and they rolled off on the floor laughing. "We must mend it," said Tommy. "Let's build the shed again."

865  "No," said Dirk at once, "don't let's waste time on the shed. You can teach me while you're here, and I can make the shed when you've gone back to school."

Tommy slowly got up from the floor, frowning. Again he felt he was being taken for granted. "Aren't you going to work on the mine

870  during the term?"

"No, I'm not going to work on the mine again. I told him I wouldn't."

"You've got to work," said Tommy, grandly.

"So I've got to work," said Dirk, threateningly. "You can go to

875  school, white boy, but I've got to work, and in the holidays I can just take time off to please you."

They fought until they were tired, and five minutes afterwards they were seated on the anthill talking. "What did you do with the five pounds?" asked Tommy.

880  "I gave them to my mother."

"What did she do with them?"

"She bought herself a dress, and then food for us all, and bought me these trousers, and she put the rest away to keep."

885 A pause. Then, deeply ashamed, Tommy asked: "Doesn't he give her any money?"

"He doesn't come any more. Not for more than a year."

"Oh, I thought he did still," said Tommy casually, whistling.

"No." Then, fiercely, in a low voice: "There'll be some more half-castes in the compound soon."

890 Dirk sat crouching, his fierce black eyes on Tommy, ready to spring at him. But Tommy was sitting with his head bowed, looking at the ground. "It's not fair," he said. "It's not fair."

"So you've discovered that, white boy?" said Dirk. It was said good-naturedly, and there was no need to fight. They went to their books

895 and Tommy taught Dirk some new sums.

But they never spoke of what Dirk would do in the future, how he would use all this schooling. They did not dare.

That was the eleventh year.

When they were twelve, Tommy returned from school to be

900 greeted by the words: "Have you heard the news?"

"What news?"

They were sitting as usual on the bench. The shed was newly built, with strong thatch, and good walls, plastered this time with mud, so as to make it harder for the ants.

905 "They are saying you are going to be sent away."

"Who says so?"

"Oh, everyone," said Dirk, stirring his feet about vaguely under the table. This was because it was the first few minutes after the return from school, and he was always cautious, until he was sure Tommy

910 had not changed towards him. And that "everyone" was explosive. Tommy nodded, however, and asked apprehensively: "Where to?"

"To the sea."

"How do they know?" Tommy scarcely breathed the word they.

"Your cook heard your mother say so…" And then Dirk added

915 with a grin, forcing the issue: "Cheek, dirty kaffirs talking about white men."

Tommy smiled obligingly, and asked: "How, to the sea, what does it mean?"

"How should we know, dirty kaffirs."

920 "Oh, shut up," said Tommy, angrily. They glared at each other, their muscles tensed. But they sighed and looked away. At twelve it was not easy to fight, it was all too serious.

That night Tommy said to his parents: "They say I'm going to sea. Is it true?"

925 His mother asked quickly: "Who said so?"

"But is it true?" Then, derisively: "Cheek, dirty kaffirs talking about us."

"Please don't talk like that, Tommy, it's not right."

"Oh, mother, please, how am I going to sea?"

930 "But be sensible Tommy, it's not settled, but Mr. Macintosh…"

"So it's Mr. Macintosh!"

Mrs. Clarke looked at her husband, who came forward and sat down and settled his elbows on the table. A family conference. Tommy also sat down.

935 "Now listen, son. Mr. Macintosh has a soft spot for you. You should be grateful to him. He can do a lot for you."

"But why should I go to sea?"

"You don't have to. He suggested it—he was in the Merchant Navy himself once."

940 "So I've got to go just because he did."

"He's offered to pay for you to go to college in England, and give you money until you're in the Navy."

"But I don't want to be a sailor. I've never even seen the sea."

"But you're good at your figures, and you have to be, so why not?"

945 "I won't," said Tommy, angrily. "I won't, I won't." He glared at them through tears. "You want to get rid of me, that's all it is. You want me to go away from here, from…"

The parents looked at each other and sighed.

"Well, if you don't want to, you don't have to. But it's not every 950 boy who has a chance like this."

"Why doesn't he send Dirk?" asked Tommy, aggressively.

"Tommy," cried Annie Clarke, in great distress.

"Well, why doesn't he? He's much better than me at figures."

"Go to bed," said Mr. Clarke suddenly, in a fit of temper. "Go 955 to bed."

Tommy went out of the room, slamming the door hard. He must be grown-up. His father had never spoken to him like that. He sat on the edge of the bed in stubborn rebellion, listening to the thudding of the stamps. And down in the compound they were dancing, the lights 960 of the fires flickered red on his window-pane.

He wondered if Dirk were there, leaping around the fires with the others.

Next day he asked him: "Do you dance with the others?" At once he knew he had blundered. When Dirk was angry, his eyes darkened 965 and narrowed. When he was hurt, his mouth set in a way which made the flesh pinch thinly under his nose. So he looked now.

"Listen, white boy. White people don't like us half-castes. Neither do the blacks like us. No one does. And so I don't dance with them."

"Let's do some lessons," said Tommy, quickly. And they went to 970 their books, dropping the subject.

Later Mr. Macintosh came to the Clarkes' house and asked for Tommy. The parents watched Mr. Macintosh and their son walk together along the edge of the great pit. They stood at the window and watched, but they did not speak.

975 Mr. Macintosh was saying easily: "Well, laddie, and so you don't want to be a sailor."

"No, Mr. Macintosh."

"I went to sea when I was fifteen. It's hard, but you aren't afraid of that. Besides, you'd be an officer."

980  Tommy said nothing.

"You don't like the idea?"

"No."

Mr. Macintosh stopped and looked down into the pit. The earth at the bottom was as yellow as it had been when Tommy was seven, but 985 now it was much deeper. Mr. Macintosh did not know how deep, because he had not measured it. Far below, in this man-made valley, the workers were moving and shifting like black seeds tilted on a piece of paper.

"Your father worked on the mines and he became an engineer 990 working at nights, did you know that?"

"Yes."

"It was very hard for him. He was thirty before he was qualified, and then he earned twenty-five pounds a month until he came to this mine."

995  "Yes."

"You don't want to do that, do you?"

"I will if I have to," muttered Tommy, defiantly.

Mr. Macintosh's face was swelling and purpling. The veins along nose and forehead were black. Mr. Macintosh was asking himself why 1000 this lad treated him like dirt, when he was offering to do him an immense favor. And yet, in spite of the look of sullen indifference which was so ugly on that young face, he could not help loving him. He was a fine boy, tall, strong, and his hair was the soft, bright brown, and his eyes clear and black. A much better man than his father, who 1005 was rough and marked by the long struggle of his youth. He said: "Well, you don't have to be a sailor, perhaps you'd like to go to university and be a scholar."

"I don't know," said Tommy, unwillingly, although his heart had moved suddenly. Pleasure—he was weakening. Then he said sudden-1010 ly: "Mr. Macintosh, why do you want to send me to college?"

And Mr. Macintosh fell right into the trap. "I have no children," he said, sentimentally. "I feel for you like my own son." He stopped. Tommy was looking away towards the compound, and his intention was clear.

1015  "Very well then," said Mr. Macintosh, harshly. "If you want to be a fool."

Tommy stood there with his eyes lowered and he knew quite well he was a fool. Yet he could not have behaved in any other way.

"Don't be hasty," said Mr. Macintosh, after a pause. "Don't throw 1020 away your chances, laddie. You're nothing but a lad, yet. Take your time." And with this tone, he changed all the emphasis of the conflict, and made it simply a question of waiting. Tommy did not move, so Mr. Macintosh went on quickly: "Yes, that's right, you just think it over." He hastily slipped a pound note from his pocket and put it into 1025 the boy's hand.

"You know what I'm going to do with it?" said Tommy, laughing suddenly, and not at all pleasantly.

"Do what you like, do just as you like, it's your money," said Mr. Macintosh, turning away so as not to have to understand.

# B2. Second Reading: Delving More Deeply

Read Section II a second time and focus on the lines indicated. Use the surrounding text and your experience to give an informed answer.

1.   *And a feeling of unwillingness grew in Tommy, because of the strain of fitting these two worlds together.* (lines 667–668) What two worlds are these? Do you think it's a natural part of growing up to have to fit two worlds together?

2.   *…and when his mother said: "What's the matter with you, why are you crying?" he said angrily, "I don't know," matching her dishonesty with his own.* (lines 714–717) What was she dishonest about? What was his dishonesty? Do you think each one knew that the other one was dishonest?

3.   *And then, when there were no more tears, there came such a storm of anger and pain that he would never forget it as long as he lived.* (lines 766–768) What is the cause of this anger and pain?

4.   *It is easy to be truthful at twenty.* (lines 786–787) Why is it easier to be twenty than forty according to the author? Do you agree with the author?

5.   *It was really funny to say that Dirk was cruel, when his very existence was a cruelty.* (lines 795–796) How was Dirk's existence a cruelty? What comment does it seem the author is making about the racial situation in this country?

6.   *"Do what you like, do just as you like, it's your money," said Mr. Macintosh, turning away so as not to have to understand.* (lines 1028–1029) What truth didn't Mr. Macintosh want to face? Do you think he lacked courage?

Now write two questions of your own about Section II that you would like to discuss with your classmates.

**FOLLOW-UP**
Discuss your answers to the First and Second Reading questions in small groups. Then discuss the questions each student wrote.

1.   _____

_____

2.   _____

_____

### Bridge 2

Discuss these questions before going on to Section III.

◆   Were you surprised that Tommy rejected Mr. Macintosh's offer to go abroad? Did Tommy act out of selfishness or out of principle?

◆   In the next section, do you think Tommy and Dirk's friendship will get stronger or weaker? Why?

◆   Which character do you think will change the most?

# A3.   First Reading: Following the Story Line

Read the following questions and keep them in mind as you read Section III. Use the questions to help you predict and follow the events of the story.

1.   What does Tommy learn about Dirk's prospects for an education? About Dirk's family?

2.   What does Tommy make for Dirk?

3.   What do Tommy and Mr. Macintosh discuss when Mr. Macintosh visits him in his bedroom?

4.   How does Mr. Macintosh act differently after this visit? What does he promise Dirk?

5.   What does Mr. Macintosh realize about himself in his mood of "sullen thoughtfulness"?

6.   How does Tommy change over the school year?

7.   How do Tommy and Dirk spend their holiday time together?

#### The Antheap (*Section III*)

1030   Tommy took the money to Dirk, who received it as if it were his right, a feeling in which Tommy was now an accomplice, and they sat together in the shed. "I've got to be something," said Tommy angrily. "They're going to make me be something."

"They wouldn't have to make me be anything," said Dirk, sardon-
1035   ically. "I know what I'd be."

"What?" asked Tommy, enviously.

"An engineer."

"How do you know what you've got to do?"

"That's what I want," said Dirk, stubbornly.

1040    After a while Tommy said: "If you went to the city, there's a school for colored children."

"I wouldn't see my mother again."

"Why not?"

"There's laws, white boy, laws. Anyone who lives with and after the 1045 fashion of the natives is a native. Therefore I'm a native, and I'm not entitled to go to school with the half-castes."

"If you went to the town, you'd not be living with the natives so you'd be classed as a colored."

"But then I couldn't see my mother, because if she came to town 1050 she'd still be a native."

There was a triumphant conclusiveness in this that made Tommy think: He intends to get what he wants another way... And then: Through me... But he had accepted that justice a long time ago, and now he looked at his own arm that lay on the rough plank of the table. 1055 The outer side was burnt dark and dry with the sun, and the hair glinted on it like fine copper. It was no darker than Dirk's brown arm, and no lighter. He turned it over. Inside, the skin was smooth, dusky white, the veins running blue and strong across the wrist. He looked at Dirk, grinning, who promptly turned his own arm over, in a challeng- 1060 ing way. Tommy said, unhappily: "You can't go to school properly because the inside of your arm is brown. And that's that!" Dirk's tight and bitter mouth expanded into the grin that was also his father's, and he said: "That is so, white boy, that is so."

"Well, it's not my fault," said Tommy aggressively, closing his fin- 1065 gers and banging the fist down again and again.

"I didn't say it was your fault," said Dirk at once.

Tommy said, in that uneasy, aggressive tone: "I've never even seen your mother."

To this, Dirk merely laughed, as if to say: You have never wanted 1070 to.

Tommy said, after a pause: "Let me come and see her now."

Then Dirk said, in a tone which was uncomfortable, almost like compassion: "You don't have to."

"Yes," insisted Tommy. "Yes, now." He got up, and Dirk rose too. 1075 "She won't know what to say," warned Dirk. "She doesn't speak English." He did not really want Tommy to go to the compound; Tommy did not really want to go. Yet they went.

In silence they moved along the path between the trees, in silence skirted the edge of the pit, in silence entered the trees on the other 1080 side, and moved along the paths to the compound. It was big, spread over many acres, and the huts were in all stages of growth and decay, some new, with shining thatch, some tumble-down, with dulled and sagging thatch, some in the process of being built, the peeled wands of the roof-frames gleaming like milk in the sun.

1085    Dirk lead the way to a big square hut. Tommy could see people watching him walking with the colored boy, and turning to laugh and whisper. Dirk's face was proud and tight, and he could feel the same

look on his own face. Outside the square hut sat a little girl of about ten. She was bronze, Dirk's color. Another little girl, quite black, perhaps six years old, was squatted on a log, finger in mouth, watching them. A baby, still unsteady on its feet, came staggering out of the doorway and collapsed, chuckling, against Dirk's knees. Its skin was almost white. Then Dirk's mother came out of the hut after the baby, smiled when she saw Dirk, but went anxious and bashful when she saw Tommy. She made a little bobbing curtsey, and took the baby from Dirk, for the sake of something to hold in her awkward and shy hands.

"This is Baas Tommy," said Dirk. He sounded very embarrassed. She made another little curtsey and stood smiling.

She was a large woman, round and smooth all over, but her legs were slender, and her arms, wound around the child, thin and knotted. Her round face had a bashful curiosity, and her eyes moved quickly from Dirk to Tommy and back, while she smiled and smiled, biting her lips with strong teeth, and smiled again.

Tommy said "Good morning," and she laughed and said "Good morning."

Then Dirk said: "Enough now, let's go." He sounded very angry. Tommy said: "Goodbye." Dirk's mother said: "Goodbye," and made her little bobbing curtsey, and she moved her child from one arm to another and bit her lip anxiously over her gleaming smile.

Tommy and Dirk went away from the square mud hut where the variously-colored children stood staring after them.

"There now," said Dirk, angrily. "You've seen my mother."

"I'm sorry," said Tommy uncomfortably, feeling as if the responsibility for the whole thing rested on him. But Dirk laughed suddenly and said: "Oh, all right, all right, white boy, it's not your fault."

All the same, he seemed pleased that Tommy was upset.

Later, with an affectation of indifference, Tommy asked, thinking of those new children: "Does Mr. Macintosh come to your mother again now?"

And Dirk answered "Yes," just one word.

In the shed Dirk studied from a geography book, while Tommy sat idle and thought bitterly that they wanted him to be a sailor. Then his idle hands protested, and he took a knife and began slashing at the edge of the table. When the gashes showed a whiteness from the core of the wood, he took a stick lying on the floor and whittled at it, and when it snapped from thinness he went out to the trees, picked up a lump of old wood from the ground, and brought it back to the shed. He worked on it with his knife, not knowing what it was he made, until a curve under his knife reminded him of Dirk's sister squatting at the hut door, and then he directed his knife with a purpose. For several days he fought with the lump of wood, while Dirk studied. Then he brought a tin of boot polish from the house, and worked the bright brown wax into the creamy white wood, and soon there was a bronze-colored figure of the little girl, staring with big, curious eyes while she squatted on spindly legs.

Tommy put it in front of Dirk, who turned it around, grinning a little. "It's like her," he said at last. "You can have it if you like," said Tommy. Dirk's teeth flashed, he hesitated, and then reached into his
1140 pocket and took out a bundle of dirty cloth. He undid it, and Tommy saw the little clay figure he had made of Dirk years ago. It was crumbling, almost worn to a lump of mud, but in it was still the vigorous challenge of Dirk's body. Tommy's mind signaled recognition—for he had forgotten he had ever made it—and he picked it up. "You kept
1145 it?" he asked shyly, and Dirk smiled. They looked at each other, smiling. It was a moment of warm, close feeling, and yet in it was the pain that neither of them understood, and also the cruelty and challenge that made them fight. They lowered their eyes unhappily. "I'll do your mother," said Tommy, getting up and running away into the trees, in
1150 order to escape from the challenging closeness. He searched until he found a thorn tree, which is so hard it turns the edge of an axe and then he took an axe and worked at the felling of the tree until the sun went down. A big stone near him was kept wet to sharpen the axe, and next day he worked on until the tree fell. He sharpened the worn axe
1155 again, and cut a length of tree about two feet, and split off the tough bark, and brought it back to the shed. Dirk had fitted a shelf against the logs of the wall at the back. On it he had set the tiny, crumbling figure of himself, and the new bronze shape of his little sister. There was a space left for the new statue. Tommy said, shyly: "I'll do it as
1160 quickly as I can so that it will be done before the term starts." Then, lowering his eyes, which suffered under this new contract of shared feeling, he examined the piece of wood. It was not pale and gleaming like almonds, as was the softer wood. It was a gingery brown, a close-fibred, knotted wood, and down its center, as he knew, was a hard
1165 black spine. He turned it between his hands and thought that this was more difficult than anything he had ever done. For the first time he studied a piece of wood before starting on it, with a desired shape in his mind, trying to see how what he wanted would grow out of the dense mass of material he held.
1170 Then he tried his knife on it and it broke. He asked Dirk for his knife. It was a long piece of metal, taken from a pile of scrap mining machinery, sharpened on stone until it was razor-fine. The handle was cloth wrapped tight around.
With this new and unwieldy tool Tommy fought with the wood for
1175 many days. When the holidays were ending, the shape was there, but the face was blank. Dirk's mother was full-bodied, with soft, heavy flesh and full, naked shoulders above a tight, sideways draped cloth. The slender legs were planted firm on naked feet, and the thin arms, knotted with work, were lifted to the weight of a child who, a small,
1180 helpless creature swaddled in cloth, looked out with large, curious eyes. but the mother's face was not yet there.
"I'll finish it next holidays," said Tommy, and Dirk set it carefully beside the other figures on the shelf. With his back turned he asked cautiously: "Perhaps you won't be here next holidays?"
1185 "Yes I will," said Tommy, after a pause. "Yes I will."
It was a promise, and they gave each other that small, warm,

unwilling smile, and turned away, Dirk back to the compound and Tommy to the house, where his trunk was packed for school.

1190     That night Mr. Macintosh came over to the Clarke's house and spoke with the parents in the front room. Tommy, who was asleep, woke to find Mr. Macintosh beside him. He sat on the foot of the bed and said: "I want to talk to you, laddie." Tommy turned the wick of the oil-lamp, and now he could see in the shadowy light that Mr. Macintosh had a look of uneasiness about him. He was sitting with his

1195 strong old body balanced behind the big stomach, hands laid on his knees, and his gray Scots eyes were watchful.

    "I want you to think about what I said," said Mr. Macintosh, in a quick, bluff good-humor. "Your mother says in two years' time you will have matriculated, you're doing fine at school. And after that you

1200 can go to college."

    Tommy lay on his elbow, and in the silence the drums came tapping from the compound, and he said: "But Mr. Macintosh, I'm not the only one who's good at his books."

    Mr. Macintosh stirred, but said bluffly: "Well, but I'm talking

1205 about you."

    Tommy was silent, because as usual these opponents were so much stronger than was reasonable, simply because of their ability to make words mean something else. And then, his heart painfully beating, he said: "Why don't you send Dirk to college? You're so rich, and Dirk

1210 knows everything I know. He's better than me at figures. He's a whole book ahead of me, and he can do sums I can't."

    Mr. Macintosh crossed his legs impatiently, uncrossed them, and said: "Now why should I send Dirk to college?" For now Tommy would have to put into precise words what he meant, and this Mr.

1215 Macintosh was quite sure he would not do. But to make certain, he lowered his voice and said: "Think of your mother, laddie, she's worrying about you, and you don't want to make her worried, do you?"

    Tommy looked towards the door, under it came a thick yellow streak of light: in that room his mother and his father were waiting in

1220 silence for Mr. Macintosh to emerge with news of Tommy's sure and wonderful future.

    "You know why Dirk should go to college," said Tommy in despair, shifting his body unhappily under the sheets, and Mr. Macintosh chose not to hear it. He got up, and said quickly: "You just

1225 think it over, laddie. There's no hurry, but by next holidays I want to know." And he went out of the room. As he opened the door, a brightly-lit, painful scene was presented to Tommy: his father and mother sat, smiling in embarrassed entreaty at Mr. Macintosh. The door shut, and Tommy turned down the light, and there was darkness.

1230     He went to school next day. Mrs. Clarke, turning out Mr. Macintosh's house as usual, said unhappily: "I think you'll find everything in its proper place," and slipped away, as if she were ashamed.

    As for Mr. Macintosh, he was in a mood which made others, besides Annie Clarke, speak to him carefully. His cookboy, who had

1235 worked for him twelve years, gave notice that month. He had been
knocked down twice by that powerful, hairy fist, and he was not a
slave, after all, to remain bound to a bad-tempered master. And when
a load of rock slipped and crushed the skulls of two workers, and the
police came out for an investigation, Mr. Macintosh met them irrita-
1240 bly, and told them to mind their own business. For the first time in
that mine's history of scandalous recklessness, after many such acci-
dents, Mr. Macintosh heard the indignant words from the police officer: "You speak as if you were above the law, Mr. Macintosh. If this
happens again, you'll see…"
1245 Worst of all, he ordered Dirk to go back to work in the pit, and
Dirk refused.

"You can't make me," said Dirk.

"Who's the boss on this mine?" shouted Mr. Macintosh.

"There's no law to make children work," said the thirteen-year-old,
1250 who stood as tall as his father, a straight, lithe youth against the bulky
strength of the old man.

The word law whipped the anger in Mr. Macintosh to the point
where he could feel his eyes go dark, and the blood pounding in that
hot darkness in his head. In fact, it was the power of this anger that
1255 sobered him, for he had been very young when he had learned to fear
his own temper. And above all, he was a shrewd man. He waited until
his sight was clear again, and then asked, reasonably: "Why do you
want to loaf around the compound, why not work and earn money?"

Dirk said: "I can read and write, and I know my figures better than
1260 Tommy—Baas Tommy," he added in a way which made the anger rise
again in Mr. Macintosh, so that he had to make a fresh effort to
subdue it.

But Tommy was a point of weakness in Mr. Macintosh, and it was
then that he spoke the words which afterwards made him wonder if
1265 he'd gone suddenly crazy. For he said: "Very well, when you're sixteen
you can come and do my books and write the letters for the mine."

Dirk said: "All right," as if this were no more than his due, and
walked off, leaving Mr. Macintosh impotently furious with himself.
For how could anyone but himself see the books? Such a person would
1270 be his master. It was impossible, he had no intention of ever letting
Dirk, or anyone else, see them. Yet he had made the promise. And so
he would have to find another way of using Dirk, or—and the words
came involuntarily—getting rid of him.

From a mood of settled bad temper, Mr. Macintosh dropped into
1275 one of sullen thoughtfulness, which was entirely foreign to his character. Being shrewd is quite different from the processes of thinking.
Shrewdness, particularly the money-making shrewdness, is a kind of
instinct. While Mr. Macintosh had always known what he wanted to
do, and how to do it, that did not mean he had known why he wanted
1280 so much money, or why he had chosen these ways of making it. Mr.
Macintosh felt like a cat whose nose has been rubbed into its own dirt,
and for many nights he sat in the hot little house, that vibrated contin-

ually from the noise of the mine-stamps, most uncomfortably considering himself and his life. He reminded himself, for instance, that he was sixty, and presumably had not more than ten or fifteen years to live. It was not a thought that an unreflective man enjoys, particularly when he had never considered his age at all. He was so healthy, strong, tough. But he was sixty nevertheless, and what would be his monument? An enormous pit in the earth, and a million pounds' worth of property. Then how should he spend ten or fifteen years? Exactly as he had the preceding sixty, for he hated being away from this place, and this gave him a caged and useless sensation, for it had never entered his head before that he was not as free as he felt himself to be.

Well, then—and this thought gnawed most closely to Mr. Macintosh's pain—why had he not married? For he considered himself a marrying sort of man, and had always intended to find himself the right sort of woman and marry her. Yet he was already sixty. The truth was that Mr. Macintosh had no idea at all why he had not married and got himself sons: and in these slow, uncomfortable ponderings the thought of Dirk's mother intruded itself only to be hastily thrust away. Mr. Macintosh, the sensualist, had a taste for dark-skinned women; and now it was certainly too late to admit as a permanent feature of his character something he had always considered as a sort of temporary whim, or makeshift, like someone who learns to enjoy an inferior brand of tobacco when better brands are not available.

He thought of Tommy, of whom he had been used to say: "I've taken a fancy to the laddie." Now it was not so much a fancy as a deep, grieving love. And Tommy was the son of his employee, and looked at him with contempt, and he, Mr. Macintosh, reacted with angry shame as if he were guilty of something. Of what? It was ridiculous.

The whole situation was ridiculous, and so Mr. Macintosh allowed himself to slide back into his usual frame of mind. Tommy's only a boy, he thought, and he'll see reason in a year or so. And as for Dirk, I'll find him some kind of a job when the time comes…

At the end of the term, when Tommy came home, Mr. Macintosh asked, as usual, to see the school report, which usually filled him with pride. Instead of heading the class with approbation from the teachers and high marks in all subjects, Tommy was near the bottom, with such remarks as Slovenly, and Lazy, and Bad-mannered. The only subject in which he got any marks at all was that called Art, which Mr. Macintosh did not take into account.

When Tommy was asked by his parents why he was not working, he replied, impatiently: "I don't know," which was quite true; and at once escaped to the anthill. Dirk was there, waiting for the books Tommy always brought for him. Tommy reached at once up to the shelf where stood the figure of Dirk's mother, lifted it down and examined the unworked space which would be the face. "I know how to do it," he said to Dirk, and took out some knives and chisels he had brought from the city.

That was how he spent the three weeks of that holiday, and when he met Mr. Macintosh he was sullen and uncomfortable. "You'll have

to be working a bit better" he said, before Tommy went back, to which he received no answer but an unwilling smile.

During that term Tommy distinguished himself in two ways besides being steadily at the bottom of the class he had so recently led. He made a fiery speech in the debating society on the iniquity of the color bar, which rather pleased his teachers, since it is a well-known fact that the young must pass through these phases of rebellion before settling down to conformity. In fact, the greater the verbal rebellion, the more settled was the conformity likely to be. In secret Tommy got books from the city library such as are not usually read by boys of his age, on the history of Africa, and on comparative anthropology, and passed from there to the history of the moment—he ordered papers from the Government Stationery Office, the laws of the country. Most particularly those affecting the relations between black and white and colored. These he bought in order to take back to Dirk. But in addition to all this ferment, there was that subject Art, which in this school meant a drawing lesson twice a week, copying busts of Julius Caesar, or it might be Nelson, or shading in fronds of fern or leaves, or copying a large vase or a table standing diagonally to the class, thus learning what he was told were the laws of Perspective. There was no modeling, nothing approaching sculpture in this school, but this was the nearest thing to it, and that mysterious prohibition which forbade him to distinguish himself in Geometry or English, was silent when it came to using the pencil.

At the end of the term his Report was very bad, but it admitted that he had An Interest in Current Events, and a Talent for Art.

And now this word Art, coming at the end of two successive terms, disturbed his parents and forced itself on Mr. Macintosh. He said to Annie Clarke: "It's a nice thing to make pictures, but the lad won't earn a living by it." And Mrs. Clarke said reproachfully to Tommy: "It's all very well, Tommy, but you aren't going to earn a living drawing pictures."

"I didn't say I wanted to earn a living with it," shouted Tommy, miserably. "Why have I got to be something, you're always wanting me to be something."

That holiday Dirk spent studying the Acts of Parliament and the Reports of Commissions and Sub-Committees which Tommy had brought him, while Tommy attempted something new. There was a square piece of soft white wood which Dirk had pilfered from the mine, thinking Tommy might use it. And Tommy set it against the walls of the shed, and knelt before it and attempted a frieze or engraving—he did not know the words for what he was doing. He cut out a great pit, surrounded by mounds of earth and rock, with the peaks of great mountains beyond, and at the edge of the pit stood a big man carrying a stick, and over the edge of the pit wound a file of black figures, tumbling into the gulf. From the pit came flames and smoke. Tommy took green ooze from leaves and mixed clay to color the mountains and edges of the pit, and he made the little figures black with charcoal, and he made the flames writhing up out of the pit red with the paint used for parts of the mining machinery.

"If you leave it here, the ants'll eat it," said Dirk, looking with grim pleasure at the crude but effective picture.

To which Tommy shrugged. For while he was always solemnly
1385   intent on a piece of work in hand, afraid of anything that might mar it, or even distract his attention from it, once it was finished he cared for it not at all.

It was Dirk who had painted the shelf which held the other figures with a mixture that discouraged ants, and it was now Dirk
1390   who set the piece of square wood on a sheet of tin smeared with the same mixture, and balanced it in a way so it should not touch any part of the walls of the shed, where the ants might climb up.

And so Tommy went back to school, still in that mood of obstinate
1395   disaffection, to make more copies of Julius Caesar and vases of flowers, and Dirk remained with his books and his Acts of Parliament. They would be fourteen before they met again, and both knew that crises and decisions faced them. Yet they said no more than the usual: Well, so long, before they parted. Nor did they ever write to each
1400   other, although this term Tommy had a commission to send certain books and other Acts of Parliament for a purpose which he entirely approved.

Dirk had built himself a new hut in the compound, where he lived alone, in the compound but not of it, affectionate to his mother, but
1405   apart from her. And to this hut at night came certain of the workers who forgot their dislike of the half-caste, that cuckoo in their nest, in their common interest in what he told them of the Acts and Reports. What he told them was what he had learnt himself in the proud loneliness of his isolation. "Education," he said, "education, that's the
1410   key"—and Tommy agreed with him, although he had, or so one might suppose from the way he was behaving, abandoned all idea of getting an education for himself. All that term parcels came to "Dirk, c/o Mr. Macintosh," and Mr. Macintosh delivered them to Dirk without any questions.

1415   In the dim and smokey hut every night, half a dozen of the workers labored with stubs of pencil and the exercise books sent by Tommy, to learn to write and do sums and understand the Laws.

One night Mr. Macintosh came rather late out of that other hut, and saw the red light from a fire moving softly on the rough ground
1420   outside the door of Dirk's hut. All the others were dark. He moved cautiously among them until he stood in the shadows outside the door, and looked in. Dirk was squatting on the floor, surrounded by half a dozen men, looking at a newspaper.

Mr. Macintosh walked thoughtfully home in the starlight. Dirk,
1425   had he known what Mr. Macintosh was thinking, would have been very angry, for all his flaming rebellion, his words of resentment were directed against Mr. Macintosh and his tyranny. Yet for the first time Mr. Macintosh was thinking of Dirk with a certain rough, amused pride. Perhaps it was because he was a Scot, after all, and in every one

1430   of his nation is an instinctive respect for learning and people with the determination to "get on." A chip off the old block, thought Mr. Macintosh, remembering how he, as a boy, had labored to get a bit of education. And if the chip was the wrong color—well, he would do something for Dirk. Something, he would decide when the time came.

1435   As for the others who were with Dirk, there was nothing easier than to sack a worker and engage another. Mr. Macintosh went to his bed, dressed as usual in vest and pajama trousers, unwashed and thrifty in candlelight.

  In the morning he gave orders to one of the overseers that Dirk 1440 should be summoned. His heart was already soft with thinking about the generous scene which would shortly take place. He was going to suggest that Dirk should teach all the overseers to read and write—on a salary from himself, of course—in order that these same overseers should be more useful in the work. They might learn to mark pay-1445 sheets, for instance.

  The overseer said that Baas Dirk spent his days studying in Baas Tommy's hut—with the suggestion in his manner that Baas Dirk could not be disturbed while so occupied, and that this was on Tommy's account.

1450   The man, closely studying the effect of his words, saw how Mr. Macintosh's big, veiny face swelled, and he stepped back a pace. He was not one of Dirk's admirers.

  Mr. Macintosh, after some moments of heavy breathing, allowed his shrewdness to direct his anger. He dismissed the man, and 1455 turned away.

  During that morning he left his great pit and walked off into the bush in the direction of the towering blue peak. He had heard vaguely that Tommy had some kind of a hut, but imagined it as a child's thing. He was still very angry because of that calculated "Baas Dirk." He 1460 walked for a while along a smooth path through the trees, and came to a clearing. On the other side was an anthill, and on the anthill a well-built hut, draped with Christmas fern around the open front, like curtains. In the opening sat Dirk. He wore a clean white shirt, and long smooth trousers. His head, oiled and brushed close, was bent over 1465 books. The hand that turned the pages of the books had a brass ring on the little finger. He was the very image of an aspiring clerk: that form of humanity which Mr. Macintosh despised most.

  Mr. Macintosh remained on the edge of the clearing for some time, vaguely waiting for something to happen, so that he might fling him-1470 self, armored and directed by his contemptuous anger, into a crisis which would destroy Dirk forever. But nothing did happen. Dirk continued to turn the pages of the book, so Mr. Macintosh went back to his house, where he ate boiled beef and carrots for his dinner.

  Afterwards he went to a certain drawer in his bedroom, and from it 1475 took an object carelessly wrapped in cloth which, exposed, showed itself as that figure of Dirk the boy Tommy had made and sold for five

pounds. And Mr. Macintosh turned and handled and pored over that crude wooden image of Dirk in a passion of curiosity, just as if the boy did not live on the same square mile of soil with him, fully available to his scrutiny at most hours of the day.

1480

If one imagines a Judgment Day with the graves giving up their dead impartially, black, white, bronze, and yellow, to a happy reunion, one of the pleasures of that reunion might well be that people who have lived on the same acre or street all their lives will look at each other with incredulous recognition. "So that is what you were like," might be the gathering murmur around God's heaven. For the glass wall between color and color is not only a barrier against touch, but has become thick and distorted, so that black men, white men, see each other through it, but see—what? Mr. Macintosh examined the image of Dirk as if searching for some final revelation, but the thought that came persistently to his mind was that the statue might be of himself as a lad of twelve. So after a few moments he rolled it again in the cloth and tossed it back into the corner of a drawer, out of sight, and with it the unwelcome and tormenting knowledge.

1485

1490

1495

Late that afternoon he left his house again and made his way towards the hut on the antheap. It was empty, and he walked through the knee-high grass and bushes till he could climb up the hard, slippery walls of the antheap and so into the hut.

# B3. Second Reading: Delving More Deeply

Read Section III a second time and focus on the lines indicated. Use the surrounding text and your experience to give an informed answer to the questions below.

1. *"I've got to be something," said Tommy angrily. "They're going to make me be something."* (lines 1032–1033) What is Tommy talking about? Why do you think he feels angry? What is Dirk's reaction to Tommy's "problem"?

2. *But he had accepted that justice a long time ago…* (line 1053) What "justice" does Tommy accept? Why does he accept it?

3. *"Let me come and see her now."* (line 1071) Why do you think Tommy suddenly decided that he wanted to see Dirk's mother?

4. *He sounded very embarrassed.* (line 1098) Why do you think Dirk was embarrassed while introducing Tommy and his mother?

5. *"I'm sorry," said Tommy uncomfortably, feeling as if the responsibility for the whole thing rested on him… "Oh, all right, all right, white boy, it's not your fault."* (lines 1114–1116) What isn't Tommy's fault? Why should Tommy feel "responsibility"?

6.   *It was a moment of warm, close feeling, and yet in it was the pain that neither of them understood, and also the cruelty and challenge that made them fight.* (lines 1146–1148) How could looking at the clay figure cause both warm feelings and pain and cruelty? What did the figure represent to the boys?

7.   *"You know why Dirk should go to college," said Tommy in despair.…* (lines 1222–1223) *As he opened the door, a brightly-lit, painful scene was presented to Tommy: his father and mother sat, smiling in embarrassed entreaty at Mr. Macintosh.* (lines 1226–1228) How does Mr. Macintosh react to Tommy's statement? Why were his parents embarrassed?

8.   *The word law whipped the anger in Mr. Macintosh to the point where he could feel his eyes go dark, and the blood pounding in that hot darkness in his head.* (lines 1252–1254) Why do you think the word "law" had such an effect on Mr. Macintosh?

9.   *And so he would have to find another way of using Dirk, or— and the words came involuntarily—getting rid of him.* (lines 1271–1273) Why would Mr. Macintosh need **another** way of using Dirk? Why had he agreed to use Dirk if he objected to the idea so strongly? How do you think he could get rid of Dirk?

10.  *And Tommy was the son of his employee, and looked at him with contempt, and he, Mr. Macintosh, reacted with angry shame as if he were guilty of something.* (lines 1308–1310) Why do you think Mr. Macintosh "reacted with angry shame" to Tommy's "contempt"? Why is it so important to Mr. Macintosh what an employee's young son thinks of him?

11.  *A chip off the old block, thought Mr. Macintosh, remembering how he, as a boy, had labored to get a bit of education.* (lines 1431–1433) In what way is Dirk "a chip off the old block" (i.e., a son just like his father)? What change does this realization signal in Mr. Macintosh? Who else noticed that Dirk was like his father? In what ways?

12.  *The overseer said that Baas Dirk spent his days studying in Baas Tommy's hut—with the suggestion in his manner that Baas Dirk could not be disturbed while so occupied…* (lines 1446–1448) Why did this report anger Mr. Macintosh? When the black overseer refers to Dirk as "Baas," is he expressing respect? Resentment? Why?

13.  What is the **unwelcome and tormenting knowledge** that Mr. Macintosh has? *(line 1494)* Do you feel any sympathy for Mr. Macintosh?

Now write two questions of your own about Section III that you would like to discuss with your classmates.

**FOLLOW-UP**
Discuss your answers to the First and Second Reading questions in small groups. Then discuss the questions each student wrote.

1. _____

_____

2. _____

_____

## Bridge 3

Discuss these questions before moving from the previous section of the story to the next one.

◆ Do you think Mr. Macintosh is really changing? Can people change? Be changed by others?

◆ At this point, which of the three main characters do you like the most?

◆ How do you suppose this story will end? Happily? Unhappily? Why?

# A4. First Reading: Following the Story Line

Read the following questions and keep them in mind as you read Section IV. Use the questions to help you predict and follow the events of the story.

1. How does Dirk spend his evenings? Does this bother Mr. Macintosh?

2. What is Mr. Macintosh trying to destroy when he burns down the hut on the antheap? Do Dirk and Tommy understand this?

3. How does Mr. Macintosh feel about the new figure of Dirk that Tommy is making?

4. What is the purpose of Mr. Macintosh's trip to town? Does Mr. Tomlinson like Mr. Macintosh?

5. Does Tommy see the opportunity to study art in college as a solution to his problems?

**6.** What displeases Dirk about the new figure Tommy is carving?

**7.** How is the dilemma among Tommy, Dirk, and Mr. Macintosh solved? Who wins in this situation? Who loses?

### The Antheap (*Section IV*)

First he looked at the books in the case. The longer he looked, the
1500 faster faded that picture of Dirk as an oiled and mincing clerk, which
he had been clinging to ever since he threw the other image into the
back of a drawer. Respect for Dirk was reborn. Complicated mathe-
matics, much more advanced than he had ever done. Geography.
History. "The Development of the Slave Trade in the Eighteenth
1505 Century." "The Growth of Parliamentary Institutions in Great
Britain." This title made Mr. Macintosh smile—the freebooting buc-
caneer examining a coastguard's notice perhaps. Mr. Macintosh lifted
down one book after another and smiled. Then, beside these books, he
saw a pile of slight, blue pamphlets, and he examined them. "The
1510 Natives Employment Act." "The Natives Juvenile Employment Act."
"The Native Passes Act." and Mr. Macintosh flipped over the leaves
and laughed, and had Dirk heard that laugh it would have been worse
to him than any whip.

For as he patiently explained these laws and others like them to his
1515 bitter allies in the hut at night, it seemed to him that every word he
spoke was like a stone thrown at Mr. Macintosh, his father. Yet Mr.
Macintosh laughed, since he despised these laws, although in a different way, as much as Dirk did. When Mr. Macintosh, on his rare trips
to the city, happened to drive past the House of Parliament, he turned
1520 on it a tolerant and appreciative gaze. "Well, why not?" he seemed to
be saying. "It's an occupation, like any other."

So to Dirk's desperate act of retaliation he responded with a smile,
and tossed back the books and pamphlets on the shelf. And then he
turned to look at the other things in the shed, and for the first time he
1525 saw the high shelf where the statuettes were arranged. He looked, and
felt his face swelling with that fatal rage. There was Dirk's mother,
peering at him in bashful sensuality from over the baby's head, and
there the little girl, his daughter, squatting on spindly legs and staring.
And there, on the edge of the shelf, a small, worn shape of clay which
1530 still held the vigorous strength of Dirk. Mr. Macintosh, breathing
heavily, holding down his anger, stepped back to gain a clearer view of
these figures, and his heel slipped on a slanting piece of wood. He
turned to look, and there was the picture Tommy had carved and colored of his mine. Mr. Macintosh saw the great pit, the black little fig-
1535 ures tumbling and sprawling over into the flames, and he saw himself,
stick in hand, astride on his two legs at the edge of the pit, his hat on
the back of his head.

And now Mr. Macintosh was so disturbed and angry that he was
driven out of the hut and into the clearing, where he walked back and
1540 forth through the grass, looking at the hut while his anger growled and

moved inside him. After some time he came close to the hut again and peered in. Yes, there was Dirk's mother, peering bashfully from her shelf, as if to say: Yes, it's me, remember? And there on the floor was the square tinted piece of wood which said what Tommy thought of him and his life. Mr. Macintosh took a box of matches from his pocket. He lit a match. He understood he was standing in the hut with a lit match in his hand to no purpose. He dropped the match and ground it out with his foot. Then he put a pipe in his mouth, filled it and lit it, gazing all the time at the shelf and at the square carving. The second match fell to the floor and lay spurting a small white flame. He ground his heel hard on it. Anger heaved up in him beyond all sanity, and he lit another match, pushed it into the thatch of the hut, and walked out of it and so into the clearing and away into the bush. Without looking behind him he walked back to his house where his supper of boiled beef and carrots was waiting for him. He was amazed, angry, resentful. Finally he felt aggrieved, and wanted to explain to someone what a monstrous injustice was Tommy's view of him. But there was no one to explain it to; and he slowly quietened to a steady dulled sadness, and for some days remained so, until time restored him to normal.

From this condition he looked back at his behavior and did not like it. Not that he regretted burning the hut, it seemed to him unimportant. He was angry at himself for allowing his anger to dictate his actions. Also he knew that such an act brings its own results.

So he waited, and thought mainly of the cruelty of fate in denying him a son who might carry on his work—for he certainly thought of his work as something to be continued. He thought sadly of Tommy, who denied him. And so, his affection for Tommy was sprung again by thinking of him, and he waited, thinking of reproachful things to say to him.

When Tommy returned from school he went straight to the clearing and found a mound of ash on the antheap that was already sifted and swept by the wind. He found Dirk, sitting on a tree-trunk in the bush waiting for him.

"What happened?" asked Tommy. And then, at once: "Did you save your books?"

Dirk said: "He burnt it."

"How do you know?"

"I know."

Tommy nodded. "All your books have gone," he said, very grieved, and as guilty as if he had burnt them himself.

"Your carvings and your statues are burnt too."

But at this Tommy shrugged, since he could not care about his things once they were finished. "Shall we build the hut again now?" he suggested.

"My books are burnt," said Dirk, in a low voice, and Tommy, looking at him, saw how his hands were clenched. He instinctively moved a little aside to give his friend's anger space.

"When I grow up I'll clear you all out, all of you, there won't be one white man left in Africa, not one."

1590　Tommy's face had a small, half-scared smile on it. The hatred Dirk was directing against him was so strong he nearly went away. He sat beside Dirk on the tree-trunk and said: "I'll try and get you more books."

"And then he'll burn them again."

1595　"But you've already got what was in them inside your head," said Tommy, consolingly. Dirk said nothing, but sat like a clenched fist, and so they remained on the tree-trunk in the quiet bush while the doves cooed and the mine-stamps thudded, all that hot morning. When they had to separate at midday to return to their different worlds, it was with deep sadness, knowing that their childhood was

1600　finished, and their playing, and something new was ahead.

And at the meal Tommy's mother and father had his school report on the table, and they were reproachful. Tommy was at the foot of his class, and he would not matriculate that year. Or any year if he went on like this.

1605　"You used to be such a clever boy," mourned his mother, "and now what's happened to you?"

Tommy, sitting silent at the table, moved his shoulders in a hunched, irritable way, as if to say: Leave me alone. Nor did he feel himself to be stupid and lazy, as the report said he was.

1610　In his room were drawing blocks and pencils and hammers and chisels. He had never said to himself he had exchanged one purpose for another, for he had no purpose. How could he, when he had never been offered a future he could accept? Now, at this time, in his fif-teenth year, with his reproachful parents deepening their reproach,

1615　and the knowledge that Mr. Macintosh would soon see that report, all he felt was a locked stubbornness, and a deep strength.

In the afternoon he went back to the clearing, and he took his chis-els with him. On the old, soft, rotted tree-trunk that he sat on that morning, he sat again, waiting for Dirk. But Dirk did not come.

1620　Putting himself in his friend's place he understood that Dirk could not endure to be with a white-skinned person—a white face, even that of his oldest friend, was too much the enemy. But he waited, sitting on the tree-trunk all through the afternoon, with his chisels and hammers in a little box at his feet in the grass, and he fingered the soft, warm

1625　wood he sat on, letting the shape and texture of it come into the knowledge of his fingers.

Next day, there was still no Dirk.

Tommy began walking around the fallen tree, studying it. It was very thick, and its roots twisted and slanted into the air to the height

1630　of his shoulder. He began to carve the root. It would be Dirk again.

That night Mr. Macintosh came to the Clarkes' house and read the report. He went back to his own, and sat wondering why Tommy was set so bitterly against him. The next day he went to the Clarkes' house again to find Tommy, but the boy was not there.

1635　He therefore walked through the thick bush to the antheap, and found Tommy kneeling in the grass working on the tree root.

Tommy said: "Good morning," and went on working, and Mr. Macintosh sat on the trunk and watched.

"What are you making?" asked Mr. Macintosh.

1640 "Dirk," said Tommy, and Mr. Macintosh went purple and almost sprang up and away from the tree-trunk. But Tommy was not looking at him. So Mr. Macintosh remained, in silence. And then the useless vigor of Tommy's concentration on that rotting bit of root goaded him, and his mind moved naturally to a new decision.

1645 "Would you like to be an artist?" he suggested.

Tommy allowed his chisel to rest, and looked at Mr. Macintosh as if this were a fresh trap. He shrugged, and with the appearance of anger, went on with his work.

"If you've a real gift, you can earn money by that sort of thing. I
1650 had a cousin back in Scotland who did it. He made souvenirs, you know, for travelers." He spoke in a soothing and jolly way.

Tommy let the souvenirs slide by him, as another of these impositions on his independence. He said: "Why did you burn Dirk's books?"

1655 But Mr. Macintosh laughed in relief. "Why should I burn his books?" It really seemed ridiculous to him, his rage had been against Tommy's work, not Dirk's.

"I know you did," said Tommy. "I know it. And Dirk does too."

Mr. Macintosh lit his pipe in good humor. For now things seemed
1660 much easier. Tommy did not know why he had set fire to the hut, and that was the main thing. He puffed smoke for a few moments and said: "Why should you think I don't want Dirk to study? It's a good thing, a bit of education."

Tommy stared disbelievingly at him.

1665 "I asked Dirk to use his education, I asked him to teach some of the others. But he wouldn't have any of it. Is that my fault?"

Now Tommy's face was completely incredulous. Then he went scarlet, which Mr. Macintosh did not understand. Why should the boy be looking so foolish? But Tommy was thinking: We were on the
1670 wrong track… And then he imagined what his offer must have done to Dirk's angry, rebellious pride, and he suddenly understood. His face still crimson, he laughed. It was a bitter, ironical laugh, and Mr. Macintosh was upset—it was not a boy's laugh at all.

Tommy's face slowly faded from crimson, and he went back to
1675 work with his chisel. He said, after a pause: "Why don't you send Dirk to college instead of me? He's much more clever than me. I'm not clever, look at my report."

"Well, laddie…" began Mr. Macintosh reproachfully—he had been going to say: "Are you being lazy at school simply to force my hand
1680 over Dirk?" He wondered at his own impulse to say it; and slid off into the familiar obliqueness which Tommy ignored: "But you know how things are, or you ought to by now. You talk as if you didn't understand."

But Tommy was kneeling with his back to Mr. Macintosh, working
1685 at the root, so Mr. Macintosh continued to smoke. Next day he returned and sat on the tree-trunk and watched. Tommy looked at him as if he considered his presence an unwelcome gift, but he did not say anything.

Slowly, the big fanged root which rose from the trunk was taking Dirk's shape. Mr. Macintosh watched with uneasy loathing. He did not like it, but he could not stop watching. Once he said: "But if there's a veld fire, it'll get burnt. And the ants'll eat it in any case." Tommy shrugged. It was the making of it that mattered, now what happened to it afterwards, and this attitude was so foreign to Mr. Macintosh's accumulating nature that it seemed to him that Tommy was touched in the head. He said: "Why don't you work on something that'll last? Or even if you studied like Dirk it would be better."

Tommy said: "I like doing it."

"But look, the ants are already at the trunk—by the time you get back from your school next time there'll be nothing left of it."

"Or someone might set fire to it," suggested Tommy. He looked steadily at Mr. Macintosh's reddening face with triumph. Mr. Macintosh found the words too near the truth. For certainly, as the days passed, he was looking at the new work with hatred and fear and dislike. It was nearly finished. Even if nothing more was done to it, it could stand as it was, complete.

Dirk's long, powerful body came writhing out of the wood like something struggling free. The head was clenched back, in the agony of the birth, eyes narrowed and desperate, the mouth—Mr. Macintosh's mouth—tightened in obstinate purpose. The shoulders were free, but the hands were held; they could not pull themselves out of the dense wood, they were imprisoned. His body was free to the knees, but below them the human limbs were uncreated, the natural shapes of the wood swelled to the perfect muscled knees.

Mr. Macintosh did not like it. He did not know what art was, but he knew he did not like this at all, it disturbed him deeply, so that when he looked at it he wanted to take an axe and cut it to pieces. Or burn it, perhaps…

As for Tommy, the uneasiness of this elderly man who watched him all day was a deep triumph. Slowly, and for the first time, he saw that perhaps this was not a sort of game that he played, it might be something else. A weapon—he watched Mr. Macintosh's reluctant face, and a new respect for himself and what he was doing grew in him.

At night, Mr. Macintosh sat in his candlelit room and he thought, or rather *felt*, his way to a decision.

There was no denying the power of Tommy's gift. Therefore, it was a question of finding the way to turn it into money. He knew nothing about such matters, however, and it was Tommy himself who directed him, for towards the end of the holidays he said: "When you're so rich you can do anything. You could send Dirk to college and not even notice it."

Mr. Macintosh, in the reasonable and persuasive voice he now always used, said, "But you know these colored people have nowhere to go."

Tommy said: "You could send him to the Cape. There are colored people in the university there. Or Johannesburg." And he insisted

against Mr. Macintosh's silence: "You're so rich you can do anything you like."

But Mr. Macintosh, like most rich people, thought not of money as things to buy, things to do, but rather how it was tied up in buildings and land.

"It would cost thousands," he said. "Thousands for a colored boy."

But Tommy's scornful look silenced him, and he said hastily: "I'll think about it." But he was thinking not of Dirk, but of Tommy. Sitting alone in his room he told himself it was simply a question of paying for knowledge.

So next morning he made his preparations for a trip to town. He shaved, and over his cotton singlet he put a striped jacket, which half concealed his long, stained khaki trousers. This was as far as he ever went in concessions to the city life he despised. He got into his big American car and set off.

In the city he took the simplest route to knowledge.

He went to the Education Department, and said he wanted to see the Minister of Education. "I'm Macintosh," he said, with perfect confidence; and the pretty secretary who had been patronizing his clothes, went at once to the Minister and said: "There is a Mr. Macintosh to see you." She described him as an old, fat, dirty man with a large stomach, and soon the doors opened and Mr. Macintosh was with the spring of knowledge.

He emerged five minutes later with what he wanted, the name of a certain expert. He drove through the deep green avenues of the city to the house he had been told to go to, which was a large and well-kept one, and comforted Mr. Macintosh in his faith that art properly used could make money. He parked his car in the road and walked in.

On the verandah, behind a table heaped with books, sat a middle-aged man with spectacles. Mr. Tomlinson was essentially a scholar with working hours he respected, and he lifted his eyes to see a big, dirty man with black hair showing above the dirty whiteness of his vest, and he said sharply: "What do you want?"

"Wait a minute, laddie," said Mr. Macintosh easily, and he held out a note from the Minister of Education, and Mr. Tomlinson took it and read it, feeling reassured. It was worded in such a way that his seeing Mr. Macintosh could be felt as a favor he was personally doing the Minister.

"I'll make it worth your while," said Mr. Macintosh, and at once distaste flooded Mr. Tomlinson, and he went pink, and said: "I'm afraid I haven't the time."

"Damn it, man, it's your job, isn't it? Or so Wentworth said."

"No," said Mr. Tomlinson, making each word clear, "I advise on ancient Monuments."

Mr. Macintosh stared, then laughed, and said: "Wentworth said you'd do, but it doesn't matter, I'll get someone else." And he left.

Mr. Tomlinson watched his hobo go off the verandah and into a magnificent car, and his thought was: "He must have stolen it." Then, puzzled and upset, he went to the telephone. But in a few moments he was smiling. Finally he laughed. Mr. Macintosh was *the* Mr.

Macintosh, a genuine specimen of the old-timer. It was the phrase "old-timer" that made it possible for Mr. Tomlinson to relent. He therefore rang the hotel at which Mr. Macintosh, as a rich man, would be bound to be staying, and he said he had made an error, he would be free the following day to accompany Mr. Macintosh.

And so next morning Mr. Macintosh, not at all surprised that the expert was at his service after all, with Mr. Tomlinson, who preserved a tolerant smile, drove out to the mine.

They drove very fast in the powerful car, and Mr. Tomlinson held himself steady while they jolted and bounced, and listened to Mr. Macintosh's tales of Australia and New Zealand, and thought of him rather as he would of an ancient Monument.

At last the long plain ended, and foothills of greenish scrub heaped themselves around the car, and then high mountains piled with granite boulders, and the heat came in thick, slow waves into the car, and Mr. Tomlinson thought: I'll be glad when we're through the mountains into the plain. But instead they turned into a high, enclosed place with mountains all around, and suddenly there was an enormous gulf in the ground, and on one side of it were two tiny tin-roofed houses, and on the other acres of kaffir huts. The mine-stamps thudded regularly, like a pulse of the heat, and Mr. Tomlinson wondered how anybody, white or black, could bear to live in such a place.

He ate boiled beef and carrots and greasy potatoes with one of the richest men in the sub-continent, and thought how well and intelligently he would use such money it he had it—which is the only consolation left to the cultivated man of moderate income. After lunch, Mr. Macintosh said: "And now, let's get it over."

Mr. Tomlinson expressed his willingness, and, smiling to himself, followed Mr. Macintosh off into the bush on a kaffir path. He did not know what he was going to see. Mr. Macintosh had said: "Can you tell if a youngster has got any talent just by looking at a piece of wood he has carved?"

Mr. Tomlinson said he would do his best.

Then they were beside a fallen tree-trunk, and in the grass knelt a big lad, with untidy brown hair falling over his face, laboring at the wood with a large chisel.

"This is a friend of mine," said Mr. Macintosh to Tommy, who got to his feet and stood uncomfortably, wondering what was happening. "Do you mind if Mr. Tomlinson sees what you are doing?"

Tommy made a shrugging movement and felt that things were going beyond his control. He looked in awed amazement at Mr. Tomlinson, who seemed to him rather like a teacher or professor, and certainly not at all what he imagined an artist to be.

"Well?" said Mr. Macintosh to Mr. Tomlinson, after a space of half a minute.

Mr. Tomlinson laughed in a way which said: "Now don't be in such a hurry." He walked around the carved tree root, looking at the figure of Dirk from this angle and that.

Then he asked Tommy: "Why do you make these carvings?"

1790

1795

1800

1805

1810

1815

1820

1825

1830

1835

Tommy very uncomfortably shrugged, as if to say: What a silly question; and Mr. Macintosh hastily said: "He gets high marks for Art at school."

Mr. Tomlinson smiled again and walked around to the other side of the trunk. From here he could see Dirk's face, flattened back on the neck, eyes half-closed and strained, the muscles of the neck shaped from natural veins of the wood.

"Is this someone you know?" he asked Tommy in an easy, intimate way, one artist to another.

"Yes," said Tommy, briefly; he resented the question.

Mr. Tomlinson looked at the face and then at Mr. Macintosh. "It has a look of you," he observed dispassionately, and colored himself as he saw Mr. Macintosh grow angry. He walked well away from the group, to give Mr. Macintosh space to hide his embarrassment. When he returned, he asked Tommy: "And so you want to be a sculptor?"

"I don't know," said Tommy, defiantly.

Mr. Tomlinson shrugged rather impatiently, and with a nod at Mr. Macintosh suggested it was enough. He said goodbye to Tommy, and went back to the house with Mr. Macintosh.

There he was offered tea and biscuits, and Mr. Macintosh asked: "Well, what do you think?"

But by now Mr. Tomlinson was certainly offended at this cash-on-delivery approach to art, and he said: "Well, that rather depends, doesn't it?"

"On what?" demanded Mr. Macintosh.

"He seems to have talent," conceded Mr. Tomlinson.

"That's all I want to know," said Mr. Macintosh, and suggested that now he could run Mr. Tomlinson back to town.

But Mr. Tomlinson did not feel it was enough, and he said: "It's quite interesting, that statue. I suppose he's seen pictures in magazines. It has quite a modern feeling."

"Modern?" said Mr. Macintosh. "What do you mean?"

Mr. Tomlinson shrugged again, giving it up. "Well," he said, practically, "what do you mean to do?"

"If you say he has talent, I'll send him to the university and he can study art."

After a long pause, Mr. Tomlinson murmured: "What a fortunate boy he is." He meant to convey depths of disillusionment and irony, but Mr. Macintosh said: "I always did have a fancy for him."

He took Mr. Tomlinson back to the city, and as he dropped him on his verandah, presented him with a check for fifty pounds, which Mr. Tomlinson most indignantly returned. "Oh, give it to charity," said Mr. Macintosh impatiently, and went to his car, leaving Mr. Tomlinson to heal his susceptibilities in any way he chose.

When Mr. Macintosh reached his mine again it was midnight, and there were no lights in the Clarkes' house, and so his need to be generous must be stifled until the morning.

Then he went to Annie Clarke and told her he would send Tommy to university, where he could be an artist, and Mrs. Clarke wept with gratitude, and said that Mr. Macintosh was much kinder than Tommy

deserved, and perhaps he would learn sense yet and go back to his books.

As far as Mr. Macintosh was concerned it was all settled.

He set off through the trees to find Tommy and announce his future to him.

But when he arrived at seeing distance there were two figures, Dirk and Tommy, seated on the trunk talking, and Mr. Macintosh stopped among the trees, filled with such bitter anger at this fresh check to his plans that he could not trust himself to go on. So he returned to his house, and brooded angrily—he knew exactly what was going to happen when he spoke to Tommy, and now he must make up his mind, there was no escape from a decision.

And while Mr. Macintosh mused bitterly in his house, Tommy and Dirk waited for him; it was now all as clear to them as it was to him.

Dirk had come out of the trees to Tommy the moment the two men left the day before. Tommy was standing by the fanged root, looking at the shape of Dirk in it, trying to understand what was going to be demanded of him. The word "artist" was on his tongue, and he tasted it, trying to make the strangeness of it fit that powerful shape struggling out of the wood. He did not like it. He did not want—but what did he want? He felt pressure on himself, the faint beginnings of something that would one day be like a tunnel of birth from which he must fight to emerge; he felt the obligations working within himself like a goad which would one day be a whip perpetually falling behind him so that he must perpetually move onwards.

His sense of fetters and debts was confirmed when Dirk came to stand by him. First he asked: "What did they want?"

"They want me to be an artist, they always want me to be something," said Tommy sullenly. He began throwing stones at the tree and shying them off along the tops of the grass. Then one hit the figure of Dirk, and he stopped.

Dirk was looking at himself. "Why do you make me like that?" he asked. The narrow, strong face expressed nothing but that familiar, sardonic antagonism, as if he said: "You, too—just like the rest!"

"Why, what's the matter with it?" challenged Tommy at once.

Dirk walked around it, then back. "You're just like all the rest," he said.

"Why? Why don't you like it?" Tommy was really distressed. Also, his feeling was: What's it got to do with him? Slowly he understood that his emotion was that belief in his right to freedom which Dirk always felt immediately, and he said in a different voice: "Tell me what's wrong with it?"

"Why do I have to come out of the wood? Why haven't I any hands or feet?"

"You have, but don't you see…" But Tommy looked at Dirk standing in front of him and suddenly gave an impatient movement: "Well, it doesn't matter, it's only a statue."

He sat on the trunk and Dirk beside him. After a while he said: "How should you be, then?"

1935 "If you made yourself, would you be half wood?"

Tommy made an effort to feel this, but failed. "But it's not me, it's you." He spoke with difficulty, and thought: But it's important, I shall have to think about it later. He almost groaned with the knowledge that here it was, the first debt, presented for payment.

1940 Dirk said suddenly: "Surely it needn't be wood. You could do the same thing if you put handcuffs on my wrists." Tommy lifted his head and gave a short, astonished laugh. "Well, what's funny?" said Dirk, aggressively. "You can't do it the easy way, you have to make me half wood, as if I was more a tree than a human being."

1945 Tommy laughed again, but unhappily. "Oh, I'll do it again," he acknowledged at last. "Don't fuss about that one, it's finished. I'll do another."

There was a silence.

Dirk said: "What did that man say about you?"

1950 "How do I know?"

"Does he know about art?"

"I suppose so."

"Perhaps you'll be famous," said Dirk at last. "In that book you gave me, it said about painters. Perhaps you'll be like that."

1955 "Oh, shut up," said Tommy roughly. "You're just as bad as he is."

"Well, what's the matter with it?"

"Why have I got to be something? First it was a sailor, and then it was a scholar, and now it's an artist."

"They wouldn't have to make me be anything," said Dirk sarcasti-
1960 cally.

"I know," admitted Tommy grudgingly. And then, passionately: I shan't go to university unless he sends you too."

"I know," said Dirk at once, "I know you won't."

They smiled at each other, that small, shy, revealed smile, which
1965 was so hard for them because it pledged them to such a struggle in the future.

Then Tommy asked: "Why didn't you come near me all this time?"

"I get sick of you," said Dirk. "I sometimes feel I don't want to see a white face again, not ever. I feel that I hate you all, every one."

1970 "I know," said Tommy, grinning. Then they laughed, and the last strain of dislike between them vanished.

They began to talk, for the first time, of what their lives would be.

Tommy said: "But when you've finished training to be an engineer, what will you do? They don't let colored people be engineers."

1975 "Things aren't always going to be like that," said Dirk.

"It's going to be very hard," said Tommy, looking at him question-ingly, and was at once reassured when Dirk said, sarcastically: "Hard, it's going to be hard? Isn't it hard now, white boy?"

Later that day Mr. Macintosh came towards them from his house.

1980 He stood in front of them, that big, shrewd, rich man, with his small, clever gray eyes, and his narrow, loveless mouth; and he said

aggressively to Tommy: "Do you want to go to the university and be an artist?"

"If Dirk comes too," said Tommy immediately.

1985 "What do you want to study?" Mr. Macintosh asked Dirk, direct.

"I want to be an engineer," said Dirk at once.

"If I pay your way through the university then at the end of it I'm finished with you. I never want to hear from you and you are never to come back to this mine once you leave it."

1990 Dirk and Tommy both nodded, and the instinctive agreement between them fed Mr. Macintosh's bitter unwillingness in the choice, so that he ground out viciously: "Do you think you two can be together in the university? You don't understand. You'll be living separate, and you can't go around together just as you like."

1995 The boys looked at each other, and then, as if some sort of pact had been made between them, simply nodded.

"You can't go to university anyway, Tommy, until you've done a bit better at school. If you go back for another year and work you can pass your matric, and go to university, but you can't go now, right at

2000 the bottom of the class."

Tommy said: "I'll work." He added at once: "Dirk'll need more books to study here till we can go."

The anger was beginning to swell Mr. Macintosh's face, but Tommy said: "It's only fair. You burnt them, and now he hasn't any

2005 at all."

"Well," said Mr. Macintosh heavily. "Well, so that's how it is!"

He looked at the two boys, seated together on the tree-trunk. Tommy was leaning forward, eyes lowered, a troubled but determined look on his face. Dirk was sitting erect, looking straight at his father

2010 with eyes filled with hate.

"Well," said Mr. Macintosh, with an effort at raillery which sounded harsh to them all: "Well, I send you both to university and you don't give me so much as a thank-you!"

At this, both faced towards him, with such bitter astonishment that

2015 he flushed.

"Well, well," he said. "Well, well…" And then he turned to leave the clearing, and cried out as he went, so as to give the appearance of dominance: "Remember, laddie, I'm not sending you unless you do well at school this year…"

2020 And so he left them and went back to his house, an angry old man, defeated by something he did not begin to understand.

As for the boys, they were silent when he had gone.

The victory was entirely theirs, but now they had to begin again, in the long and difficult struggle to understand what they had won, and

2025 how they would use it.

# B4.  Second Reading: Delving More Deeply

Read Section IV a second time and focus on the lines indicated. Use the surrounding text and your experience to give an informed answer.

1.   *…and Mr. Macintosh flipped over the leaves and laughed, and had Dirk heard that laugh it would have been worse to him than any whip.* (lines 1511–1513) Why would this laugh have been so unbearable to Dirk? Can another person's laughter hurt as much as or more than criticism?

2.   *Anger heaved up in him beyond all sanity…* (line 1551) What did this anger provoke him to do? What was the source of this anger? Is his anger justifiable?

3.   *"When I grow up I'll clear you all out, all of you, there won't be one white man left in Africa, not one."* (lines 1588–1589) Dirk was angry at his father. Why did he lash out at (attack) *all* whites?

4.   *It was a bitter, ironical laugh, and Mr. Macintosh was upset—it was not a boy's laugh at all.* (lines 1672–1673) Mr. Macintosh seemed relieved during the conversation with Tommy about the fire until he noticed Tommy's rage. What was the source of Mr. Macintosh's relief and Tommy's rage?

5.   *Mr. Macintosh did not like it. He did not know what art was, but he knew he did not like this at all…* (lines 1715–1716) Why was Mr. Macintosh so disturbed by the new figure Tommy was making of Dirk?

6.   *Sitting alone in his room he told himself it was simply a question of paying for knowledge.* (lines 1745–1746) What knowledge did Mr. Macintosh want? Why do you think Mr. Macintosh was so desperate for Tommy to go to college?

7.   *He… thought how well and intelligently he would use such money if he had it—which is the only consolation left to the cultivated man of moderate income.* (lines 1809–1812) What was it about Mr. Macintosh that Mr. Tomlinson disliked?

8.   *…it was now all as clear to them as it was to him.* (line 1899) What was clear to Tommy, Dirk, and Mr. Macintosh?

9.   *"You're just as bad as he is."* (line 1955) How was Dirk like his father according to Tommy? Do you agree?

**FOLLOW-UP**
Discuss your answers to First and Second Reading questions in small groups.

10.   *"Things aren't always going to be like that…"* (line 1975) What does Kirk mean when he says this? Do you agree?

# III. STRENGTHENING SKILLS THROUGH THE TEXT

## A.  Responding to the Reading

Write at least 75 words on *one* of the following topics. When you finish, choose a classmate to listen to what you have written.

1.  Did you like this story? Why or why not?

2.  Which character in the story do you sympathize with the most? Explain why?

_____

_____

_____

_____

_____

_____

_____

_____

_____

_____

_____

_____

_____

_____

_____

_____

_____

# B. Global Comprehension Check: Chronological Order of Events

Number the following sentences in chronological order from first (number 1) to last (number 16). Number 1 is done for you.

_____ Tommy began to teach Dirk how to read.

_____ Dirk began to teach other natives about the laws that controlled their lives.

_____ Tommy began a figure of Dirk's mother, but he was unable to finish it.

_____ Mr. Macintosh set fire to the hut that contained Dirk's books and Tommy's figures.

_____ Tommy got five pounds from Mr. Macintosh for the figure of Dirk and gave it to Dirk.

___1___ Tommy's mother forbade Tommy to go to the compound to play.

_____ Tommy realized who Dirk's father was.

_____ Tommy and Dirk had their first fight.

_____ Tommy gave Dirk the figure he had made of him.

_____ Dirk became very upset at the unfinished figure Tommy made of him.

_____ Tommy began to make figures.

_____ Mr. Macintosh agreed to send both Dirk and Tommy to a university.

_____ Tommy went away to school for the first time.

_____ Tommy met Dirk's mother and saw her other children.

_____ Tommy told Mr. Macintosh that he should send Dirk to college and that Mr. Macintosh knows why this is so.

**FOLLOW-UP**
Compare your answers in pairs or small groups.

_____ Tommy made a fiery speech on the inequity of the color bar in his debating society.

# C.    Text-based Focus on Vocabulary: Key Words

Skim the text for 12 key words that recall for you the important incidents and themes of "The Antheap." Be able to explain what each of your words means and why you chose it as a key word.

EXAMPLE:  *half-cast*

**a.**    *Half-cast* refers to a person who is an equal combination of two races, such as black and white, like Dirk in the story.

**FOLLOW-UP**
Share your words, their meanings if necessary, and your reasons for choosing them with a partner or small group.

**b.**    *Half-cast* is an important key word for me because it explains why Dirk's father did not claim him as a son. Although the word *discrimination* is not mentioned in the story, we know Dirk faces discrimination from both his parents' races. I feel the author is making a statement against discrimination through the character of Dirk.

# IV.  MOVING BEYOND THE TEXT

# A.   Discussion and Writing

Discuss the following topics as a class or in groups. Your teacher may assign a different topic to each group and ask a group leader to summarize its discussion for the class. Write on *one or more* of the topics as instructed by your teacher.

**1.**    Two contradictory sayings about friendship are:

*"Opposites attract."*

*"Birds of a feather flock together."*

What does each saying mean? Which saying characterizes Dirk and Tommy's friendship? Why do you think so?

**2.**    What does the future hold for Dirk and Tommy? Will their friendship continue or falter? What will each one be doing in ten years' time? (Suggestion for writing: Continue the story, starting ten years after it ends.)

**3.**    Which of the three main characters do you admire the most? Why?

**4.** A major theme of "The Antheap" is racial discrimination. What message does the author give about discrimination? What incidents or descriptions support this message?

**5.** *"If all men were just, there would be no need of courage."*
Plutarch, *Life of Agesilaus*

What does this quotation about courage mean to you? How does it apply to "The Antheap"?

**6.** The clay and wood figures that Tommy makes are important in the story. Choose one of the questions below to discuss:

**a.** The figures of Dirk and his family sometimes please Dirk, and at other times upset him. Why?

**b.** The figure of the pit and the third figure of Dirk drove Mr. Macintosh to actions and decisions he would not have taken otherwise. Why did they affect him so much?

**c.** Do you consider Tommy an artist or merely a craftsman? Why?

_____

_____

_____

_____

_____

_____

_____

_____

_____

_____

_____

_____

_____

# B. Roleplay Interview

*Four students will take the roles of Tommy, Dirk, Mrs. Clarke, and Mr. Macintosh. Each of the other class members will direct at least one question about what a character has done or said in the story to one of the four characters. Begin the interview as shown:*

CLASS MEMBER #1: Tommy, why did you make figures of clay and wood?

TOMMY: (answers as he wishes but in keeping with the story)

CLASS MEMBER #2: Mrs. Clarke, are you happy that both Tommy and Dirk will go away to college?

MRS. CLARKE: (etc.)